The Ultimate Air Fryer Cookbook

An Amazing Collection With 500 Most Wanted Healthy and Tasty Recipes for your Air Fryer

Lucy Miles

Table Of Contents

DESCRIPTION

The history of Air fryers dates back to a few years ago; exactly during the third quarter of the year 2010 and it was a completely revolutionary invention that was invented by Philips Electronics Company. Philips introduced the Air Fryer to the world and changed the conception of the culinary world all at once.

The Air Fryer is used as a substitute for your oven, stovetop, and deep fryer. It comes with various handy parts and other tools that you can buy to use your Air Fryer for different cooking styles, which include the following:

- Grilling. It provides the same heat to grill food ingredients without the need to flip them continuously. The hot air goes around the fryer, giving heating on all sides. The recipes include directions of how many times you ought to shake the pan during the cooking process.

To make the process of grilling faster, you can use a grill pan or a grill layer. They will soak the excess fat from the meat that you are cooking to give you delicious and healthy meals.

- Baking. The Air Fryer usually comes with a baking pan (or you can buy or use your ownto make treats that are typically done using an oven. You can bake goodies, such as cakes, bread, cupcakes, muffins, and brownies in your Air Fryer.
- Roasting. It roasts food ingredients, which include vegetables and meat, faster than when you do it in the oven.
- Frying is its primary purpose – to cook fried foods with little or no oil.

You can cook most food items in an Air Fryer. There are some foods that you should refrain from cooking in the fryer because they will taste better when cooked in the traditional ways — they include fried foods with batter and steamed veggies, such as beans and carrots.

Despite this, you will never run out of ingredients to cook using your Air Fryer – from veggies to seafood, chicken, egg, turkey, and a lot more. The most common component that is prepared using this appliance is potatoes.

The Air Fryer also comes with a separator, and this allows you to cook multiple dishes at the same time. You need to choose recipes that can be prepared at the same temperature setting.

This book covers the following topics:

- Breakfast
- Mains
- Sides
- Seafood
- Poultry
- Meat
- Vegetables
- Snacks
- Desserts and more!!!

INTRODUCTION

There are many kinds of foods that you can cook using an air fryer, but there are also certain types that are not suited for it. Avoid cooking ingredients, which can be steamed, like beans and carrots. You also cannot fry foods covered in heavy batter in this appliance.

Aside from the above mentioned, you can cook most kinds of ingredients using an air fryer. You can use it to cook foods covered in light flour or breadcrumbs. You can cook a variety of vegetables in the appliance, such as cauliflower, asparagus, zucchini, kale, peppers, and corn on the cob. You can also use it to cook frozen foods and home prepared meals by following a different set of instructions for these purposes.

An air fryer also comes with another useful feature - the separator. It allows you to cook multiple dishes at a time. Use the separator to divide ingredients in the pan or basket. You have to make sure that all ingredients have the same temperature setting so that everything will cook evenly at the same time.

The Benefits of Air fryer

It is important to note that air fried foods are still fried. Unless you've decided to eliminate the use of oils in cooking, you must still be cautious about the food you eat. Despite that, it clearly presents a better and healthier option than deep-frying. It helps you avoid unnecessary fats and oils, which makes it an ideal companion when you intend to lose weight. It offers a lot more benefits, which include the following:

- It is convenient and easy to use, plus, it’s easy to clean.
- It doesn’t give off unwanted smells when cooking.
- You can use it to prepare a variety of meals.
- It can withstand heavy cooking.
- It is durable and made of metal and high-grade plastic.
- Cooking using this appliance is not as messy as frying in a traditional way. You don’t have to worry about greasy spills and stains in the kitchen.

CHAPTER 1

BREAKFAST

1. Strawberry and Nut Cereal

Preparation time: 10 minutes • Cooking time: 12 minutes • Servings: 12

INGREDIENTS

- 1 cup almonds, chopped finely
- ½ cup walnuts, chopped finely
- ½ cup dried strawberries
- 1 cup pecans, chopped finely
- 1/3 cup pumpkin seeds
- 1/3 cup hemp seeds
- ½ cup ground flaxseeds
- 1 tsp vanilla
- 1 egg white, whisked
- ¼ cup butter, melted

DIRECTIONS:

1. Preheat your air fryer to 325 degrees F.
2. Line your air fryer basket with parchment.
3. Place the chopped nuts in a large bowl and then add the pumpkin seeds, hemp seeds and flaxseed. Toss well.

Add the remaining ingredients and toss well.

4. Pour the nut mix into the air fryer basket and bake for 18 minutes, tossing halfway through to bake evenly.
5. Empty the granola onto a try and let cool completely. Enjoy with milk or own its own.

NUTRITION: Calories 298, Total Fat 27, Saturated Fat 18g, Total Carbs 11g, Net Carbs 6g, Protein 7g, Sugar 3g, Fiber 5g, Sodium 187mg, Potassium 54g

2. Seedy Breakfast Granola

Preparation time: 10 minutes • Cooking time: 18 minutes • Servings: 12

INGREDIENTS

- 1 cup almonds, chopped finely
- ½ cup walnuts, chopped finely
- ½ cup hazelnuts, peeled, chopped finely
- 1 cup pecans, chopped finely
- 1/3 cup pumpkin seeds
- 1/3 cup hemp seeds
- 1/3 cup chia seeds
- ½ cup ground flaxseeds
- 1 tsp vanilla

- 1 egg white, whisked
- ¼ cup butter, melted

DIRECTIONS:

1. Preheat your air fryer to 325 degrees F.
2. Line your air fryer basket with parchment.
3. Place the chopped nuts in a large bowl and then add the pumpkin seeds, hemp seeds, chia seeds and flaxseed. Toss well.
4. Add the remaining ingredients and toss well.
5. Pour the nut mix into the air fryer basket and bake for 18 minutes, tossing halfway through to bake evenly.
6. Empty the granola onto a try and let cool completely. Enjoy with milk or own its own.

NUTRITION: Calories 342, Total Fat 32, Saturated Fat 22g, Total Carbs 7g, Net Carbs 2g, Protein 9g, Sugar 1g, Fiber 5g, Sodium 187mg, Potassium 54g

3. Pepper Stuffed Spinach Parmesan Baked Eggs

Preparation time: 5 minutes • Cooking time: 14 minutes • Servings: 2

INGREDIENTS

- 4 eggs
- 2 Tbsp heavy cream
- 2 Tbsp frozen, chopped spinach, thawed
- 2 Tbsp grated parmesan cheese
- ½ tsp salt
- 1/8 tsp ground black pepper
- 1 large red pepper, cut in half vertically, seeds removed

DIRECTIONS:

1. Preheat your air fryer to 330 degrees F.
2. Place red pepper halves in the air fryer basket and cook for 5 minutes.
3. In a small bowl, whisk together all the ingredients
4. Pour the eggs into the partially cooked peppers and bake for 7 minutes.
5. Enjoy straight out of the baking cup!

NUTRITION: Calories 189, Total Fat 11g, Saturated Fat 4g, Total Carbs 5g, Net Carbs 3g, Protein 14g, Sugar 2g, Fiber 2g, Sodium 134mg, Potassium 148g

4. Pepper Stuffed Spinach and Feta Eggs

Preparation time: 5 minutes • Cooking time: 14 minutes • Servings: 2

INGREDIENTS

- 4 eggs

- 2 Tbsp heavy cream
- 2 Tbsp frozen, chopped spinach, thawed
- ¼ cup feta crumbles
- ½ tsp salt
- 1/8 tsp ground black pepper
- 1 large red pepper, cut in half vertically, seeds removed

DIRECTIONS:

1. Preheat your air fryer to 330 degrees F.
2. Place red pepper halves in the air fryer basket and cook for 5 minutes.
3. In a small bowl, whisk together all the ingredients
4. Pour the eggs into the partially cooked peppers and bake for 7 minutes.
5. Enjoy straight out of the baking cup!

NUTRITION: Calories 192, Total Fat 11g, Saturated Fat 6g, Total Carbs 5g, Net Carbs 3g, Protein 14g, Sugar 2g, Fiber 2g, Sodium 156mg, Potassium 148g

5. Egg Stuffed Peppers and Cheese

Preparation time: 5 minutes • Cooking time: 14 minutes • Servings: 2

INGREDIENTS

- 4 eggs
- 2 Tbsp heavy cream
- 2 Tbsp grated cheddar cheese
- 2 Tbsp grated parmesan cheese
- ½ tsp salt
- 1/8 tsp ground black pepper
- 1 large red pepper, cut in half vertically, seeds removed

DIRECTIONS:

1. Preheat your air fryer to 330 degrees F.
2. Place red pepper halves in the air fryer basket and cook for 5 minutes.
3. In a small bowl, whisk together all the ingredients
4. Pour the eggs into the partially cooked peppers and bake for 7 minutes.
5. Enjoy straight out of the baking cup!

NUTRITION: Calories 178, Total Fat 16g, Saturated Fat 8g, Total Carbs 5g, Net Carbs 3g, Protein 10g, Sugar 2g, Fiber 2g, Sodium 134mg, Potassium 148g

6. Bacon and Egg Stuffed Peppers

Preparation time: 5 minutes • Cooking time: 14 minutes • Servings: 2

INGREDIENTS

- 4 eggs
- 2 Tbsp heavy cream
- 2 Tbsp chopped cooked bacon

- 2 Tbsp grated cheddar cheese
- ½ tsp salt
- 1/8 tsp ground black pepper
- 1 large red pepper, cut in half vertically, seeds removed

DIRECTIONS:

1. Preheat your air fryer to 330 degrees F.
2. Place red pepper halves in the air fryer basket and cook for 5 minutes.
3. In a small bowl, whisk together all the ingredients
4. Pour the eggs into the partially cooked peppers and bake for 7 minutes.
5. Enjoy straight out of the baking cup!

NUTRITION: Calories 210, Total Fat 19g, Saturated Fat 9, Total Carbs 9g, Net Carbs 4g, Protein 14g, Sugar 2g, Fiber 5g, Sodium 198mg, Potassium 148g

7. Peppers and Eggs

Preparation time: 5 minutes • Cooking time: 14 minutes • Servings: 2

INGREDIENTS

- 4 eggs
- 2 Tbsp heavy cream
- 1 jalapeno, sliced
- 2 Tbsp grated cheddar cheese
- ½ tsp salt
- 1/8 tsp ground black pepper
- 1 large red pepper, cut in half vertically, seeds removed

DIRECTIONS:

1. Preheat your air fryer to 330 degrees F.
2. Place red pepper halves in the air fryer basket and cook for 5 minutes.
3. In a small bowl, whisk together all the ingredients
4. Pour the eggs into the partially cooked peppers and bake for 7 minutes.
5. Enjoy straight out of the baking cup!

NUTRITION: Calories 154, Total Fat 11g, Saturated Fat 4g, Total Carbs 5g, Net Carbs 3g, Protein 9g, Sugar 2g, Fiber 2g, Sodium 126mg, Potassium 154g

8. Pepper Stuffed Spinach Parmesan Baked Eggs

Preparation time: 5 minutes • Cooking time: 14 minutes • Servings: 2

INGREDIENTS

- 4 eggs
- 2 Tbsp heavy cream

- ¼ zucchini, sliced and chopped thinly
- 2 Tbsp grated parmesan cheese
- ½ tsp salt
- 1/8 tsp ground black pepper
- 1 large red pepper, cut in half vertically, seeds removed

DIRECTIONS:

1. Preheat your air fryer to 330 degrees F.
2. Place red pepper halves in the air fryer basket and cook for 5 minutes.
3. In a small bowl, whisk together all the ingredients
4. Pour the eggs into the partially cooked peppers and bake for 7 minutes.
5. Enjoy straight out of the baking cup!

NUTRITION: Calories 172, Total Fat 7g, Saturated Fat 3g, Total Carbs 8g, Net Carbs 4g, Protein 14g, Sugar 2g, Fiber 4g, Sodium 117mg, Potassium 154g

9. Brussels Hash

Preparation time: 10 minutes • Cooking time: 25 minutes • Servings: 4

INGREDIENTS

- 6 slices bacon, chopped, cooked
- ½ cup chopped white onion
- 1 pound Brussel sprouts, sliced in quarters
- ½ tsp salt
- ½ tsp ground black pepper
- 2 cloves garlic, minced
- 4 eggs, whisked

DIRECTIONS:

1. Preheat your air fryer to 350 degrees F.
2. Toss the bacon, onion, Brussels, salt, pepper and garlic together in a large bowl.
3. Pour the mix into a seven inch pan that will fit in your air fryer basket.
4. Place in the air fryer and cook for 15 minutes.
5. Pour the whisked eggs in the basket and return the pan to the air fryer to cook for 10 more minutes.
6. Mix well to break up the hash and enjoy while hot.

NUTRITION: Calories 238, Total Fat 12g, Saturated Fat 7g, Total Carbs 6g, Net Carbs 3g, Protein 12g, Sugar 1g, Fiber 3g, Sodium 189mg, Potassium 217g

10. Zucchini Hash

Preparation time: 10 minutes • Cooking time: 25 minutes • Servings: 4

INGREDIENTS

- 6 slices bacon, chopped,

cooked
- ½ cup chopped white onion
- 1 pound shredded zucchini, water squeezed out
- ½ tsp salt
- ½ tsp ground black pepper
- 2 cloves garlic, minced
- 4 eggs, whisked

DIRECTIONS:

1. Preheat your air fryer to 350 degrees F.
2. Toss the bacon, onion, zucchini, salt, pepper and garlic together in a large bowl.
3. Pour the mix into a seven inch pan that will fit in your air fryer basket.
4. Place in the air fryer and cook for 15 minutes.
5. Pour the whisked eggs in the basket and return the pan to the air fryer to cook for 10 more minutes.
6. Mix well to break up the hash and enjoy while hot.

NUTRITION: Calories 215, Total Fat 11g, Saturated Fat 7g, Total Carbs 8g, Net Carbs 5g, Protein 10g, Sugar 3g, Fiber 3g, Sodium 189mg, Potassium 211g

11. Vegetable Hash

Preparation time: 10 minutes • Cooking time: 25 minutes • Servings: 4

INGREDIENTS

- 6 slices bacon, chopped, cooked
- ½ cup chopped white onion
- 2 cups Brussel sprouts, sliced in quarters
- 2 cups diced green bell peppers
- ½ tsp salt
- ½ tsp ground black pepper
- 2 cloves garlic, minced
- 4 eggs, whisked

DIRECTIONS:

1. Preheat your air fryer to 350 degrees F.
2. Toss the bacon, onion, Brussels, bell peppers, salt, pepper and garlic together in a large bowl.
3. Pour the mix into a seven inch pan that will fit in your air fryer basket.
4. Place in the air fryer and cook for 15 minutes.
5. Pour the whisked eggs in the basket and return the pan to the air fryer to cook for 10 more minutes.
6. Mix well to break up the hash and enjoy while hot.

NUTRITION: Calories 238, Total Fat 12g, Saturated Fat 7g, Total Carbs 6g, Net Carbs 3g, Protein 12g, Sugar 1g, Fiber 3g, Sodium 189mg, Potassium 217g

12. Ham, Cheese and Mushroom Melt

Preparation time: 12 minutes • Cooking time: 18 minutes • Servings: 4

INGREDIENTS

- 2 Tbsp butter

- ½ pound sliced mushrooms
- 1 clove garlic, minced
- ¼ cup white onion, diced
- 1-16 oz ham steak, cooked
- ¼ cup cooked, crumbled bacon
- 1 Tbsp fresh parsley, chopped
- 1 cup grated gruyere cheese

DIRECTIONS:

1. Preheat your air fryer to 350 degrees F.
2. In a pan that will fit inside your air fryer, combine the butter and diced onion. Place in the preheated air fryer and cook for 5 minutes.
3. Remove the pan from the air fryer and stir in the garlic and mushrooms. Return to the air fryer for another 5 minutes.
4. Remove the pan again and add the ham steak, pushing it toward the bottom of the pan. Top with the bacon and grated cheese and place in the air fryer for another 8 minutes.
5. Move the ham steak and pan contents to a plate, garnish with the parsley and serve while hot.

NUTRITION: Calories 352, Total Fat 22g, Saturated Fat 11g, Total Carbs 5g, Net Carbs 4g, Protein 34g, Sugar 2g, Fiber 1g, Sodium 1576mg, Potassium 387g

13. Ham and Pepper Melt

Preparation time: 10 minutes • Cooking time: 18 minutes • Servings: 4

INGREDIENTS

- 2 Tbsp butter
- 1 cup diced red peppers
- 1 clove garlic, minced
- ¼ cup white onion, diced
- 1-16 oz ham steak, cooked
- ¼ cup cooked, crumbled bacon
- 1 Tbsp fresh parsley, chopped
- 1 cup blue cheese

DIRECTIONS:

1. Preheat your air fryer to 350 degrees F.
2. In a pan that will fit inside your air fryer, combine the butter, bell peppers and diced onion. Place in the preheated air fryer and cook for 5 minutes.
3. Remove the pan from the air fryer and stir in the garlic and mushrooms. Return to the air fryer for another 5 minutes.
4. Remove the pan again and add the ham steak, pushing it toward the

bottom of the pan. Top with the bacon and blue cheese and place in the air fryer for another 8 minutes.

5. Move the ham steak and pan contents to a plate, garnish with the parsley and serve while hot.

NUTRITION: Calories 382, Total Fat 25g, Saturated Fat 13g, Total Carbs 5g, Net Carbs 4g, Protein 35g, Sugar 2g, Fiber 1g, Sodium 1576mg, Potassium 387g

14. Veggie Melt

Preparation time: 10 minutes • Cooking time: 14 minutes • Servings: 4

INGREDIENTS

- 2 Tbsp butter
- ½ pound sliced mushrooms
- 1 clove garlic, minced
- ¼ cup white onion, diced
- 1 cup diced green bell peppers
- 1 cup diced zucchini
- 1 cup chopped baby spinach
- 1 Tbsp fresh parsley, chopped
- 1 cup grated gruyere cheese

DIRECTIONS:

1. Preheat your air fryer to 350 degrees F.
2. In a pan that will fit inside your air fryer, combine the butter, bell pepper and diced onion. Place in the preheated air fryer and cook for 5 minutes.
3. Remove the pan from the air fryer and stir in the garlic, zucchini and mushrooms. Return to the air fryer for another 5 minutes.
4. Remove the pan again and add the baby spinach and grated cheese and place in the air fryer for another 4 minutes.
5. Move the ham steak and pan contents to a plate, garnish with the parsley and serve while hot.

NUTRITION: Calories 268, Total Fat 11g, Saturated Fat 7g, Total Carbs 8g, Net Carbs 5g, Protein 34g, Sugar 2g, Fiber 3g, Sodium 452mg, Potassium 254g

15. Blueberry Breakfast Cake

Preparation time: 10 minutes • Cooking time: 24 minutes • Servings:12

INGREDIENTS

- 1 cup almond flour
- 1 Tbsp powdered stevia
- ¼ cup whole milk
- 1 egg
- ¼ tsp salt
- ¼ tsp ground cinnamon

- 2 tsp baking powder
- ½ cup frozen or fresh blueberries

DIRECTIONS:

1. Preheat your air fryer to 350 degrees F.
2. Spray a cake pan lightly with cooking spray. A seven inch pan will fit in most air fryers.
3. In a large bowl, stir together the almond flour, stevia, salt, cinnamon, and baking powder.
4. Add the eggs and milk and stir well.
5. Fold in the blueberries.
6. Pour the batter into the prepared pan and place into the air fryer basket and cook for 24 minutes or until a toothpick comes out cleanly when inserted into the center.
7. Remove from the air fryer and let cool.
8. Serve and enjoy!

NUTRITION: Calories 42, Total Fat 3g, Saturated Fat 1g, Total Carbs 3g, Net Carbs 2g, Protein 2g, Sugar 0g, Fiber 1g, Sodium 36mg, Potassium 68g

16. Red Pepper Breakfast Cake

Preparation time: 10 minutes • Cooking time: 24 minutes • Servings: 12

INGREDIENTS

- 1 cup almond flour
- 1 Tbsp powdered stevia
- ¼ cup whole milk
- 1 egg
- ¼ tsp salt
- ¼ tsp ground cayenne
- 2 tsp baking powder
- ½ cup sauted red peppers, diced

DIRECTIONS:

1. Preheat your air fryer to 350 degrees F.
2. Spray a cake pan lightly with cooking spray. A seven inch pan will fit in most air fryers.
3. In a large bowl, stir together the almond flour, stevia, salt, cayenne, and baking powder.
4. Add the eggs and milk and stir well.
5. Fold in the red peppers.
6. Pour the batter into the prepared pan and place into the air fryer basket and cook for 24 minutes or until a toothpick comes out cleanly when inserted into the center.
7. Remove from the air fryer and let cool.
8. Serve and enjoy!

NUTRITION: Calories 32, Total Fat 3g, Saturated Fat 1g, Total Carbs 2g, Net Carbs 2g, Protein 2g, Sugar 0g, Fiber 1g, Sodium 36mg, Potassium 68g

17. Zucchini Breakfast Cake

Preparation time: 10 minutes • Cooking time: 28 minutes • Servings: 12

INGREDIENTS

- 1 cup almond flour

- 1 Tbsp powdered stevia
- ¼ cup whole milk
- 1 egg
- ¼ tsp salt
- ¼ tsp ground cinnamon
- 2 tsp baking powder
- ½ cup shredded zucchini, water squeezed out

DIRECTIONS:

1. Preheat your air fryer to 350 degrees F.
2. Spray a cake pan lightly with cooking spray. A seven inch pan will fit in most air fryers.
3. In a large bowl, stir together the almond flour, stevia, salt, cinnamon, and baking powder.
4. Add the eggs and milk and stir well.
5. Fold in the zucchini.
6. Pour the batter into the prepared pan and place into the air fryer basket and cook for 24 minutes or until a toothpick comes out cleanly when inserted into the center.
7. Remove from the air fryer and let cool.
8. Serve and enjoy!

NUTRITION: Calories 42, Total Fat 3g, Saturated Fat 1g, Total Carbs 3g, Net Carbs 2g, Protein 2g, Sugar 0g, Fiber 1g, Sodium 36mg, Potassium 68g

18. Strawberry Breakfast Bread

Preparation time: 10 minutes • Cooking time: 24 minutes • Servings: 12

INGREDIENTS

- 1 cup almond flour
- 1 Tbsp powdered stevia
- ¼ cup whole milk
- 1 egg
- ¼ tsp salt
- ¼ tsp ground cinnamon
- 2 tsp baking powder
- ½ cup chopped fresh strawberries

DIRECTIONS:

1. Preheat your air fryer to 350 degrees F.
2. Spray a cake pan lightly with cooking spray. A seven inch pan will fit in most air fryers.
3. In a large bowl, stir together the almond flour, stevia, salt, cinnamon, and baking powder.
4. Add the eggs and milk and stir well.
5. Fold in the strawberries.
6. Pour the batter into the prepared pan and place into the air fryer basket and cook for 24 minutes or until a toothpick comes out cleanly when inserted into the center.
7. Remove from the air fryer and let cool.

8. Serve and enjoy!

NUTRITION: Calories 42, Total Fat 3g, Saturated Fat 1g, Total Carbs 3g, Net Carbs 2g, Protein 2g, Sugar 0g, Fiber 1g, Sodium 36mg, Potassium 68g

19. Raspberry Breakfast Cake

Preparation time: 10 minutes • Cooking time: 24 minutes • Servings: 12

INGREDIENTS

- 1 cup almond flour
- 1 Tbsp powdered stevia
- ¼ cup whole milk
- 1 egg
- ¼ tsp salt
- ¼ tsp ground cinnamon
- 2 tsp baking powder
- ½ cup frozen or fresh raspberries

DIRECTIONS:

1. Preheat your air fryer to 350 degrees F.
2. Spray a cake pan lightly with cooking spray. A seven inch pan will fit in most air fryers.
3. In a large bowl, stir together the almond flour, stevia, salt, cinnamon, and baking powder.
4. Add the eggs and milk and stir well.
5. Fold in the raspberries.
6. Pour the batter into the prepared pan and place into the air fryer basket and cook for 24 minutes or until a toothpick comes out cleanly when inserted into the center.
7. Remove from the air fryer and let cool.
8. Serve and enjoy!

NUTRITION: Calories 42, Total Fat 3g, Saturated Fat 1g, Total Carbs 7g, Net Carbs 4g, Protein 2g, Sugar 4g, Fiber 3g, Sodium 36mg, Potassium 68g

20. Cheesy Bacon Pancake

Preparation time: 10 minutes • Cooking time: 9 minutes • Servings: 2

INGREDIENTS

- 2 eggs
- ½ cup whole milk
- 2 Tbsp butter, melted
- 1 tsp vanilla extract
- 1 ¼ cup almond flour
- 2 Tbsp granulated erythritol
- 1 tsp baking powder
- 1/8 tsp salt
- ½ cup crumbled, cooked bacon
- ¼ cup grated cheddar cheese

DIRECTIONS:

1. Preheat your air fryer to 400 degrees F and line a baking pan with parchment paper. Be sure the pan will fit in your air fryer- typically a seven inch round pan will

work perfectly.
2. Place the eggs, milk, butter and vanilla extract in a blender and puree for about thirty seconds.
3. Add the remaining ingredients to the blender and puree until smooth.
4. Pour the pancake batter into the prepared pan and stir in the cheese and bacon.
5. Place in the air fryer.
6. Cook for 9 minutes or until the pancake is puffed and the top is golden brown.
7. Slice and serve with keto, sugar free syrup!

NUTRITION: Calories 278, Total Fat 28g, Saturated Fat 12g, Total Carbs 15g, Net Carbs 10g, Protein 15g, Sugar 3g, Fiber 5g, Sodium 125mg, Potassium 111g

21. Cheesy Pancake

Preparation time: 10 minutes • Cooking time: 9 minutes • Servings: 2

INGREDIENTS

- 2 eggs
- ½ cup whole milk
- 2 Tbsp butter, melted
- 1 tsp vanilla extract
- 1 ¼ cup almond flour
- 2 Tbsp granulated erythritol
- 1 tsp baking powder
- 1/8 tsp salt
- ½ cup grated cheddar cheese

DIRECTIONS:

1. Preheat your air fryer to 400 degrees F and line a baking pan with parchment paper. Be sure the pan will fit in your air fryer- typically a seven inch round pan will work perfectly.
2. Place the eggs, milk, butter and vanilla extract in a blender and puree for about thirty seconds.
3. Add the remaining ingredients to the blender and puree until smooth.
4. Pour the pancake batter into the prepared pan and stir in the cheese.
5. Place in the air fryer.
6. Cook for 9 minutes or until the pancake is puffed and the top is golden brown.
7. Slice and serve with keto, sugar free syrup!

NUTRITION: Calories 261, Total Fat 28g, Saturated Fat 12g, Total Carbs 12g, Net Carbs 9g, Protein 9g, Sugar 3g, Fiber 5g, Sodium 125mg, Potassium 111g

22. Strawberry Feta Pancake

Preparation time: 10 minutes • Cooking time: 9 minutes • Servings: 2

INGREDIENTS

- 2 eggs
- ½ cup whole milk
- 2 Tbsp butter, melted

- 1 tsp vanilla extract
- 1 ¼ cup almond flour
- 2 Tbsp granulated erythritol
- 1 tsp baking powder
- 1/8 tsp salt
- ¼ cup chopped strawberries
- ¼ cup feta cheese

DIRECTIONS:

1. Preheat your air fryer to 400 degrees F and line a baking pan with parchment paper. Be sure the pan will fit in your air fryer- typically a seven inch round pan will work perfectly.
2. Place the eggs, milk, butter and vanilla extract in a blender and puree for about thirty seconds.
3. Add the remaining ingredients to the blender and puree until smooth.
4. Pour the pancake batter into the prepared pan and stir in the feta and strawberries.
5. Place in the air fryer.
6. Cook for 9 minutes or until the pancake is puffed and the top is golden brown.
7. Slice and serve with keto, sugar free syrup!

NUTRITION: Calories 262, Total Fat 22g, Saturated Fat 10g, Total Carbs 15g, Net Carbs 10g, Protein 15g, Sugar 3g, Fiber 5g, Sodium 145mg, Potassium 109g

23. Pepper Pancake

Preparation time: 10 minutes • Cooking time: 9 minutes • Servings: 2

INGREDIENTS

- 2 eggs
- ½ cup whole milk
- 2 Tbsp butter, melted
- 1 tsp vanilla extract
- 1 ¼ cup almond flour
- 2 Tbsp granulated erythritol
- 1 tsp baking powder
- 1/8 tsp salt
- ½ cup diced bell pepper

DIRECTIONS:

1. Preheat your air fryer to 400 degrees F and line a baking pan with parchment paper. Be sure the pan will fit in your air fryer- typically a seven inch round pan will work perfectly.
2. Place the eggs, milk, butter and vanilla extract in a blender and puree for about thirty seconds.
3. Add the remaining ingredients to the blender and puree until smooth.
4. Pour the pancake batter into the prepared pan and stir in the bell pepper.

5. Place in the air fryer.
6. Cook for 9 minutes or until the pancake is puffed and the top is golden brown.
7. Slice and serve with keto, sugar free syrup!

NUTRITION: Calories 189, Total Fat 16g, Saturated Fat 8g, Total Carbs 12g, Net Carbs 7g, Protein 9g, Sugar 3g, Fiber 5g, Sodium 125mg, Potassium 111g

24. Sausage Omelette

Preparation time: 5 minutes • Cook time:11 minutes • Servings: 4

INGREDIENTS

- 4 eggs
- 3 Tbsp heavy whipping cream
- ¼ cup cheddar cheese, grated
- ½ cup cooked, chopped sausage
- ½ tsp salt
- ¼ tsp ground black pepper

DIRECTIONS:

1. Preheat your air fryer to 350 degrees F and line a baking pan with parchment paper. Be sure the pan will fit in your air fryer- typically a seven inch round pan will work perfectly.
2. In a small bowl, whisk together the eggs, cream, salt and pepper. Stir in the sausage.
3. Pour the mix into the prepared baking pan and then place the pan in your preheated air fryer.
4. Cook for about 10 minutes or until the eggs are completely set.
5. Sprinkle the cheese across the cooked eggs and return the pan to the air fryer for another minute to melt the cheese.
6. Fold the omelet in half.
7. Slice into wedges and serve while hot.

NUTRITION: Calories 210, Total Fat 22g, Saturated Fat 14g, Total Carbs 6g, Net Carbs 3g, Protein 7g, Sugar 1g, Fiber 3g, Sodium 863mg, Potassium 125g

25. Ham and Cheese Omelet

Preparation time: 5 minutes • Cook time:11 minutes • Servings: 4

INGREDIENTS

- 4 eggs
- 3 Tbsp heavy whipping cream
- ¼ cup cheddar cheese, grated

- ½ cup chopped, cooked ham
- ½ tsp salt
- ¼ tsp ground black pepper

DIRECTIONS:

1. Preheat your air fryer to 350 degrees F and line a baking pan with parchment paper. Be sure the pan will fit in your air fryer- typically a seven inch round pan will work perfectly.
2. In a small bowl, whisk together the eggs, cream, salt and pepper. Stir in the ham.
3. Pour the mix into the prepared baking pan and then place the pan in your preheated air fryer.
4. Cook for about 10 minutes or until the eggs are completely set.
5. Sprinkle the cheese across the cooked eggs and return the pan to the air fryer for another minute to melt the cheese.
6. Fold the omelet in half.
7. Slice into wedges and serve while hot.

NUTRITION: Calories 218, Total Fat 19g, Saturated Fat 9g, Total Carbs 6g, Net Carbs 2g, Protein 7g, Sugar 1g, Fiber 4g, Sodium 890mg, Potassium 343g

26. Air fried Cheese Sandwich

Preparation Time: 13 Minutes • Servings: 2

INGREDIENTS

- Bread slices-4
- Butter softened -4 tsp.
- Cheddar cheese slices -4

DIRECTIONS

1. Layer the top of bread slices with butter.
2. Place two cheese slices each on 2 slices of bread.
3. Cover it with remaining two slices of bread then cut in half diagonally.
4. Place the sandwiches in the Air fryer basket and seal it.
5. Cook for 8 minutes at 370 o F on Air fryer mode.
6. Serve fresh.

NUTRITION: Calories: 200, Fat: 3g, Fiber: 5g, Carbs: 12g, Protein: 4g

27. Green Beans Egg Bake

Preparation Time: 15 Minutes • Servings: 4

INGREDIENTS

- Eggs, whisked-4
- Soy sauce -1 tbsp.
- Olive oil-1 tbsp.

- Garlic cloves, minced-4
- Green beans, trimmed and halved-3 ounces
- Salt and black pepper -to taste

DIRECTIONS

1. Whisk everything in a bowl except oil and beans.
2. Let your Air fryer preheat and grease its pan with oil.
3. Add beans to the pan and sauté for 3 minutes.
4. Pour the prepared mixture over then seal the Fryer.
5. Cook for 8 minutes at the same temperature on Air fryer mode.
6. Slice and serve to enjoy.

NUTRITION: Calories: 212, Fat: 8g, Fiber: 6g, Carbs: 8g, Protein: 6g

28. Cod Corn Burritos

Preparation Time: 27 Minutes • Servings: 4

INGREDIENTS

- Tortillas -4
- Olive oil- a drizzle
- Green bell pepper, chopped-1
- Red onion, chopped -1
- Corn -1 cup
- Cod fillets, skinless and boneless -4
- Salsa -½ cup
- Baby spinach - a handful
- Parmesan cheese, grated -4 tbsp.

DIRECTIONS

1. Place the fish in the Air fryer's basket.
2. Secure the Fryer and cook for 6 minutes at 350 o F on Air fryer mode.
3. Meanwhile, preheat a pan with oil and sauté bell peppers, corn, and onions in it.
4. After 5 minutes put off the heat.
5. Spread the tortillas on a working surface then divide the fish, salsa, spinach, sautéed veggies and parmesan over each tortilla.
6. Roll them into a burrito then place them in the Air fryer basket.
7. Seal it and cook for 6 minutes at 350 o F on Air fryer mode.
8. Serve warm.

NUTRITION: Calories: 230, Fat: 12g, Fiber: 7g, Carbs: 14g, Protein: 5g

29. Cheese and Ham Pockets

Preparation Time: 20 Minutes • Servings: 4

INGREDIENTS

- Puff pastry sheet -1
- Mozzarella cheese, grated -4 handfuls

- Mustard -4 tsp.
- Ham slices, chopped-8

DIRECTIONS

1. Spread the puff pastry on a working surface and slice it into 12 squares.
2. Top the half of the pieces with an equal amount of cheese, mustard, and ham.
3. Place the remaining halves on top and seal their edges.
4. Place these pockets in the Air fryer's basket then seal the Fryer.
5. Cook for 10 minutes at 370 o F on Air fryer mode.
6. Serve warm and fresh.

NUTRITION: Calories: 212, Fat: 12g, Fiber: 7g, Carbs: 14g, Protein: 8g

30. Tuna Mayo Sandwiches

Preparation Time: 14 Minutes • Servings: 4

INGREDIENTS

- Canned tuna, drained-16 ounces
- Mayonnaise -¼ cup
- Mustard -2 tbsp.
- Lime juice -1 tbsp.
- Spring onions, chopped -2
- Bread slices -6
- Butter, melted-3 tbsp.
- Provolone cheese slices -6

DIRECTIONS

1. Toss tuna with lime juice, mayo, spring onions and mustard in a bowl.
2. Layer the bread slices with butter then place them in the Air fryer basket.
3. Seal the fryer and cook for 5 minutes at 350 o F on Air fryer.
4. Top the half of the bread slices with tuna mixture and cheese.
5. Place the remaining slices on top and place the sandwich in the Air fryer basket.
6. Seal the fryer and cook for 4 minutes at Air fryer mode at 350 o F.
7. Serve warm.

NUTRITION: Calories: 212, Fat: 8g, Fiber: 7g, Carbs: 8g, Protein: 6g

31. Mint & Peas Omelet

Preparation Time: 15 Minutes • Servings: 8

INGREDIENTS

- Baby peas-½ pound
- Avocado oil-3 tbsp.
- Yogurt -1½ cups

- Eggs, whisked-8
- Mint, chopped -½ cup
- Salt and black pepper -to taste

DIRECTIONS

1. Add oil to a pan, suitable to fit the Air fryer and place it over medium heat.
2. Add peas and sauté for 4 minutes.
3. Whisk yogurt with mint, eggs, pepper, and salt in a bowl.
4. Add the mixture over the peas and toss well.
5. Place this pea pan in the Air fryer and seal the fryer.
6. Cook for 7 minutes at 350 o F on Air fryer mode.
7. Slice and serve.

NUTRITION: Calories: 212, Fat: 9g, Fiber: 4g, Carbs: 13g, Protein: 7g

32. Vanilla Steel Cut Oats

Preparation Time: 22 Minutes • Servings: 4

INGREDIENTS

- Milk -1 cup
- Steel cut oats -1 cup
- Water -2½ cups
- Brown sugar -2 tbsp.
- Vanilla extract -2 tsp.

DIRECTIONS

1. Take a pan, suitable to fit the Air Fryer.
2. Add everything to this pan and mix well.
3. Place this pan in the Air fryer and seal it.
4. Cook for 17 minutes at 360 o F on Air fryer mode.
5. Serve fresh.
6. Enjoy!

NUTRITION: Calories: 161, Fat: 7g, Fiber: 6g, Carbs: 9g, Protein: 6g

33. Pear Cinnamon Oatmeal

Preparation Time:
17 Minutes •
Servings: 4

INGREDIENTS

- Milk -1 cup
- Butter, softened -1 tbsp.
- Brown sugar -¼ cups
- Cinnamon powder -½ tbsp.
- Old fashioned oats -1 cup
- Walnuts, chopped-½ cup
- Pear, peeled and chopped-2 cups

DIRECTIONS

1. Take a pan, suitable to fit the Air Fryer.
2. Add everything to the pan and mix well.
3. Place this pan in the Air fryer and seal it.
4. Cook for 12 minutes at 360 o F on Air fryer mode.
5. Serve right away.

NUTRITION: Calories: 210, Fat: 9g, Fiber: 11g, Carbs: 12g, Protein: 5g

34. Maple Rice Pudding

Preparation Time: 25 Minutes • Servings: 4

INGREDIENTS

- Brown rice-1 cup
- Coconut, shredded-½ cup
- Almond milk-3 cups
- Maple syrup -½ cup
- Almonds, chopped -½ cup

DIRECTIONS

1. Add rice to a pan, suitable to the Air Fryer.
2. Stir in remaining things and toss them well.
3. Place this pan in the Air fryer basket and seal it.
4. Cook at 360 o F for 20 minutes on Air fryer mode.
5. Serve right away.

NUTRITION: Calories: 201, Fat: 6, Fiber: 8, Carbs: 19, Protein: 6

35. Squash Mushroom Mix

Preparation Time: 15 Minutes • Servings: 4

INGREDIENTS

- Red bell pepper, roughly chopped-1
- White mushrooms, sliced-1 cup
- Yellow squash, cubed -1
- Green onions, sliced-2
- Butter, softened-2 tbsp.
- Feta cheese, crumbled-½ cup

DIRECTIONS

1. Add everything to a bowl except feta cheese.
2. Spread this mixture in the Air fryer pan then seal it.
3. Cook for 10 minutes at 350 o F on Air fryer mode.
4. Garnish with feta cheese.
5. Serve fresh.

NUTRITION: Calories: 202, Fat: 12g, Fiber: 4g, Carbs: 7g, Protein: 2g

36. Tarragon Cheese Omelet

Preparation Time: 20 Minutes • Servings: 4

INGREDIENTS

- Eggs, whisked-6
- Parsley, a chopped-1 tbsp.
- Tarragon, chopped -1 tbsp.
- Chives, chopped-2 tbsp.
- Salt and black pepper -to taste
- Parmesan cheese, grated-2 tbsp.
- Heavy cream-4 tbsp.

DIRECTIONS

1. Mix everything in a b owl except parmesan.
2. Add this mixture to a pan, suitable to fit in the Air fryer basket.
3. Seal it and cook for 15 minutes at 350 o F on Air fryer mode.
4. Slice and serve with parmesan cheese on top.
5. Enjoy.

NUTRITION: Calories: 251, Fat: 8g, Fiber: 4g, Carbs: 15g, Protein: 4g

37. Zucchini Chicken Burritos

Preparation Time: 12 Minutes • Servings: 4

INGREDIENTS

- Tortillas -4
- Butter softened -4 tbsp.
- Rotisserie chicken, cooked and shredded- 6 ounces
- Zucchini, shredded-1 cup
- Mayonnaise-⅓ cup
- Mustard -2 tbsp.
- Parmesan cheese, grated-1 cup

DIRECTIONS

1. Layer the tortillas with butter then place then in the Air fryer's basket.
2. Seal it and cook for 3 minutes at 400 o F on Air fryer mode.
3. Toss chicken with mustard, mayo, and zucchini in a bowl.
4. Divide this prepared mixture in the tortillas and top them with cheese.
5. Roll each tortilla and place them in the Air fryer basket.
6. Seal it and cook for 4 minutes at 400 o F on Air fryer mode.
7. Serve.

NUTRITION: Calories: 212, Fat: 8g, Fiber: 8g, Carbs: 9g, Protein: 4g

38. Kale & Pumpkin Seeds Sandwich

Preparation Time: 11 Minutes • Servings: 1

INGREDIENTS

- Olive oil-1 tbsp.
- Kale, torn-2 cups
- Salt and black pepper - a pinch

- Pumpkin seeds-2 tbsp.
- Small shallot, chopped-1
- Mayonnaise-1½ tbsp.
- Avocado slice -1
- English muffin, halved-1

DIRECTIONS

1. Let you Air fryer preheat at 360 o F with its pan greased with oil.
2. Add salt, pepper, kale, shallots and pumpkin seeds.
3. Toss well then seal the fryer and cook for 6 minutes at Air fryer mode.
4. Shake it well once cooked half way through.
5. Layer the English muffin halves with mayo.
6. Top the half of them with avocado slice and kale mixture.
7. Place the remaining muffin halves on top.
8. Serve fresh.

NUTRITION: Calories: 162, Fat: 4g, Fiber: 7g, Carbs: 9g, Protein: 4g

39. Apple Cinnamon Pancakes

Preparation Time: 30 Minutes • Servings: 4

INGREDIENTS

- White flour-1¾ cups
- Sugar-2 tbsp.
- Baking powder-2 tsp.
- Vanilla extract -¼ tbsp.
- Cinnamon powder-2 tsp.
- Milk -1¼ cups
- Egg whisked -1
- Apple, peeled, cored and chopped-1 cup
- Cooking spray

DIRECTIONS

1. Mix everything in a bowl except cooking spray.
2. Grease the Air fryer's pan with cooking spray.
3. Pour ¼ of the batter in the Air fryer pan and place it in the Fryer.
4. Seal it and cook for 5 minutes at 360 o F.
5. Once cooked half way through then flip it.
6. Cook the remaining pancakes following the same steps.
7. Serve fresh.

NUTRITION: Calories: 172, Fat: 4g, Fiber: 4g, Carbs: 8g, Protein: 3g

40. Romanesco Tofu Quinoa

Preparation Time: 25 Minutes • Servings: 4

INGREDIENTS

- Firm tofu, cubed-12 ounces
- Maple syrup-3 tbsp.
- Soy sauce-¼ cup

- Olive oil -2 tbsp.
- Lime juice -2 tbsp.
- Fresh Romanesco, torn-1 pound
- Carrots, chopped-3
- Red bell pepper, chopped-1
- Baby spinach, torn-8 ounces
- Red quinoa, cooked-2 cups

DIRECTIONS

1. Toss tofu with maple syrup, oil, lime juice and soy sauce in a bowl.
2. Add this tofu to the Air fryer basket and seal it.
3. Cook for 15 minutes at 370 o F on Air fryer mode.
4. Shake it halfway through.
5. Once done, add the tofu to a bowl.
6. Add carrots, Romanesco, quinoa, bell pepper and spinach.
7. Mix well then serve.
8. Enjoy.

NUTRITION: Calories: 209, Fat: 7g, Fiber: 6g, Carbs: 8g, Protein: 4g

41. Black Bean Cheese Burritos

Preparation Time: 19 Minutes • Servings: 2

INGREDIENTS

- Canned black beans, drained-2 cups
- Olive oil- a drizzle
- Red bell pepper, sliced -½
- Small avocado, peeled, pitted and sliced- 1
- Mild salsa -2 tbsp.
- Salt and black pepper- to taste
- Mozzarella cheese, shredded- ⅛ cup
- Tortillas -2

DIRECTIONS

1. Grease your Air fryer pan with oil.
2. Add beans, salsa, salt, pepper, and bell peppers.
3. Seal the fryer and cook for 6minutes at 400 o F on Air fryer mode.
4. Spread the tortillas on the working surface then divide the beans mixture on top.
5. Add avocado and cheese, then roll the burritos.
6. Place the burritos in the Air fryer basket and seal the fryer.
7. Cook for 3 minutes at 300 o F on Air fryer mode.
8. Serve.

NUTRITION: Calories: 189, Fat: 3g, Fiber: 7g, Carbs: 12g, Protein: 5g

42. Mushroom Tofu Casserole

Preparation Time: 35 Minutes • Servings: 2

INGREDIENTS

- Yellow onion, chopped -1

- Garlic, minced-1 tbsp.
- Olive oil-1 tbsp.
- Carrot, chopped -1
- Celery stalks, chopped-2
- White mushrooms, chopped-½ cup
- Red bell pepper, chopped -½ cup
- Salt and black pepper- to taste
- Oregano, a dried-1 tbsp.
- Cumin, a ground-½ tbsp.
- Firm tofu, cubed-7 ounces
- Lemon juice -1 tbsp.
- Water -2 tbsp.
- Quinoa, already cooked-½ cup
- Cheddar cheese, grated-2 tbsp.

DIRECTIONS

1. Choose a pan and grease it with oil. Place it over medium heat.
2. Add onion and garlic. Sauté for 3 minutes.
3. Stir in celery, carrots, bell peppers, salt, mushrooms, pepper, cumin, and oregano.
4. Sauté for 6 minutes then take it off the heat.
5. Add tofu to the food processor along with cheese, quinoa, water, and lemon juice.
6. Blend until it is smooth then add this mixture to the sautéed veggies.
7. Mix well then add these veggies to the Air fryer pan.
8. Seal the Air fryer and cook for 15 minutes at 350 o F on Air fryer mode.
9. Serve warm.

NUTRITION: Calories: 230, Fat: 11g, Fiber: 7g, Carbs: 14g, Protein: 5g

43. Cinnamon Yam Pudding

Preparation Time: 13 Minutes Servings: 4

INGREDIENTS

- Canned candied yams, drained-16 ounces
- Cinnamon powder-½ tbsp.
- Allspice, a ground-¼ tbsp.
- Coconut sugar -½ cup
- Eggs, whisked-2
- Heavy cream -2 tbsp.
- Maple syrup-½ cup
- Cooking spray

DIRECTIONS

1. Toss yams with allspice and cinnamon in a bowl.
2. Mash them with a fork and keep it aside.
3. Grease the Air fryer pan with pan and preheat it at 400 o F.
4. Spread the yams mixture at the bottom of the pan.
5. Whisk eggs with maple syrup, and cream in a separate bowl.
6. Pour this mixture over the yams layer.

7. Seal the fryer and cook for 8 minutes at 400 o F on Air fryer mode.
8. Serve fresh.

NUTRITION: Calories: 251, Fat: 11g, Fiber: 7g, Carbs: 9g, Protein: 5g

44. Tangy Cauliflower Hash

Preparation Time: 25 Minutes • Servings: 4

INGREDIENTS

- Cauliflower head stems discarded, florets separated and steamed -1
- Olive oil -2 tbsp.
- Salt and black pepper -to taste
- Hot paprika -1 tbsp.
- Sour cream -4 ounces

DIRECTIONS

1. Add everything to a pan, suitable to fit the Air Fryer.
2. Place this pan in the Air fryer basket then seal it.
3. Cook at 360 o F for 20 minutes on Air fryer mode.
4. Serve warm.

NUTRITION: Calories: 150, Fat: 3g, Fiber: 2g, Carbs: 10g, Protein: 3g

45. Nutmeg Mushroom Fritters

Preparation Time: 2hrs. 11 Minutes • Servings: 8

INGREDIENTS

- Mushrooms, chopped -4 ounces
- Red onion, chopped-1
- Salt and black pepper -to taste
- Nutmeg, a ground-¼ tbsp.
- Olive oil- 2 tbsp
- Panko breadcrumbs -1 tbsp.
- Milk -10 ounces

DIRECTIONS

1. Add 1 tbsp oil to a suitable pan and place it over medium-high heat.
2. Stir in mushrooms and onions, sauté for 3 minutes.
3. Add nutmeg, pepper, salt, and milk.
4. Take it off the heat and keep it aside for 2 hours.
5. Mix remaining oil with breadcrumbs in a separate plate.
6. Take a tbsp of the mushroom mixture and roll it.

7. Coat this ball with breadcrumbs mixture then flatten it.
8. Place it in the Air fryer basket.
9. Repeat the same steps and place the fritters in the basket.
10. Seal it and cook for 8 minutes at 400 o F on Air fryer mode.
11. Serve warm.

NUTRITION: Calories: 202, Fat: 8g, Fiber: 1g, Carbs: 11g, Protein: 6g

46. Tofu & Bell Peppers Medley

Preparation Time: 15 Minutes • Servings: 8

INGREDIENTS

- Yellow bell pepper, cut into strips-1
- Orange bell pepper, cut into strips -1
- Green bell pepper, cut into strips -1
- Salt and black pepper -to taste
- Firm tofu, crumbled-3 ounces
- Green onion, chopped-1
- Parsley, chopped-2 tbsp.

DIRECTIONS

1. Take a pan, suitable to fit your Air fryer.
2. Add bell pepper strips along with remaining things.
3. Toss well then place the pan in the Air fryer basket.
4. Seal it and cook for 10 minutes at 400 o F on Air fryer mode.
5. Serve warm.

NUTRITION: Calories: 135, Fat: 2g, Fiber: 2g, Carbs: 8g, Protein: 3g

47. Stuffed Feta Cheese Peppers

Preparation Time: 13 Minutes • Servings: 8

INGREDIENTS

- Small bell peppers, tops cut off and seeds removed-8
- Avocado oil -1 tbsp.
- Salt and black pepper -to taste
- Feta cheese, cubed-3½ ounces

DIRECTIONS

1. Toss cheese with oil, salt, and pepper in a bowl.
2. Stuff the peppers with cheese mixture then place these peppers in the Air fryer basket.
3. Seal the fryer and cook for 8 minutes at 400 o F on Air fryer mode.
4. Serve warm.

NUTRITION: Calories: 210, Fat: 2g, Fiber: 1g, Carbs: 6g, Protein: 5g

48. Citrus Pepper Salad

Preparation Time: 15 Minutes • Servings: 4

INGREDIENTS

- Lime juice -1 tbsp.
- Red bell peppers-4
- Lettuce head, torn-1
- Salt and black pepper- to taste
- Heavy cream-3 tbsp.
- Olive oil -2 tbsp.
- Rocket leaves -2 ounces

DIRECTIONS

1. Add bell peppers to the Air fryer's basket and seal it.
2. Cook at 400 o F on Air fryer mode for 10 minutes.
3. Remove the peppers from the Fryer.
4. Peel them and slice them into strips.
5. Toss the peppers with remaining things in a bowl.
6. Enjoy fresh.

NUTRITION: Calories: 200, Fat: 5g, Fiber: 3g, Carbs: 7g, Protein: 6g

49. Spinach Egg Pie

Preparation Time: 34 Minutes • Servings: 4

INGREDIENTS

- White flour-7 ounces
- Spinach, torn-7 ounces
- Olive oil-2 tbsp.
- Eggs whisked -2
- Milk-2 tbsp.
- Mozzarella cheese, crumbled-3 ounces
- Salt and black pepper -to taste
- Red onion, chopped -1

DIRECTIONS

1. Add flour, eggs, milk, pepper, salt and 1 tbsp oil to a food processor.
2. Blend well to form a dough then knead it.
3. Place the dough in a bowl and cover it. Refrigerate for 10 minutes.
4. Add 1 tbsp oil to a suitable pan and place it over medium heat.
5. Stir in remaining things and sauté for 4 minutes then take it off the heat.
6. Divide the dough into 4 pieces and spread each into a circle.
7. Place one dough circle in a ramekin.
8. Divide the prepared spinach mixture in the ramekin.

9. Place the ramekins in the Air fryer's basket and seal it.
10. Cook for 15 minutes on Air fryer mode at 350 o F.

NUTRITION: Calories: 200, Fat: 12g, Fiber: 2g, Carbs: 13g, Protein: 5g

50. Eggplant & Zucchini Mix

Preparation Time: 55 Minutes • Servings: 4

INGREDIENTS

- Eggplant, sliced-8 ounces
- Zucchini, sliced-8 ounces
- Bell peppers, chopped -8 ounces
- Garlic cloves, minced-2
- Olive oil-5 tbsp.
- Yellow onions, chopped-2
- Tomatoes, cut into quarters -8 ounces
- Salt and black pepper -to taste

DIRECTIONS

1. Add 1 tbsp oil to a pan, suitable to fit the Air fryer and place it over medium heat.
2. Stir in eggplant, pepper and salt. Sauté for 5 minutes.
3. Keep it aside in a bowl.
4. Add 1 tbsp oil more to the pan then add bell peppers and zucchini.
5. Stir cook for 4 minutes then add them to the sautéed eggplant.
6. Now add the remaining of the oil to the same pan and stir in onions.
7. Sauté for 3 minutes then add garlic, tomatoes, salt, and pepper.
8. Place this mixture along with all the sautéed veggie to the Air fryer pan.
9. Seal it and cook for 30 minutes at 300 o F on Air fryer mode.
10. Serve warm.

NUTRITION: Calories: 210, Fat: 1g, Fiber: 3g, Carbs: 14g, Protein: 6g

CHAPTER 2

MAINS

51. Cedar Planked Salmon

Cooking Time: 15 minutes • Servings: 6

INGREDIENTS

- 4untreated cedar planks
- ½ cup olive oil
- 1½ tablespoons of rice vinegar
- 1teaspoon sesame oil
- 2lbs. of salmon fillets, skin removed
- 1teaspoon garlic, minced
- 1tablespoon ginger root, fresh, grated
- ¼ cup green onions, chopped
- ½ cup soy sauce

DIRECTIONS

1. Start by soaking the cedar planks for 2- hours. Take a shallow baking dish and stir in the olive oil, the rice vinegar, the sesame oil, soy sauce, ginger, and green onions. Place the salmon fillets in the prepared marinade for at least 20- minutes. Place the planks in the basket of your air fryer. Cook the salmon fillets for 15-minutes at 360°Fahrenheit.

NUTRITION: Calories: 273, Total Fat: 7.5g, Carbs: 5.2g, Protein: 34.2g

52. Crested Halibut

Cooking Time: 30 minutes Servings: 4

INGREDIENTS

- 4halibut fillets
- ¾ cup of pork rinds
- ½ cup of parsley, fresh, chopped
- ¼ cup dill, fresh, chopped
- ¼ cup chives, fresh, chopped
- 1tablespoon olive oil
- 1teaspoon lemon zest, finely grated
- Sea salt and black pepper to taste

DIRECTIONS

1. Preheat your air fryer to 390°Fahrenheit. In a mixing bowl, combine the pork rinds, parsley, dill, chives, olive oil, lemon zest, sea salt and black pepper. Rinse the halibut fillets and dry them on a paper towel. Arrange the halibut fillets and dry them on a paper towel.

Arrange the halibut fillets onto a baking sheet. Spoon the pork rind crumb mixture onto fish fillets. Lightly press the mixture on the fillets. Bake the fillets in your preheated air fryer basket for 30- minutes. Serve warm.

NUTRITION: Calories: 272, Total Fat: 10.3g, Carbs: 9.4g, Protein: 32.2g

53. Creamy Halibut

Cooking Time: 20 minutes • Servings: 6

INGREDIENTS

- 2lbs. of halibut fillets, cut into 6 pieces
- 1teaspoon dill weed, dried
- ½ cup light sour cream
- ½ cup light mayonnaise
- 4chopped green onions

DIRECTIONS

1. Preheat the air fryer to 390°Fahrenheit. Season the halibut with salt and pepper. In a bowl, mix the onions, sour cream, mayonnaise, and dill. Spread the onion mixture evenly over the halibut fillets. Cook in air fryer for 20- minutes. Serve warm.

NUTRITION: Calories: 286, Total Fat: 11.3g, Carbs: 6.9, Protein: 29.8g

54. Air Fried Catfish

Cooking Time: 20 minutes Servings: 2

INGREDIENTS

- 5catfish filets
- 1pinch of salt
- 1teaspoon garlic powder
- 1teaspoon crab seasoning
- 1cup almond flour
- 2tablespoons olive oil for spraying
- 2tablespoons hot sauce
- 1cup buttermilk
- Black pepper as needed

DIRECTIONS

1. Season catfish fillets on both sides with salt and pepper. In a dish, combine the buttermilk with hot sauce. Add the catfish fillets and cover them with liquid. Let the ingredients soak while you prepare the rest of the ingredients. Whisk the flour, crab seasoning, and garlic powder in a casserole dish. Remove the catfish from the buttermilk and allow excess liquid to drip off. Dredge the

catfish on both sides in the flour mixture. Place fillets into air fryer and drizzle with oil. Cook at 390°Fahrenheit for 15-minutes. When cooking is completed remove basket and gently turn the fillets over, spray some oil on them, and cook for an additional 5-minutes.

NUTRITION: Calories: 283, Total Fat: 8.6g, Carbs: 6.5g, Protein: 34.3g

55. Air Fried Spinach Fish

Cooking Time: 12 minutes • Servings: 2

INGREDIENTS

- 4ounces of spinach leaves
- 1large egg, beaten
- 2tablespoons olive oil
- 2cups almond flour
- 2white fish fillets
- Pinch of sea salt
- Black pepper to taste

DIRECTIONS

1. In a deep bowl, place the beaten egg, almond flour, sea salt, black pepper, and spinach leaves. Marinate the fish for 2- hours in the fridge. Transfer the fish to air fryer and cook for 12-minutes at 370°Fahrenheit. Serve with lemon slices.

NUTRITION: Calories: 286, Total Fat: 11.2g, Carbs: 5.2g, Protein: 29.7g

56. Roly Poly Air Fried White Fish

Cooking Time: 10 minutes • Servings: 4

INGREDIENTS

- 4lbs. of white fish fillets
- 2½ teaspoons of sea salt
- 4mushrooms, sliced
- 1teaspoon liquid stevia
- 2tablespoons of Chinese winter pickle
- 2tablespoons of vinegar
- 2teaspoons chili powder
- 2onions, thinly sliced
- 1cup vegetable stock
- 2tablespoons soy sauce

DIRECTIONS

1. Fill the fish fillets with mushrooms and pickle. Cut the onions into thinly sliced pieces. Spread the onions over the fish

fillets. Combine the stock, soy sauce, vinegar, sea salt, and stevia. Sprinkle the mixture over the fish fillets. Place the fish fillets into your air fryer and cook at 350°Fahrenheit for 10-minutes. Serve warm.

NUTRITION: Calories: 278, Total Fat: 9.2g, Carbs: 7.4g, Protein: 33.2g

57. Air Fried Dragon Shrimp

Cooking Time: 15 minutes Servings: 2

INGREDIENTS

- ½ lb. shrimp
- ¼ cup almond flour
- Pinch of ginger
- 1cup chopped green onions
- 2tablespoons olive oil
- 2eggs, beaten
- ½ cup soy sauce

DIRECTIONS

1. Boil the shrimps for 5-minutes. Prepare a paste made of ginger and onion. Now, beat the eggs, add the ginger paste, soya sauce and almond flour and combine well. Add the shrimps to the mixture then place them in a baking dish and spray with oil. Cook shrimps at 390°Fahrenheit for 10-minutes.

NUTRITION: Calories: 278, Total Fat: 8.6g, Carbs: 6.2g, Protein: 28.6g

58. Lasagna Zucchini Cups

Cooking Time: 25 minutes • Servings: 6

INGREDIENTS

- Chopped parsley, for garnish
- ¼ cup parmesan, freshly grated
- ½ cup mozzarella, shredded
- ½ cup ricotta
- 1-14.5-ounce can of crushed tomatoes
- Black pepper and salt to taste
- ½ teaspoon oregano, dried
- ½ lb. ground beef
- 2garlic cloves, minced
- ½ onion, chopped
- 1tablespoon olive oil
- 3zucchinis

DIRECTIONS

1. n a large pan over medium heat, add the

oil. Add onion and garlic and cook for 5- minutes. Add in the ground beef and cook for 10-minutes stirring often. Season with oregano, salt, pepper, cook until meat is no longer pink. Add crushed tomatoes and simmer mixture for 5-minutes. Stir in the ricotta and remove from heat. Cut zucchini in half crosswise in two. Using a spoon scoop out zucchini flesh to create wells. Fill wells with meat mixture. Top with mozzarella and parmesan cheese. Place directly in air fryer and cook at 350°Fahrenheit for 15-minutes. Garnish with parsley and parmesan.

59. Spinach Artichoke Stuffed Peppers

Cooking Time: 15 minutes • Servings: 4

INGREDIENTS

- 4assorted bell peppers,
- halved and seeded
- Salt and black pepper to taste
- Olive oil for drizzling
- 2cups shredded rotisserie chicken
- Fresh parsley, chopped for garnish
- 2cloves garlic, minced
- ¼ cup mayonnaise
- ¼ cup sour cream
- ½ cup mozzarella, shredded, divided
- 6-ounces cream cheese, softened
- 1(10-ouncepackage frozen spinach, thawed, well-drained, and chopped
- 1(14-ouncecan artichoke hearts, drained and chopped

DIRECTIONS

1. On a large, rimmed baking sheet, place bell peppers cut side-up and drizzle with olive oil, then season with salt and pepper. In a large bowl, combine chicken, artichoke hearts, spinach, cream cheese, ½ cup mozzarella, parmesan, sour cream, mayo and garlic. Season with more salt and pepper and mix until well blended. Divide the chicken mixture between pepper halves, top with remaining mozzarella, and bake in air fryer at 400°Fahrenheit for 15- minutes. Garnish with parsley and serve.

NUTRITION: Calories: 284, Total Fat: 13.4g, Carbs: 9.2g, Protein: 34.3g

60. Cauliflower Shepherd's Pie

Cooking Time: 43 minutes • Servings: 4

INGREDIENTS

- 1medium head of cauliflower, cut into florets
- ¼ cup whole milk
- 3-ounces cream cheese, softened
- 1tablespoon parsley, chopped for garnish
- 2/3 cup chicken broth
- 2tablespoons almond flour
- 1cup frozen peas
- 1lb. ground beef
- 2cloves garlic, minced
- 2carrots, peeled, and chopped
- 1large onion, chopped
- 1tablespoon olive oil
- Salt and black pepper to taste

DIRECTIONS:

1. Make mashed cauliflower. Bring a pot of water to boil, add the florets and cook for 10-minutes. Drain pot and then use paper towel to absorb excess water. Return florets to pot and mash with potato masher until smooth. Stir in cream cheese, milk and season with salt and pepper. Set aside. Make the beef mixture: in large pan over medium heat, heat oil. Add onion, garlic and cook for 5- minutes.
2. Add ground beef for 5- minutes or until meat is no longer pink. Stir in frozen peas and corn and cook another 3- minutes. Sprinkle meat mixture with almond flour and stir to even distribute. Cook for another minute then add chicken broth. Bring to a simmer and let mixture thicken slightly, for 5- minutes. Place beef mixture in air fryer baking dish. Top beef mixture with an even layer of cauliflower and bake in air fryer at 400°Fahrenheit for 15- minutes. Garnish with parsley and serve.

NUTRITION: Calories: 279, Total Fat: 13.2g, Carbs: 10.2g, Protein: 34.2g

61. Coconut Lime Skirt Steak

Cooking Time: 5 minutes • Servings: 2

INGREDIENTS

- ½ cup coconut oil, melted
- Zest of one lime

- 2-1lb. grass fed skirt steaks
- ¾ teaspoon sea salt
- 1teaspoon red pepper flakes
- 1teaspoon ginger, fresh, grated
- 1tablespoon garlic, minced
- 2tablespoons freshly squeezed lime juice

DIRECTIONS

1. In a mixing bowl, combine lime juice, coconut oil, garlic, ginger, red pepper, salt, and zest. Add the steaks and toss and rub with marinade. Allow the meat to marinate for about 20-minutes at room temperature. Transfer steaks to your air fryer directly on the rack. Cook steaks in air fryer at 400°Fahrenhet for 5-minutes.

NUTRITION: Calories: 312, Total Fat: 12.3g, Carbs: 6.4g, Protein: 42.1g

62. Spicy Chicken Enchilada Casserole

Cooking Time: 40 minutes • Servings: 2

INGREDIENTS

- 1lb. of chicken breasts, skinless and boneless
- Salt and pepper to taste
- ½ cup cilantro, fresh, minced
- Olive oil spray
- 2cups cheddar cheese, shredded
- Lime wedges (optional
- Sour cream (optional
- 1(4-ouncecan of green chilies, chopped
- 1cup feta cheese, finely crumbled
- 1½ cup enchilada sauce

DIRECTIONS

1. Pat the chicken breasts dry and season with salt and pepper. Combine the chicken and enchilada sauce in a pan and simmer for 15-minutes over medium-low heat. Flip chicken over and cover and cook for an additional 15-minutes. Remove the chicken from pan and shred into bite-size pieces. Combine shredded chicken, feta cheese, enchilada sauce, chiles, and cilantro in a bowl. Add salt and pepper. Spray the air fryer basking dish with olive oil. Coat the entire bottom and sides. Evenly spread a cup of shredded cheese on the bottom of baking dish.

Add the chicken mixture, then add another cup of cheese on top. Bake in your air fryer at 350°Fahrenheit for 10-minutes. Serve with optional lime wedges and sour cream.

NUTRITION: Calories: 338, Total Fat: 12.3g, Carbs: 8.3g, Protein: 32.2g

63. Kale & Ground Beef Casserole

Cooking Time: 16 minutes • Servings: 4

INGREDIENTS

- 4-ounces mozzarella, shredded
- 2cups marinara sauce
- 10-ounces kale, fresh
- 1teaspoon oregano
- 1teaspoon onion powder
- ½ teaspoon sea salt
- 1lb. lean ground beef
- 2tablespoons olive oil

DIRECTIONS

1. in a deep skillet, heat the olive oil for 2- minutes, add in the ground beef and cook for an additional 8-minutes or until meat is browned. stir in salt, pepper, garlic powder, onion powder and oregano. in batches, stir the kale into beef mixture, cooking for another 2-minutes. stir in the marinara sauce and cook for 2-minutes more. mix in half the cheese into mixture. transfer mixture into the air fryer baking dish. sprinkle the remaining cheese on top. broil in air fryer at 400°fahrenheit for 2-minutes. allow to rest for 5-minutes before serving.

NUTRITION: Calories: 312, Total Fat: 13.2, Carbs: 9.2g, Protein: 43.2g

64. Cauliflower-Cottage Pie

Cooking Time: 40 minutes • Servings: 4

INGREDIENTS

- Half a cup of bacon bits
- 2cups cauliflower rice
- ¼ cup tomato puree
- 1tablespoon coconut oil
- ½ white onion, chopped
- 2lbs. lean ground beef
- 1tablespoon mixed spice blend

DIRECTIONS

1. In the frying pan add coconut oil and onions cook for 2-minutes. Add the ground beef into pan and cook for an additional 5-minutes or until meat is browned. Add spices and stir to combine. Add the tomato puree and mix well and cook for another 10-minutes. Transfer to air fryer baking dish. Top with cauliflower rice and bacon bits. Bake in air fryer at 350°Fahrenheit for 20-minutes. Serve warm.

NUTRITION: Calories: 367, Total Fat: 13.4g, Carbs: 11.2g, Protein: 43.1g

65. Roasted Asian Shrimp & Brussels Sprouts

Cooking Time: 19 minutes • Servings: 4

INGREDIENTS

- 1lb. jumbo frozen shrimp, thawed and drained
- 1lb. brussels sprouts
- 2tablespoons olive oil
- Salt and pepper to taste
- Asian Marinade Sauce:
- 2tablespoons rice vinegar
- 2tablespoons Splenda
- 2teaspoons liquid stevia
- 1tablespoon Asian sesame oil
- ½ teaspoon garlic powder
- 1/3 cup soy sauce

DIRECTIONS

1. About 20-minutes before you start cooking, place the shrimp into a colander and place it in the sink and let shrimp drain. Mix the soy sauce, stevia, rice vinegar, sesame oil, and garlic powder to make marinade mixture. After the shrimp have drained well, layer them on a paper towel an blot dry, so they are as dry as you can get them. Place dried shrimp into Ziploc bag with half of the marinade and allow the shrimp to marinate while you cook the brussels sprouts. Trim the stem ends off each brussels sprout and cut in half. Place brussels sprouts into a bowl and toss with desired amount of olive oil, salt and pepper.
2. Spread brussels sprouts out in a single layer in your air fryer and roast at 400°Fahrenheit for 15-minutes. Keep brussels sprouts in air fryer and move to one side. Add shrimp beside them in air fryer. Roast for an additional 4- minutes. Remove from air fryer and

place into serving bowl, add remaining marinade into bowl and give dish a stir. Serve immediately.

NUTRITION: Calories: 267, Total Fat: 11.2g, Carbs: 8.3g, Protein: 9.2g

66. Grilled Chicken with Garlic Sauce

Cooking Time: 15-minutes • Servings: 4

INGREDIENTS

- 1lb. chicken breast, cut into large cubes
- 2bell peppers, chopped
- 1zucchini
- 1onion, chopped
- For Garlic Sauce:
- 1head garlic, peeled
- ¼ cup lemon juice
- 1cup olive oil
- 1teaspoon salt
- Additional ingredients for the marinade:
- 1teaspoon salt
- ½ cup olive oil

DIRECTIONS

1. Soak 4 wooden skewers in water. For your garlic sauce, place garlic cloves and salt into blender. Then, add in about 1/8 of a cup of lemon juice and ½ a cup of olive oil. Blend for about 10- seconds. Keep half of the garlic sauce to serve with. Take the other half of garlic sauce and add an additional ½ cup of olive oil and a teaspoon of salt and mix well—this will make your marinade. Chop up the chicken, onion, bell peppers, and zucchini into 1-inch cubes or squares. Mix them in a bowl with the marinade. Place the cubes onto the skewers and cook them directly on the air fryer rack at 400°Fahrenheit for 15-minutes. Serve warm.

NUTRITION: Calories: 321, Total Fat: 12.5g, Carbs: 9.2g, Protein: 32.1g

67. Bacon-Wrapped Stuffed Zucchini Boats

Cooking Time: 15 minutes • Servings: 4

INGREDIENTS

- ½ a teaspoon of fresh ground black pepper
- 1teaspoon sea salt

- 5-ounces cream cheese
- 8-mushrooms, finely chopped
- 1tablespoon Italian parsley, chopped
- 1tablespoon finely chopped dill
- 3garlic cloves, peeled, pressed
- 1sweet red pepper, finely chopped
- 2large zucchinis
- 12bacon strips
- 1medium onion, chopped

DIRECTIONS

1. Preheat your air fryer to 350°Fahrenheit. Trim the ends off zucchini. Cut zucchini in half length- wise. Scoop out pulp, leaving ¼-inch thick shells. Stir pulp in mixing bowl. Add onion, garlic, herbs, pepper, cream cheese, salt, and pepper. Mix well to combine. Fill individual shells with the same amount of stuffing. Wrap three bacon strips around each zucchini boat such that the ends end up underneath. Place them directly on the air fryer rack and bake turning the temperature up to 375°Fahrenheit for 15-minutes. Remove and serve immediately.

NUTRITION: Calories: 282, Total Fat: 9.1g, Carbs: 6.3g, Protein: 24.2g

68. Parmesan Chicken Wings

Cooking Time: 22 minutes • Servings: 4

INGREDIENTS

- 2lbs. chicken wings
- 2tablespoons olive oil
- 1teaspoon sea salt
- 1teaspoon black pepper
- 3tablespoons butter
- 3tablespoons olive oil
- 3garlic cloves, minced
- 4tablespoons parmesan cheese
- 1/8 teaspoon smoked paprika
- ¼ teaspoon red pepper flakes
- Salt and pepper to taste

DIRECTIONS

1. Add chicken to a bowl and pat the chicken dry. Drizzle with 2 tablespoons of olive oil, 1 teaspoon of sea salt, and 1 teaspoon black pepper. Gently toss to coat chicken. Place chicken wings into air fryer directly on the rack. Bake at 400°Fahrenheit for 20-minutes, flipping wings half-way through cook time. In a pan over medium heat add butter and 3 tablespoons olive

oil and melt the butter down, for about 3-minutes. Add 2 tablespoons of parmesan cheese, smoked paprika, red pepper flakes, salt and pepper to taste. Cook sauce for about 2- minutes. Remove the wings from air fryer and place in large bowl. Pour the garlic parmesan sauce over the wings toss to coat. Serve wings topped with additional a2 tablespoons of parmesan cheese.

NUTRITION: Calories: 324, Total Fat: 12.3g, Carbs: 9.3g, Protein: 39.3g

69. Beef Burgers

Cooking Time: 10 minutes Servings: 4

INGREDIENTS

- 1lb. ground beef
- 1teaspoon parsley, dried
- ½ teaspoon oregano, dried
- ½ teaspoon ground black pepper
- ½ teaspoon salt
- ½ teaspoon onion powder
- ½ teaspoon garlic powder
- 1tablespoon Worcestershire sauce
- Olive oil cooking spray

DIRECTIONS

1. In a mixing bowl, mix the seasonings. Add the seasoning to beef in a bowl. Mix well to combine. Divide the beef into four patties, put an indent in the middle of patties with your thumb to prevent patties from bunching up in the middle. Place burgers into air fryer and spray the tops of them with olive oil. Cook for 10-minutes at 400°Fahrenheit, no need to flip patties. Serve on a bun with a side dish of your choice.

NUTRITION: Calories: 312, Total Fat: 11.3g, Carbs: 7.2g, Protein: 39.2g

70. Bacon Wrapped Avocado

Cooking Time: 10 minutes • Servings: 2

INGREDIENTS

- 2avocados, fresh and firm
- Chili powder
- Ground cumin
- 4thick slices of hickory smoked bacon

DIRECTIONS

1. Slice the avocados into wedges and peel off the skin. Stretch the bacon strips this will help to elongate them. Slice avocados in half. Next, take half a bacon strip and wrap one around each avocado wedge and tuck the ends under the bottom. Sprinkle wedges with chili powder and cumin. Bake the bacon wrapped avocado wedges in air fryer at 400°Fahrenheit for 10-minutes. Serve with your favorite salad!

NUTRITION: Calories: 276, Total Fat: 7.3g, Carbs: 6.3g, Protein: 21g

71. Buffalo Chicken Meatballs

Cooking Time: 20 minutes • Servings: 4

INGREDIENTS

- 1lb. ground chicken
- 1egg, beaten
- 1celery stalk, trimmed and finely diced
- 1cup buffalo wing sauce
- 1teaspoon black pepper
- 1teaspoon pink sea salt
- 1teaspoon garlic powder
- 1teaspoon onion powder
- 1tablespoon mayonnaise
- 1tablespoon almond flour
- 2sprigs of green onion, finely chopped

DIRECTIONS

1. Place the baking pan in air fryer and spray with olive oil. In a bowl, combine all ingredients, except buffalo sauce. Mix well. Use your hands to form 2-inch balls. Place the meatballs in air fryer and bake at 350°Fahrenheit for 15-minutes. Remove the meatballs from the air fryer. Add them to a pan over medium-low heat. Coat meatballs with buffalo sauce and stir cooking in pan for 5-minutes. Serve.

NUTRITION: Calories: 302, Total Fat: 12.4g, Carbs: 7.6g, Protein: 32.1g

72. Caprese Grilled Chicken with Balsamic Vinegar

Cooking Time: 20 minutes • Servings: 6

INGREDIENTS

- 6grilled chicken breasts, boneless, skinless
- 6large basil leaves
- 6slices of tomato
- 6slices of mozzarella cheese
- 1tablespoon butter
- ¼ cup balsamic vinegar

DIRECTIONS

1. Prepare chicken in air fryer at 400°Fahrenheit for 15-minutes or until chicken is cooked. As chicken is cooking, pour balsamic vinegar into the pan and cook until reduced by half, for about 5- minutes. Add in the butter and stir with a flat whisk until well combined. Set aside. Top chicken with mozzarella cheese slices, basil leaves, and tomato slice each. Drizzle with balsamic reduction and serve warm.

NUTRITION: Calories: 289, Total Fat: 11.3g, Carbs: 7.2g, Protein: 28g

73. Philly Cheese Steak Stuffed Peppers

Cooking Time: 40 minutes • Servings: 2

INGREDIENTS

- 8-ounces of roast beef, thinly sliced
- 8-slices of provolone cheese
- 2large green bell peppers
- 1medium sweet onion, diced
- 1(6-ounce) package of baby Bella mushrooms
- 1tablespoon garlic, minced
- 2tablespoons olive oil
- 2tablespoons butter

IRECTIONS

1. Cut your peppers in half lengthwise, removing ribs and seeds. Slice onions and mushrooms. Sautė over medium heat with butter, olive oil, a dash of salt, pepper, and minced garlic. Cook for 20-minutes or until the mushrooms and onions are sweet and caramelized. Slice the roast beef into thin strips and add to the onion/mushroom mixture. Allow cooking for 10-minutes. In the inside of each pepper line it with a slice of provolone cheese. Fill each pepper with meat mixture. Garnish top of each pepper with another slice of provolone cheese. Bake in the air fryer at 375°Fahrenhiet for 10-minutes.

NUTRITION: Calories: 298, Total Fat: 11.5g, Carbs: 8.2g, Protein: 39.2g

74. Parmesan, Garlic, Lemon Roasted Zucchini

Cooking Time: 10 minutes • Servings: 4

INGREDIENTS

- 1½ lbs. zucchini (about 4 small zucchini)
- Salt and pepper to taste

- ¾ cup parmesan cheese, finely shredded
- 2cloves garlic, minced
- Zest of 1 lemon
- 2tablespoons olive oil

DIRECTIONS

1. Cut zucchini into thick wedges or halves (cut each zucchini in half then that half in half, so you have 4 wedges from each zucchini. In a bowl, stir olive oil, garlic, and lemon zest. Align zucchini in air fryer space them evenly apart. Brush olive oil mixture over tops of zucchini. Sprinkle tops with parmesan cheese and season lightly with salt and pepper. Bake in air fryer at 375°Fahrenheit for 10-minutes. Serve warm.

75. Chicken Filet Stuffed with Sausage

Cooking Time: 15 minutes • Servings: 4

INGREDIENTS

- 4chicken fillets
- 4sausages, casings removed

DIRECTIONS

1. Place the sausage inside the chicken filets and roll the fillets. Seal with 2 toothpicks each. Air fry the chicken filets at 375°Fahrenheit for 15-minutes. Serve warm.

NUTRITION: Calories: 276, Total Fat: 12.2g, Carbs: 8.2g, Protein: 28g

76. Bourbon Chicken

Cooking Time: 22 minutes • Servings: 4

INGREDIENTS

- 3lbs. of chicken wings
- ¾ cups ketchup
- ¼ teaspoon cayenne
- ¼ cup Bourbon
- 2teaspoons smoked paprika
- ½ cup water
- 2garlic cloves, crushed
- ¼ cup onion, minced
- 2teaspoons stevia
- 1tablespoon liquid smoke
- 1teaspoon salt
- ½ teaspoon black pepper

DIRECTIONS

1. In a bowl, mix liquid smoke, onion, garlic, ketchup, stevia and cook for 5-minutes in an electric pressure cooker on Sautė function. Combine the rest of your ingredients and

cook on high pressure for 5-minutes. Do a quick release of pressure and then transfer the chicken wings into the air fryer basket. Cook wings in air fryer for 6-minutesat 400°Fahrenheit. Dip wings into sauce and air fry for another 6-minutes. Serve hot!

NUTRITION: Calories: 302, Total Fat: 12.5g, Carbs: 8.4g, Protein: 32.4g

77. Roasted Chicken Legs

Cooking Time: 35 minutes • Servings: 2

INGREDIENTS

- 2chicken legs
- 2teaspoons sweet smoked paprika
- 1teaspoon honey
- Salt and pepper to taste
- ½ teaspoon garlic powder
- Fresh parsley, chopped for garnish
- 1lime sliced for garnish

DIRECTIONS

1. Combine all the ingredients except the chicken in a bowl. Rub the mixture over the chicken and preheat your air fryer for 3-minutes. Cook the chicken in air fryer at 390°Fahrenheit for 35-minutes. Serve with a favorite salad of your choice.

NUTRITION: Calories: 232, Total Fat: 9.3g, Carbs: 7.5g, Protein: 22.1g

78. Mongolian Chicken

Cooking Time: 17 minutes Servings: 4

INGREDIENTS

- 4chicken breasts, boneless, skinless, chopped small pieces
- 1yellow onion, thinly sliced
- Olive oil for frying
- 1Chili Padi, chopped
- 3garlic cloves, minced
- 5curry leaves
- 1teaspoon ginger, grated
- ¾ cup evaporated milk
- Marinade:
- 1egg
- 1tablespoon light soy sauce
- Self-raising flour to coat
- ½ tablespoon cornstarch
- Seasonings:
- 1teaspoon liquid stevia
- 1tablespoon chili sauce
- ½ teaspoon sea salt
- Dash of black pepper

DIRECTIONS

1. Combine all of you marinade ingredients in a bowl and marinate the chicken with it for an hour. Dredge the chicken in the self-raising flour and spray some oil over. Cook in air fryer for 10-minutes at 390°Fahrenheit. Heat a wok and sautė the ginger, garlic, chili padi, curry leaves and onions for 2-minutes. Add the chicken and seasonings, stirring to combine well. Add your milk and cook until thickened. Serve hot!

NUTRITION: Calories: 286, Total Fat: 11.3g, Carbs: 6.4g, Protein: 28g

79. Chicken Drumsticks with Spinach Sauce

Preparation time: 15 minutes • Cooking time: 20 minutes • Servings: 4

INGREDIENTS

- 15oz chicken drumsticks
- 1up fresh spinach
- 1tablespoon olive oil
- ½ teaspoon minced garlic
- 1tablespoon walnuts
- 1teaspoon coconut oil
- ½ teaspoon thyme

DIRECTIONS

1. Pour the coconut oil into the air fryer basket.
2. Sprinkle the chicken drumsticks with the minced garlic and thyme and place them in the air fryer basket.
3. Cook the chicken for 5 minutes at 400 F.Stir it frequently.
4. Meanwhile, blend together the fresh spinach, olive oil, and walnuts.
5. Transfer the blended mixture over the drumsticks and cook them for 15 minutes at 370 F.
6. When the time is over and the chicken drumsticks are cooked – let them chill little.
7. Enjoy!

NUTRITION: Calories 234, Fat 11.9, Fiber 0.4, Carbs 0.7, Protein 30

80. Parsley Meatballs

Preparation time: 10 minutes • Cooking time: 10 minutes • Servings: 3

INGREDIENTS

- 1tablespoon fresh parsley, chopped

- 1teaspoon dried parsley
- 1cup ground pork
- ¼ teaspoon cayenne pepper
- ½ teaspoon salt
- 1tablespoon olive oil

DIRECTIONS

1. olive oil.
2. Add the meatballs and cook them for 10 minutes at 380 F. Stir the meatballs half-way.
3. Serve the cooked meatballs immediately!
4. Blend the chopped parsley and combine it together with the dried parsley, ground pork, cayenne pepper, and salt.
5. Mix the mixture up and make the medium meatballs.
6. Spray the air fryer with the

NUTRITION: calories 122, fat 6.7, fiber 0.1, carbs 0.2, protein 14.9

81. Paprika Beef Short Ribs

Preparation time: 20 minutes • Cooking time: 18 minutes • Servings: 8

INGREDIENTS

- 2-pound beef short ribs
- 1teaspoon salt
- 1tablespoon ground paprika
- 1teaspoon cilantro
- ½ teaspoon basil, dried
- 1tablespoon olive oil

DIRECTIONS

1. Sprinkle the ribs with the salt, ground paprika, cilantro, basil, and olive oil.
2. Stir the meat carefully and leave for 10 minutes to marinate.
3. After this, put the beef short ribs in the air fryer and cook at 400 F for 18 minutes. Stir the meat every 4 minutes.
4. Then transfer the cooked short ribs in the serving bowl and serve immediately!

NUTRITION: Calories 250, Fat 12.1, Fiber 0.3, Carbs 0.5, Protein 32.9

82. Lamb Burger

Preparation time: 15 minutes • Cooking time: 20 minutes • Servings: 6

INGREDIENTS

- 10oz lamb fillet
- 1teaspoon thyme
- ½ teaspoon minced garlic

- ½ teaspoon ground paprika
- ½ teaspoon salt
- 1teaspoon olive oil

DIRECTIONS

1. Chop the lamb fillet into the tiny pieces.
2. Sprinkle the meat with the thyme, minced garlic, ground paprika, and salt.
3. Stir it carefully until homogenous/
4. After this, make the medium burgers from the lamb meat mixture.
5. Pour the olive oil in the air fryer basket and add the lamb burgers.
6. Cook the lamb burgers for 20 minutes (10 minutes from each sideat 375 F.
7. Enjoy!

NUTRITION: Calories 271, Fat 11.2, Fiber 0.1, Carbs 0.3, Protein 39.8

83. Pesto Chicken

Preparation time: 10 minutes • Cooking time: 15 minutes • Servings: 6

INGREDIENTS

- 1tablespoon cashews
- 2cups fresh basil
- 1cup fresh spinach
- 2garlic cloves, chopped
- 4tablespoon olive oil
- ¼ teaspoon salt
- 2-pound chicken breast
- 1teaspoon ground black pepper
- 1teaspoon coconut oil
- ½ teaspoon cayenne pepper

DIRECTIONS

1. Place the cashews, fresh basil, fresh spinach, chopped garlic, olive oil, salt, ground black pepper, and coconut oil in the blender.
2. Add cayenne pepper and blend the mixture until smooth.
3. Place the chicken breast in the air fryer basket.
4. Then pour the blended pesto mixture over the chicken breast and stir it gently.
5. Cook the chicken breast for 15 minutes at 380 F. Stir it time to time.
6. Check if the chicken is cooked and let it rest for 10 minutes.
7. Slice the chicken breast and serve it!

NUTRITION: Calories 273, Fat 14.7, Fiber 0.4, Carbs 1.5, Protein 32.8

84. Lemon Trout

Preparation time: 10 minutes •Cooking time: 12 minutes • Servings: 4

INGREDIENTS

- 1-pound trout
- ½ lemon

- ¼ teaspoon chili flakes
- ½ teaspoon salt
- ½ teaspoon ground coriander
- 1tablespoon olive oil
- 1tablespoon basil

DIRECTIONS

1. Slice the lemon.
2. Rub the fish with the chili flakes, salt, ground coriander, basil, and olive oil carefully.
3. Then fill the fish with the sliced lemon and transfer it to the air fryer basket.
4. Cook the trout for 12 minutes at 375 F.
5. When the trout is cooked – serve it hot!

NUTRITION: Calories 248, Fat 13.1, Fiber 0.2, Carbs 0.7, Protein 30.3

85. Stuffed Salmon Fillet with Tomatoes

Preparation time: 15 minutes • Cooking time: 15 minutes • Servings: 6

INGREDIENTS

- 2-pound salmon fillet
- 1teaspoon minced garlic
- ¼ cup fresh basil
- ¼ cup cherry tomatoes
- 1tablespoon olive oil
- ½ teaspoon dried dill

DIRECTIONS

1. Blend the fresh basil until smooth.
2. Then sprinkle the salmon fillet with the dried dill, olive oil, and minced garlic.
3. Make the cut in the salmon fillet and fill it with the blended basil and cherry tomatoes.
4. Secure the cut with the toothpicks if desired.
5. Place the salmon in the air fryer basket and cook it for 15 minutes at 385 F.
6. When the salmon is cooked – serve it only hot!

NUTRITION: Calories 222, Fat 11.7, Fiber 0.1, Carbs 0.5, Protein 29.5

86. Tomato Beef Brisket

Preparation time: 35 minutes • Cooking time: 30 minutes • Servings: 6

INGREDIENTS

- 17oz beef brisket

- ½ cup tomato
- 1cup fresh basil
- 1teaspoon cayenne pepper
- 1tablespoon olive oil
- 1teaspoon turmeric

DIRECTIONS

1. Put the tomatoes in the blender and blend them well.
2. Add fresh basil and blend the mixture until smooth.
3. After this, pour the tomato mixture over the beef brisket.
4. Sprinkle it with the cayenne pepper, olive oil, and turmeric and stir carefully.
5. Let it marinate for 20 minutes.
6. Then place the beef brisket in the air fryer basket and cook it at 370 F for 30 minutes. Stir the beef every 5 minutes.
7. When the meat is cooked – let it chill for 5 minutes and serve it!

NUTRITION: Calories 175, Fat 7.5, Fiber 0.4, Carbs 1.1, Protein 24.7

87. Seafood Bowl

Preparation time: 10 minutes • Cooking time: 11 minutes • Servings: 4

INGREDIENTS

- 10oz shrimps, peeled
- 8oz salmon fillet
- 7oz scallops
- 1teaspoon ground coriander
- 1teaspoon minced garlic
- 1tablespoon lemon juice
- 1tablespoon olive oil
- ¼ onion, diced

DIRECTIONS

1. Combine together the ground coriander, minced garlic, lemon juice, olive oil, and diced onion in the mixing bowl.
2. Stir the mixture well.
3. Then separate the mixture into 3 bowls.
4. Chop the salmon fillet and sprinkle with the 1 part of the spicy mixture.
5. Stir well and place in the air fryer basket.
6. Cook the salmon for 5 minutes at 400 F. Stir it after 3 minutes of cooking.
7. Then mix up together the shrimps and spice mixture.
8. After this, mix the scallops and spice mixture.
9. Add the shrimps and scallops in the air fryer basket and cook for 6 minutes. Stir the meal frequently.
10. Then let the cooked meal chill little and serve it!

NUTRITION: Calories 238, Fat 8.6, Fiber 0.2, Carbs 3.2, Protein 35.6

88. Spicy Meat Bowl

Preparation time: 15 minutes • Cooking time: 16 minutes • Servings: 6

INGREDIENTS

- 1cup ground pork
- 8oz bacon, chopped
- 1tablespoon chives
- 1teaspoon salt
- ½ teaspoon ground black pepper
- ½ teaspoon minced garlic
- ¼ teaspoon chili flakes
- 1tablespoon olive oil
- ¼ cup almond milk

DIRECTIONS

1. Pour the olive oil into the air fryer basket.
2. Add ground pork, chopped bacon, chives, salt, ground black pepper, minced garlic, chili flakes, and almond milk.
3. Stir the mixture well and cook it at 380 F for 16 minutes. Stir the meat every 5 minutes.
4. When the meat is cooked – stir it one more time and serve!

NUTRITION: Calories 289, Fat 21.5, Fiber 0.3, Carbs 1.3, Protein 21.7

89. Stuffed Sweet Potato

Preparation time: 10 minutes •Cooking time: 10 minutes • Servings: 6

INGREDIENTS

- 3sweet potatoes
- 6teaspoon almond milk
- 1teaspoon minced garlic
- 12oz ground chicken
- 1teaspoon chives
- 1tablespoon olive oil
- 1tablespoon turmeric
- 1teaspoon avocado oil

DIRECTIONS

1. Cut the sweet potatoes into the halves and remove the meat.
2. Then mix up together the almond milk, minced garlic, ground chicken, chives, olive oil, and turmeric.
3. Stir the mixture.
4. Sprinkle the sweet potato halves with the avocado oil.
5. Then fill the sweet potatoes with the meat mixture and wrap them in foil.

6. Place the sweet potatoes in the air fryer basket and cook at 380 F for 30 minutes.
7. When the time is over – discard the foil from the sweet potatoes and serve!

NUTRITION: Calories 145, Fat 7.9, Fiber 0.4, Carbs 1.3, Protein 16.7

90. Basil Beef Shank

Preparation time: 15 minutes • Cooking time: 30 minutes • Servings: 4

INGREDIENTS

- 1-pound beef shank
- 1teaspoon paprika
- 1teaspoon chili flakes
- 1tablespoon olive oil
- ½ cup fresh basil
- 1teaspoon minced garlic

DIRECTIONS

1. Sprinkle the beef shank with the paprika, chili flakes, and minced garlic.
2. Combine together the fresh basil and olive oil.
3. Blend it and rub the beef shank with the green mixture.
4. Transfer the beef shank in the air fryer and cook it for 30 minutes at 380 F.
5. Stir the meat time to time.
6. When the time is over – check if the meat is cooked and serve it immediately!

NUTRITION: Calories 244, Fat 10.7, Fiber 0.3, Carbs 0.6, Protein 34.6

91. Sesame Pork Cubes

Preparation time: 10 minutes • Cooking time: 15 minutes • Servings: 4

INGREDIENTS

- 1tablespoon avocado oil
- 16oz pork fillet
- 1tablespoon sesame seeds
- 1teaspoon ground black pepper
- 1teaspoon paleo mayo

DIRECTIONS

1. Chop the pork fillet into the cubes.
2. Sprinkle the pork cubes with the ground black pepper and Paleo mayo.
3. Stir the meat.
4. Then add avocado oil and stir it one more time.
5. After this, place the meat in the air fryer basket and cook it

for 10 minutes at 370 F.

6. Then stir the meat and add sesame seeds.
7. Cook the meat for 5 minutes more at 365 F.
8. When the meat is cooked – let it chill little and serve!

NUTRITION: Calories 291, Fat 17, Fiber 0.6, Carbs 1.1, Protein 32.1

92. Thai Chicken

Preparation time: 10 minutes • Cooking time: 15 minutes • Servings: 4

INGREDIENTS

- 12oz chicken fillet
- 1tablespoon curry
- 1oz lemongrass
- ½ cup almond milk
- ¾ cup chicken stock
- ½ teaspoon salt
- 1teaspoon minced garlic

DIRECTIONS

1. Chop the chicken fillet roughly.
2. Then sprinkle the chicken with the curry, salt, and minced garlic.
3. Stir the meat and place it in the air fryer basket.
4. Add almond milk and lemongrass.
5. Cook the chicken for 15 minutes at 380 F.
6. When Thai chicken is cooked – let it chill little and serve!

NUTRITION: Calories 246, Fat 13.8, Fiber 1.2, Carbs 4.7, Protein 25.8

93. Vegetable and Chicken Bowl

Preparation time: 10 minutes • Cooking time: 10 minutes • Servings: 3

INGREDIENTS

- 6oz broccoli florets
- ½ red onion, chopped
- 1teaspoon ground cumin
- ½ teaspoon cilantro
- 1sweet pepper, roughly chopped
- 12oz chicken wings
- ½ cup chicken stock
- 1tablespoon coconut oil

DIRECTIONS

1. Place the broccoli florets in the air fryer basket.
2. Sprinkle them with the ground cumin, cilantro, and coconut oil.
3. Stir it carefully and add the chopped red onion.

4. After this, add chicken stock and cook the vegetables for 7 minutes at 400 F.
5. Then transfer the vegetables to the bowl.
6. Place the chicken wings in the air fryer basket and cook them for 10 minutes at 400 F.
7. Add the sweet pepper after 8 minutes of cooking/
8. When the time is over – transfer the chicken wings and sweet pepper in the vegetable bowl and serve.
9. Enjoy!

NUTRITION: Calories 298, Fat 13.5, Fiber 2.5, Carbs 8.9, Protein 35.2

94. Stuffed Cabbage

Preparation time: 20 minutes • Cooking time: 40 minutes • Servings: 6

INGREDIENTS

- 1zucchini, grated
- 1cup ground pork
- 1teaspoon ground nutmeg
- ½ teaspoon salt
- 1tomato, chopped
- 1tablespoon olive oil
- 1cup almond milk
- 1-pound cabbage

DIRECTIONS

1. Make the big hole in the cabbage.
2. Combine together the ground pork and grated zucchini.
3. Add ground nutmeg and salt.
4. After this, add chopped tomato and almond milk.
5. Stir the mixture well.
6. Spray the cabbage with the olive oil from all sides.
7. Then fill the cabbage hole with the ground pork mixture.
8. Wrap the cabbage in the foil and transfer it to the air fryer basket.
9. Cook the cabbage for 40 minutes at 380 F.
10. When the time is over – let it chill little and serve!

NUTRITION: Calories 180, Fat 13.2, Fiber 3.3, Carbs 8.3, Protein 9.8

95. Chili

Preparation time: 15 minutes • Cooking time: 25 minutes • Servings: 4

INGREDIENTS

- 1cup ground beef

- 1tablespoon avocado oil
- 1sweet pepper, chopped
- 1red onion, chopped
- 3garlic cloves, chopped
- ¼ teaspoon cumin
- 1teaspoon cayenne pepper
- ½ teaspoon chili pepper
- 2tomatoes, chopped
- 1cup beef broth
- 1teaspoon salt

DIRECTIONS

1. Place the ground beef in the air fryer basket and add avocado oil.
2. Cook the meat for 5 minutes at 400 F.
3. Then add the chopped sweet pepper, onion, garlic clove, cumin, cayenne pepper, chill pepper, chopped tomato, beef broth, and salt.
4. Stir the chili and cook for 25 minutes at 375 F.
5. When the chili is cooked – let it rest for 15 minutes.
6. Serve it!

NUTRITION: Calories 52, Fat 1.2, Fiber 2.1, Carbs 8.8, Protein 2.8

96. Lime Chicken with Pistachio

Preparation time: 10 minutes • Cooking time: 17 minutes • Servings: 4

INGREDIENTS

- 1-pound chicken breast, boneless
- ¼ cup pistachios, crushed
- 1tablespoon avocado oil
- ¼ lime
- 2tablespoons Paleo mayo
- ¼ cup chicken stock

DIRECTIONS

1. Squeeze the juice from the lime.
2. Sprinkle the chicken breast with the lime juice.
3. Then rub the chicken with Paleo mayo and crushed pistachios.
4. Place the chicken in the air fryer basket and sprinkle with the avocado oil.
5. Cook the chicken for 10 minutes at 365 F.
6. After this, add the chicken stock and cook the chicken for 7 minutes more at 375 F.
7. When the chicken is cooked – let it chill little and serve!

NUTRITION: Calories 206, Fat 11.1, Fiber 0.7, Carbs 1.7, Protein 24.9

97. Turkey Dill Meatballs

Preparation time: 10 minutes • Cooking time: 6 minutes • Servings: 6

INGREDIENTS:

- 2-pound ground turkey
- ¼ cup fresh dill

- 1egg
- 1tablespoon almond flour
- 1teaspoon salt

DIRECTIONS

1. Blend the dill in the blender until smooth.
2. Then beat the egg in the blended dill and combine it with the almond flour, salt, and ground turkey.
3. Mix the mixture carefully with the help of the spoon.
4. After this, make the small meatballs.
5. Place the meatballs in the air fryer basket and cook them for 3 minutes from each side at 400 F.
6. Then chill the meatballs and serve!

NUTRITION: Calories 337, Fat 19.8, Fiber 0.8, Carbs 2.2, Protein 43.7

98. Mango Turkey

Preparation time: 8 minutes • Cooking time: 15 minutes • Servings: 3

INGREDIENTS

- 5oz mango, chopped
- 10oz ground turkey
- ¼ cup onion, grated
- ½ teaspoon salt
- 1teaspoon olive oil
- 1teaspoon paprika

DIRECTIONS

1. Place the chopped mango in the air fryer basket.
2. Add grated onion, salt, paprika, and olive oil.
3. Stir the mango mixture and cook it for 5 minutes at 375 F.
4. Then stir the mango mixture and add the ground turkey.
5. Stir the mixture well and cook it for 10 minutes at 375 F. Stir the meal frequently.
6. Transfer the cooked turkey to the serving bowl and serve!

NUTRITION: Calories 232, Fat 12.2, Fiber 1.2, Carbs 8.4, Protein 26.5

99. Turkey Burger with Jalapeno

Preparation time: 15 minutes • Cooking time: 15 minutes • Servings: 4

INGREDIENTS

- 13oz ground turkey
- 1jalapeno

- 1teaspoon olive oil
- 1tablespoon coconut flour
- ½ teaspoon paprika
- ¼ teaspoon nutmeg
- 1tablespoon chives

DIRECTIONS

1. Chop the jalapeno and blend it.
2. Combine together jalapeno and ground turkey.
3. Add coconut flour, paprika, nutmeg, and chives.
4. Stir the mixture well and make the medium burgers.
5. Place the burgers in the air fryer basket and spray them with the olive oil.
6. Cook the burgers for 15 minutes at 375 F.
7. When the burgers are cooked – chill them little and serve!

NUTRITION: Calories 208, Fat 11.9, Fiber 1.5, Carbs 2.5, Protein 25.8

100. Fennel Fish Fillet

Preparation time: 10 minutes • Cooking time: 15 minutes • Servings: 4

INGREDIENTS

- 1-pound white fish fillet
- 8oz fennel
- ½ teaspoon sea salt
- 1tablespoon vinegar
- 1teaspoon ground black pepper
- 1teaspoon olive oil

DIRECTIONS

1. Chop the fennel roughly.
2. Chop the white fish and place it in the air fryer.
3. Sprinkle the fish with the sea salt, vinegar, ground black pepper, and olive oil.
4. Stir the fish gently with the help of the spatula.
5. Cook the white fish for 5 minutes at 400F.
6. Then add the chopped fennel and stir the fish.
7. Cook the fish for 10 minutes more at 360 F.
8. When the meal is cooked – transfer it directly to the serving plate and serve!

NUTRITION: Calories 225, Fat 9.8, Fiber 1.9, Carbs 4.5, Protein 28.5

101. Shrimp Chowder

Preparation time: 10 minutes • Cooking time: 21 minutes • Servings: 4

INGREDIENTS:

- 10oz shrimps, peeled
- 3oz bacon, chopped, cooked
- 1tablespoon chives

- ½ carrot, chopped
- 1onion, diced
- 2potatoes, chopped
- 1teaspoon olive oil
- 4cups chicken stock
- ½ teaspoon ground coriander
- 1teaspoon salt

DIRECTIONS

1. Place the shrimps, bacon, chives, chopped carrot, and onion in the air fryer basket.
2. Add chopped potato and olive oil.
3. Sprinkle the mixture with the ground coriander and salt.
4. Stir it carefully and cook at 400 F for 5 minutes.
5. After this, stir the mixture and add the chicken stock.
6. Cook the chowder for 16 minutes more at 345 F.
7. When the chowder is cooked – let it rest for 10 minutes.
8. Enjoy!

NUTRITION: Calories 307, Fat 12, Fiber 3.4, Carbs 22.2, Protein 26.9

102. Ground Beef Bowl

Preparation time: 10 minutes • Cooking time: 15 minutes • Servings: 4

INGREDIENTS

- 2tablespoons chives
- 1onion, chopped
- 16oz ground beef
- 1teaspoon olive oil
- 1teaspoon paprika
- 1teaspoon cumin
- ½ teaspoon ground black pepper

DIRECTIONS

1. Put the ground beef in the air fryer basket.
2. Sprinkle the meat with the cumin, paprika, ground black pepper, and olive oil.
3. Stir it and cook for 7 minutes at 380 F. Stir the meat time to time.
4. After this, add chopped onion and chives.
1. Stir the meat mixture and cook it at 380 F for 8 minutes more or until all the ingredients are cooked.
5. Transfer the ground beef to the bowl and serve!

NUTRITION: Calories 236, Fat 8.5, Fiber 1, Carbs 3.3, Protein 35

103. Turmeric Chicken Liver

Preparation time: 10 minutes • Cooking time: 7 minutes • Servings: 5

INGREDIENTS

- 17oz chicken liver
- 2tablespoons almond flour
- 1tablespoon coconut oil

- ½ teaspoon salt
- ¼ teaspoon minced garlic
- ¾ cup chicken stock

DIRECTIONS

1. Place the coconut oil in the air fryer basket and preheat it for 20 seconds.
2. Then add chicken liver.
3. Stir it and cook for 2 minutes at 400 F.
4. Then sprinkle the chicken liver with the almond flour, salt, and minced garlic.
5. Add the chicken stock and stir liver and cook it for 5 minutes more or until cooked.
6. Serve the meal immediately!

NUTRITION: Calories 250, Fat 14.7, Fiber 1.2, Carbs 3.4, Protein 26.1

104. Chicken Burgers

Preparation time: 15 minutes • Cooking time: 12 minutes • Servings: 3

INGREDIENTS

- ¼ cup fresh parsley, chopped
- 1garlic clove, chopped
- 1tablespoon olive oil
- 1egg
- 10oz ground chicken
- 1teaspoon paprika
- 1teaspoon almond flour

DIRECTIONS

1. Place the ground chicken in the mixing bowl.
2. Beat the egg into the mixture and sprinkle it with the paprika, almond flour, chopped garlic clove, and chopped parsley.
3. Stir the meat mixture until homogenous.
4. Then make the medium burgers from the mixture.
5. Spray the air fryer basket with the olive oil inside and place the chicken burgers there.
6. Cook the meal for 12 minutes at 390 F. Turn the burgers into another side after 6 minutes of cooking.
7. Chill the cooked burgers little and serve!

NUTRITION: Calories 299, Fat 17.9, Fiber 1.5, Carbs 3.2, Protein 31.5

105. Zucchini Casserole

Preparation time: 10 minutes • Cooking time: 20 minutes • Servings: 5

INGREDIENTS

- 1carrot, sliced
- 1onion, sliced
- 1zucchini, sliced
- 1cup chicken stock
- 1cup kale, chopped
- 1teaspoon paprika

- 1teaspoon salt
- 3oz bacon, chopped, cooked
- 1tablespoon olive oil

DIRECTIONS

1. Combine together the carrot, onion, zucchini, and chopped kale in the mixing bowl.
2. Stir the mixture well.
3. Then add salt and paprika. Stir it.
4. Pour the olive oil into the air fryer basket.
5. Add the vegetable mixture and chopped bacon.
6. Stir it well.
7. Then add the chicken stock and cook the casserole for 20 minutes at 375 F. Stir it gently time to time.

When the time is over – check if all the ingredients are cooked.

8. Chill the casserole to the room temperature and serve!

NUTRITION: Calories 146, Fat 10.2, Fiber 1.6, Carbs 6.6, Protein 7.7

106. Cherry Tuscan Pork Loin

Preparation time: 15 minutes • Cooking time: 40 minutes • Servings: 5

INGREDIENTS

- -pound pork loin
- ½ lemon
- 1cup cherry tomatoes
- 1teaspoon chili pepper
- 1tablespoon olive oil
- 1onion, chopped
- 1garlic clove, chopped

DIRECTIONS

1. Pour the olive oil into the air fryer basket.
2. Sprinkle the pork loin with the chili pepper and garlic clove.
3.
4. Place the pork loin in the air fryer basket and cook it for 20 minutes from one side at 360 F.
5. After this, turn the pork loin into another side and cook it for 10 minutes more.
6. Add the cherry tomatoes.
7. Squeeze the lemon juice over the meat and tomatoes and cook the meal for 10 minutes more at 360 F.
8. When the meat is cooked – let it chill for 5 minutes.
9. Enjoy!

NUTRITION: Calories 262, Fat 15.6, Fiber 1.1, Carbs 4.3, Protein 25.5

107. Ground Chicken and Ground Pork Mix

Preparation time: 10 minutes • Cooking time: 20 minutes • Servings: 4

INGREDIENTS

- 7oz ground chicken
- 9oz ground pork
- 3oz cherry tomatoes
- 1onion, chopped
- ¼ teaspoon minced garlic

- 1oz fresh cilantro, chopped
- 1tablespoon olive oil
- ¼ teaspoon nutmeg

DIRECTIONS

1. Pour the olive oil into the air fryer basket.
2. Add ground pork and sprinkle the meat with the nutmeg and minced garlic.
3. Stir the mixture well and cook it for 5 minutes at 370 F.
4. After this, stir the ground pork and add the ground chicken.
5. Then add the chopped onion.
6. Chop the cherry tomatoes and add them too.
7. Add the chopped cilantro and stir the mix.
8. Cook the ground meat mix for 15 minutes more at 360 F.
9. Stir the mixture every 4 minutes.
10. When the time is over and all the ingredients are cooked – let it chill well.
11. Enjoy!

NUTRITION: Calories 233, Fat 9.6, Fiber 1.1, Carbs 3.8, Protein 31.7

108. Shrimp Salad with Greens and Avocado

Preparation time: 10 minutes • Cooking time: 5 minutes • Servings: 3

INGREDIENTS

- 8oz shrimps, peeled
- 1avocado, pitted
- 1cup fresh basil, chopped
- 1garlic clove, diced
- 1teaspoon olive oil
- 1teaspoon ground paprika
- 1teaspoon avocado oil
- 1cup fresh parsley, chopped

DIRECTIONS

1. Sprinkle the peeled shrimps with the olive oil and ground paprika.
2. Stir the mixture.
3. Place the shrimps in the air fryer basket and cook them for 5 minutes at 400 F. Stir them after 3 minutes of cooking.
4. Meanwhile, peel the avocado and chop it.
5. Place the chopped avocado in the mixing bowl.
6. Add diced garlic and chopped fresh basil.
7. After this, add the chopped parsley and avocado oil.
8. Stir salad well.
9. When the shrimps are cooked – place them over the salad and serve immediately!

NUTRITION: Calories 252, Fat 16.2, Fiber 5.6, Carbs 9.1, Protein 19.5

109. Cauliflower Fritters with Carrot

Preparation time: 10 minutes • Cooking time: 10 minutes • Servings: 6

INGREDIENTS

- 1-pound cauliflower head
- 1carrot, grated
- 1tablespoon almond flour

- 1egg, beaten
- 1tablespoon chopped dill
- 1tablespoon chopped parsley
- ½ teaspoon salt
- 1tablespoon olive oil
- ½ teaspoon chili flakes
- 1tablespoon coconut flakes

DIRECTIONS

1. Chop the cauliflower and place it in the blender.
2. Blend the cauliflower carefully.
3. Then place the blended cauliflower in the mixing bowl.
4. Add the grated carrot and almond flour.
5. After this, add the egg, chopped dill, chopped parsley, salt, coconut flakes, and chili flakes.
6. Stir the mixture carefully until smooth and homogenous.
7. Preheat the air fryer and pour the olive oil into the air fryer basket.
8. Then make the medium fritters from the cauliflower mixture with the help of the hands and place them in the air fryer basket.
9. Cook the fritters for 10 minutes at 400 F.
10. Turn the fritters into another side after 5 minutes of cooking.
11. When the fritters are cooked – chill them little.
12. Serve!

NUTRITION: Calories 85, Fat 5.8, Fiber 2.8, Carbs 6.5, Protein 3.7

110. Lamb Fillet with Tomato Gravy

Preparation time: 20 minutes • Cooking time: 10 minutes • Servings: 3

INGREDIENTS

- 9oz lamb fillet
- 2tomatoes, chopped
- 1orange
- 1teaspoon salt
- 1tablespoon vinegar
- 1tablespoon avocado oil
- 1teaspoon chili flakes
- 11tablespoon almond flour

DIRECTIONS

1. Place the chopped tomatoes in the blender.
2. Peel the orange and add it to the blender too.
3. After this, add the salt, avocado oil, vinegar, chili flakes, and almond flour.
4. Blend the mixture until smooth.
5. Then chop the lamb fillet roughly.
6.

7. Pour the blended tomato mixture in the chopped lamb and stir it carefully.
8. Marinate the lamb fillet for 10 minutes.
9. After this, transfer the lamb fillet in the air fryer basket.
10. Sprinkle it with the remaining tomato mixture.
11. Cook the meat for 10 minutes at 400 F.
12. Stir the meat every 3 minutes.
13. When the meat is tender – transfer it in the serving bowls and sprinkle with the cooked gravy.
14. Serve it!

NUTRITION: Calories 262, Fat 11.7, Fiber 3.7, Carbs 12.7, Protein 27.3

111. Chicken Strips with Orange Zest

Preparation time: 10 minutes • Cooking time: 10 minutes • Servings: 4

INGREDIENTS

- 1-pound chicken fillet
- 1orange
- 1tablespoon dried oregano
- 1tablespoon olive oil
- ½ teaspoon salt

DIRECTIONS

1. Cut the chicken fillet into the strips.
2. Then sprinkle the chicken strips with the dried oregano and salt.
3. Squeeze the juice from the orange and pour it into the chicken strips.
4. Stir the mixture.
5. Pour the olive oil into the air fryer basket.
6. Add the chicken strips and cook the meal for 10 minutes at 390 F.
7. Stir the chicken strips after 5 minutes of cooking.
8. When the time is over – check if the meat is cooked and transfer it to the serving plate.
9. Serve it!

NUTRITION: Calories 271, Fat 12.1, Fiber 1.6, Carbs 6.1, Protein 33.4

112. Broccoli Casserole

Preparation time: 15 minutes • Cooking time: 15 minutes • Servings: 6

INGREDIENTS

- 12oz broccoli, chopped
- 1sweet potato, grated
- 1sweet pepper, chopped

- 1cup chicken stock
- ½ teaspoon dried basil
- ½ teaspoon salt
- 1tomato, chopped
- 8oz pork chop

DIRECTIONS

1. Chop the pork chops and place them in the air fryer basket.
2. Add salt, dried basil, and chicken stock.
3. Stir the mixture gently and cook it at 400 F for 8 minutes.
4. Meanwhile, combine together the chopped broccoli, grated sweet potato, and chopped sweet pepper.
5. Stir the vegetable mixture.
6. Add chopped tomato and shake it gently.
7. When the time is over – add the vegetable mixture in the air fryer basket and cook it for 7 minutes more.
8. Then check if all the ingredients are cooked and chill the casserole till the room temperature.
9. Serve it!

NUTRITION: Calories 167, Fat 9.8, Fiber 2.5, Carbs 9.7, Protein 10.9

113. Coconut Sour Shrimps with Greens

Preparation time: 20 minutes • Cooking time: 5 minutes • Servings: 4

INGREDIENTS

- 1tablespoon chives, chopped
- 1tablespoon fresh parsley, chopped
- 11oz shrimps, peeled
- 1/3 lemon
- 3tablespoons coconut milk
- 1tablespoon olive oil
- ¼ teaspoon salt

DIRECTIONS

1. Combine together the olive oil, salt, coconut milk, and chopped fresh parsley.
2. Add the chives and transfer the mixture to the blender.
3. Blend it well.
4. Then place the mixture in the mixing bowl and add the shrimps.
5. Stir the mixture with the help of the hands or spoon.
6. After this, squeeze the juice of the lemon.
7. Add the lemon juice to the shrimp mixture.

8. Marinate the shrimps for 10 minutes and transfer them to the air fryer basket.
9. Cook the shrimps for 5 minutes at 400 F.
10. Turn the shrimps into another side after 3 minutes of cooking.
11. Then let the cooked shrimps chill little and serve them!

NUTRITION: Calories 150, Fat 7.5, Fiber 0.4, Carbs 2.3, Protein 18.1

114. Seafood Casserole

Preparation time: 15 minutes • Cooking time: 12 minutes • Servings: 6

INGREDIENTS

- 1-pound salmon fillet
- 1teaspoon minced garlic
- ¼ cup almond milk
- 1onion, chopped
- 7oz broccoli, chopped
- 1sweet pepper, chopped
- 1teaspoon olive oil
- 1teaspoon salt
- 1teaspoon chili flakes

DIRECTIONS

1. Chop the salmon fillet into the medium cubes and sprinkle them with the minced garlic.
2. Then pour the olive oil into the air fryer basket.
3. Place the salmon in the air fryer.
4. Add the chopped onion and broccoli.
5. Then sprinkle the mixture with the salt, chili flakes, and add the sweet pepper.
6. Then pour the almond milk and cook the casserole for 12 minutes at 380 F.
7. You can stir the casserole during the cooking.
8. When the time is over and the meal is cooked – let it chill little and serve!

NUTRITION: Calories 155, Fat 8, Fiber 1.8, Carbs , Protein 16.3

115. Stuffed Chicken Breast with Avocado

Preparation time: 20 minutes • Cooking time: 13 minutes • Servings: 4

INGREDIENTS

- 1-pound chicken breast, boneless
- 1cup spinach, chopped
- 1tablespoon olive oil
- 3oz almonds, crushed
- ½ teaspoon salt
- ½ teaspoon ground black pepper
- 1onion, chopped

DIRECTIONS

1. Make a cut the chicken breast.
2. Place the fresh spinach in the blender and blend it well.
3. Add olive oil and crushed almond.

4. Blend the mixture for 10 seconds more.
5. Then transfer the mixture to the mixing bowl.
6. Add salt and ground black pepper.
7. Add onion and stir the mixture.
8. Fill the chicken breast with the spinach mixture and secure the cut with the help of the toothpicks.
9. Spread the chicken breast with the remaining spinach mixture and place in the air fryer basket.
10. Cook the chicken breast for at 380 F for 13 minutes.
11. Turn the chicken into another side after 7 minutes of cooking.
12. When the time is over – check if the chicken is cooked and transfer it to the serving plate.
13. Slice it and serve with the greens!

NUTRITION: Calories 296, Fat 17, Fiber 3.5, Carbs 7.6, Protein 29.1

116. Spiralized Casserole

Preparation time: 15 minutes • Cooking time: 15 minutes • Servings: 3

INGREDIENTS

- 1carrot, spiralized
- 1zucchini, spiralized
- 1onion, sliced
- ½ teaspoon ground black pepper
- 1teaspoon ground paprika
- 1tablespoon coconut flakes
- 1tablespoon almond flour
- 1tablespoon olive oil
- ¼ cup chicken stock

DIRECTIONS

1. Spray the air fryer basket with the olive oil inside.
2. After this, combine together the spiralized carrot, zucchini, and sliced onion.
3. Stir the mixture gently and sprinkle it with the ground black pepper, ground paprika, and coconut flakes.
4. Then add almond flour.
5. Stir the vegetable mixture with the help of 2 forks and transfer it to the air fryer basket.
6. Pour the chicken stock and cook the casserole for 15 minutes at 380 F.
7. When the casserole is cooked – all the vegetables should be soft.
8. Serve it!

NUTRITION: Calories 136, Fat 10.2, Fiber 3.5, Carbs 10.5, Protein 3.6

117. Crunchy Chicken Fingers

Preparation time: 15 minutes • Cooking time: 12 minutes • Servings: 4

INGREDIENTS

- 12oz chicken fillet
- ½ cup coconut flakes
- 2eggs
- ¼ cup almond milk
- 1tablespoon almond flour
- ½ teaspoon chili flakes
- ½ teaspoon salt
- ½ teaspoon ground black pepper
- 1tablespoon olive oil

DIRECTIONS

1. Cut the chicken fillet in the shape of the fingers.
2. Then take the bowl and beat the eggs in it.
3. Whisk the eggs and add almond milk and almond flour.
4. Then add the chili flakes and salt.
5. Sprinkle the mixture with the ground black pepper and whisk it well until homogenous.
6. Dip the chicken fingers in the egg batter and after this, coat them in the coconut flakes.
7. Pour the olive oil into the air fryer basket and place the chicken fingers there too.
8. Cook the meal for 12 minutes (6 minutes from each sideat 380 F.
9. When the meal is cooked – let it chill little and serve!

NUTRITION: Calories 334, Fat 22.4, Fiber 2.1, Carbs 4.2, Protein 29.6

118. Egg Salad with Avocado

Preparation time: 12 minutes • Cooking time: 15 minutes • Servings: 6

INGREDIENTS

- 2sweet peppers, chopped
- 1red onion, sliced
- 1avocado, chopped
- 3eggs
- 1tomato, chopped
- 1tablespoon olive oil
- 1teaspoon minced garlic

DIRECTIONS

1. Place the eggs on the air fryer rack and cook them at 250 F for 15 minutes.
2. After this, place them in the ice water to chill.
3. Then place the chopped sweet peppers in the bowl.

4. Add the sliced onion and chopped avocado.
5. After this, add the minced garlic.
6. Peel the eggs and chop them roughly.
7. Add the eggs to the vegetable bowl.
8. Sprinkle the salad with the olive oil and stir gently.
9. Serve it immediately!

NUTRITION: Calories 142, Fat 11.2, Fiber 3.3, Carbs 8.3, Protein 4.1

119. Juicy Scallops

Preparation time: 15 minutes • Cooking time: 6 minutes • Servings: 2

INGREDIENTS

- 11oz scallops
- 1orange
- ¼ lime
- 1tablespoon olive oil
- ½ teaspoon dried rosemary
- ¼ teaspoon salt
- ¼ teaspoon ground black pepper

DIRECTIONS

1. Grate the orange zest and squeeze the juice.
2. Mix up together the orange juice and orange zest.
3. Stir it carefully and add dried rosemary and salt.
4. Sprinkle the mixture with the ground black pepper.
5. Squeeze the juice from the lime and add it to the mixture.
6. Whisk it well.
7. Pour the liquid mixture over the scallops and leave them for at least 6 minutes to marinate.
8. After this, pour the olive oil in the air fryer basket and add the marinated scallops.
9. Cook the seafood for 6 minutes at 400 F. Flip the scallops into another side after 3 minutes of cooking.
10. Serve the cooked meal immediately.

NUTRITION: Calories 245, Fat 8.4, Fiber 2.6, Carbs 15.7, Protein 27.1

120. Stuffed Pepper Halves with Ground Meat

Preparation time: 15 minutes • Cooking time: 13 minutes • Servings: 6

INGREDIENTS

- 3sweet peppers, halved
- 8oz ground pork
- 1teaspoon chili flakes

- 1tablespoon fresh parsley, chopped
- 1tablespoon olive oil
- 1teaspoon ground black pepper
- ½ onion, diced

DIRECTIONS

1. Remove the seeds from the pepper halves.
2. Then combine together the ground pork, chili flakes, chopped parsley, ground black pepper, and diced onion in the mixing bowl.
3. Stir it carefully.
4. Pour the olive oil into the air fryer basket and add the meat mixture.
5. Stir it carefully and cook the mixture for 7 minutes at 380F.
6. Stir the mixture twice during the cooking.
7. After this, transfer the cooked ground pork in the mixing bowl.
8. Fill the pepper halves with the pork mixture.
9. Transfer the pepper halves in the air fryer basket and cook them for 6 minutes at 400 F (depend on the size of the vegetables).
10. When the time is over – let the cooked meal chill little and serve it.

NUTRITION: Calories 98, Fat 3.8, Fiber 1.1, Carbs 5.6, Protein 10.7

121. Pear Bowl with Nuts and Flax Seeds

Preparation time: 10 minutes • Cooking time: 10 minutes • Servings: 6

INGREDIENTS

- 2pears
- 4oz walnuts
- 2tablespoons flax seeds
- ¼ teaspoon ground cinnamon
- 1teaspoon vanilla extract
- 5oz bacon, chopped
- 1tablespoon sesame seeds

DIRECTIONS

1. Cut the pears into the halves and remove the seeds.
2. Then chop the pears and place them in the air fryer basket.
3. Sprinkle the fruits with the vanilla extract and ground cinnamon.
4. Stir the fruits and cook them for 4 minutes at 400 F.
5. After this, transfer the fruits in the bowl.
6. Place the chopped

bacon in the air fryer and cook it at 400 F for 6 minutes.
7. Stir it time to time.
8. Meanwhile, sprinkle the cooked pears with the sesame seeds and flax seeds.
9. Stir the mixture gently.
10. Crush the walnuts and add them to the pear bowl.
11. After this, add the cooked sesame seeds and stir the mixture.
12. Serve it immediately!

NUTRITION: Calories 308, Fat 22.6, Fiber 4.3, Carbs 14, Protein 14.3

122. Sweet Potato Toasts

Preparation time: 15 minutes • Cooking time: 11 minutes • Servings: 4

INGREDIENTS

- 1avocado, pitted
- 6oz bacon, chopped
- 2sweet potatoes, peeled
- 1onion, sliced
- ¼ teaspoon salt
- 1teaspoon ground paprika
- 1tablespoon avocado oil

DIRECTIONS

1. Slice the sweet potatoes into the medium slices.
2. Then place the chopped bacon in the air fryer basket and cook it for 6 minutes at 400 F. Stir it after 3 minutes of cooking.
3. Then transfer the cooked bacon to the mixing bowl.
4. Place the sliced sweet potato in the air fryer basket and sprinkle it with the avocado oil.
5. Cook the sweet potato slices for 4 minutes from one side and for 4 minutes from another side at 400 F.
6. Meanwhile, mash the avocado well and combine it together with the chopped bacon, salt, ground paprika, and sliced onion.
7. Stir the mixture carefully until homogenous.
8. When the sliced sweet potato is cooked – let it chill for 4 minutes.
9. Then spread each slice of the sweet potato with the avocado mash and make the sandwiches.
10. Serve the meal warm!

NUTRITION: Calories 345, Fat 27.7, Fiber 4.2, Carbs 7.9, Protein 17.1

123. Bacon Red Potato Halves

Preparation time: 10 minutes • Cooking time: 14 minutes • Servings: 5

INGREDIENTS

- 1-pound red potato
- 8oz bacon
- 1tablespoon dried dill

- 1teaspoon dried basil
- 1teaspoon salt
- 1tablespoon olive oil

DIRECTIONS

1. Wash the red potatoes carefully and cut them into the halves.
2. Then sprinkle the red potatoes with the dried basil, dried dill, and salt.
3. Stir the potatoes carefully.
4. After this, chop the bacon and place it in the air fryer basket.
5. Cook the bacon for 4 minutes at 380 F. Stir it after 2 minutes of cooking.
6. After this, add the red potato halves and stir the mixture carefully.
7. Cook the meal at 400 F for 10 minutes.
8. Stir the potatoes every 3 minutes.
9. Then check if the meal is cooked and transfer it to the serving plates.
10. Serve it!

NUTRITION: Calories 335, Fat 21.9, Fiber 1.6, Carbs 15.4, Protein 18.6

124. Hash Brown

Preparation time: 10 minutes Cooking time: 10 minutes Servings: 3

INGREDIENTS:

- 3potatoes, peeled
- 1tablespoon olive oil
- ¼ teaspoon ground white pepper
- ¾ teaspoon salt
- 1teaspoon ground paprika

DIRECTIONS

1. Grate the peeled carrot and combine it together with the ground white pepper, salt, and ground paprika.
2. Stir the mixture well.
3. Pour the olive oil into the air fryer basket and place the grated potato mixture there with the help of the spoon.
4. Cook the potato hash brown for 10 minutes at 400 F.
5. Stir the hashbrown after 6 minutes of cooking. The cooked meal should have light brown color.
6. Chill the hash brown to the room temperature and serve!

NUTRITION: Calories 189, Fat 5, Fiber 5.4, Carbs 34, Protein 3.7

125. Mixed Meat Sausages

Preparation time: 15 minutes • Cooking time: 13 minutes • Servings: 6

INGREDIENTS

- 11oz ground chicken
- 8oz ground pork
- 1teaspoon minced garlic

- 1onion, grated
- ½ teaspoon salt
- ½ teaspoon ground nutmeg
- ½ teaspoon turmeric
- 1teaspoon olive oil
- 1tablespoon almond flour

DIRECTIONS

1. Place the ground chicken and ground pork in the mixing bowl.
2. Add the minced garlic and grated onion.
3. After this, sprinkle the meat mixture with the salt, ground nutmeg, and turmeric.
4. Add almond flour and stir the mixture with the help of the spoon until homogenous.
5. Make the medium sausages from the meat mixture with the help of the hands.
6. Spray the air fryer basket with the olive oil inside.
7. Place the sausages in the air fryer basket and cook them at 380 F for 13 minutes.
8. Turn the sausages into another side after 6 minutes of cooking.
9. When the sausages are cooked – let them chill little and transfer in the serving plate.
10. Serve the meal with the fresh vegetables.

NUTRITION: Calories 196, Fat 8.4, Fiber 1, Carbs 3.1, Protein 26.2

126. Asparagus with Chicken

Preparation time: 10 minutes • Cooking time: 14 minutes • Servings: 5

INGREDIENTS

- 9oz asparagus
- 8oz chicken breast
- 1tablespoon olive oil
- 1sweet pepper, chopped
- ½ teaspoon salt
- 1tablespoon chicken stock

DIRECTIONS

1. Wash the asparagus carefully and chop it roughly.
2. Then sprinkle the chicken breast with the salt and olive oil.
3. Place the chicken breast in the air fryer basket and cook it for 9 minutes at 380 F.
4. Flip the chicken to another side after 5 minutes of cooking.
5. After this, add the asparagus and chicken stock.

6. Stir the mixture and cook it at 400 F for 5 minutes more.
7. When the time is over – let the cooked meal chill little and serve it.

NUTRITION: Calories 94, Fat 4.1, Fiber 1.4, Carbs 3.8, Protein 11

CHAPTER 3

SIDES

127. Curried Cauliflower Florets

Cooking Time: 10 minutes • Servings: 4

INGREDIENTS:

- 1/4 cup sultanas or golden raisins
- ¼ teaspoon salt
- 1tablespoon curry powder
- 1head cauliflower, broken into small florets
- ¼ cup pine nuts
- ½ cup olive oil

DIRECTIONS

1. In a cup of boiling water, soak your sultanas to plump. Preheat your air fryer to 350°Fahrenheit. Add oil and pine nuts to air fryer and toast for a minute or so. In a bowl toss the cauliflower and curry powder as well as salt, then add the mix to air fryer mixing well. Cook for 10- minutes. Drain the sultanas, toss with cauliflower, and serve.

NUTRITION: Calories: 275, Total Fat: 11.3g, Carbs: 8.6g, Protein: 9.5g

128. Parsnip Fries

Cooking Time: 12 minutes • Servings: 2

INGREDIENTS

- 2tablespoons of olive oil
- A pinch of sea salt
- 1large bunch of parsnips

DIRECTIONS

1. Wash and peel the parsnips, then cut them into strips. Place the parsnips in a bowl with the olive oil and sea salt and coat well. Preheat your air fryer to 360°Fahrenheit. Place the parsnip and oil mixture into the air fryer basket. Cook for 12- minutes. Serve with sour cream or ketchup.

NUTRITION: Calories: 262g, Total Fat: 11.3g, Carbs: 10.4g, Protein: 7.2g

129. Coconut Chips

Cooking Time: 5 minutes • Servings: 2

INGREDIENTS

- 2cups large pieces of shredded coconut
- 1/3 teaspoon liquid Stevia
- 1tablespoon chili powder

DIRECTIONS

1. Preheat your air fryer to 390°Fahrenheit. Combine the shredded coconut pieces with spices. Cook for 5- minutes in air fryer and enjoy!

NUTRITION: Calories: 261, Total Fat: 9.2g, Carbs: 7.3g, Protein: 6.2g

130. Sweet Potato Chips

Cooking Time: 15 minutes • Servings: 2

INGREDIENTS

- 2large sweet potatoes, thinly sliced with Mandoline
- 2tablespoons olive oil
- Salt to taste

DIRECTIONS

1. Preheat your air fryer to 350°Fahrenheit. Stir the sweet potato slices, in a large bowl with the oil. Arrange slices in your air fryer and cook them until crispy, for about 15- minutes.

NUTRITION: Calories: 253, Total Fat: 11.2g, Carbs: 8.4g, Protein: 6.5g

131. Vegetable Spring Rolls

Cooking Time: 23 minutes • Servings: 10

INGREDIENTS

- 10spring roll wrappers
- 2tablespoons cornstarch
- Water
- 3green onions, thinly sliced
- 1tablespoon black pepper
- 1teaspoon soy sauce
- Pinches of salt
- 2tablespoons cooking oil, plus more for brushing
- 8-cloves of garlic, minced
- ½ bell pepper, cut into thin matchsticks
- 2large onions, cut into thin matchsticks
- 1large carrot, cut into thin matchsticks
- 2cups cabbage, shredded
- 2-inch piece of ginger, grated

DIRECTIONS

1. To prepare the filling: add to a large bowl the carrot, bell pepper, onion, cabbage, ginger, and garlic. Gently add two tablespoons of olive oil in a pan over high heat. Add the filling mixture and stir in salt and a dash of stevia sweetener if you like. Cook for 3-minutes. Add soy sauce, black pepper and mix well.
2. Add green onions, stir and set aside. In a small bowl, combine enough water and cornstarch to make a creamy paste. Fill the rolls with a tablespoon of filling in center of each wrapper and roll tightly, dampening the edges with cornstarch paste to ensure a good seal. Repeat until all wrappers and filling are used. Preheat your air fryer to 350°Fahrenheit. Brush the rolls with oil, and arrange them in the air fryer, and cook them until crisp and golden for about 20-minutes. Halfway through the cook time flip them over.

NUTRITION: Calories: 263, Total Fat: 11.2g, Carbs: 8.6g, Protein: 8.2g

132. Onion Pakora

Cooking Time: 6 minutes • Servings: 6

INGREDIENTS:

- 1cup graham flour
- ¼ teaspoon turmeric powder
- Salt to taste
- 1/8 teaspoon chili powder
- ¼ teaspoon carom
- 1tablespoon fresh coriander, chopped
- 2green chili peppers, finely chopped
- 4onions, finely chopped
- 2teaspoons vegetable oil
- ¼ cup rice flour

DIRECTIONS

1. Combine the flours and oil in a mixing bowl. Add water as needed to create a dough-like consistency. Add peppers, onions, coriander, carom, chili powder, and turmeric. Preheat air fryer to 350°Fahrenheit. Roll vegetable mixture into small balls, add to the fryer and cook for about 6-minutes. Serve with hot sauce!

NUTRITION: Calories: 253, Total Fat: 12.2g, Carbs: 11.4g, Protein: 7.6g

133. Semolina Veggie Cutlets

Cooking Time: 23 minutes • Servings: 2

INGREDIENTS

- 1cup semolina
- Olive oil for frying
- Salt and pepper to taste

- 1½ cups of your favorite veggies(suggestion: carrot, peas, green beans, bell pepper and cauliflower
- 5cups milk

DIRECTIONS:

1. Stir and warm the milk in a saucepan over medium heat. Add vegetables when it becomes hot and cook until they are softened for about 3-minutes. Season with salt and pepper. Add the semolina to milk mixture and cook for another 10-minutes. Remove from heat and spread thin across a piece of parchment on a baking sheet, and chill for 4 hours in the fridge. Take out the baking sheet from the fridge, cut semolina mixture into cutlets. Preheat your air fryer to 350°Fahrenheit. Brush the cutlets with oil and bake for 10-minutes in your air fryer and serve with hot sauce!

NUTRITIONAL Value per serving: Calories: 252, Total Fat: 11.2g, Carbs: 10.3g, Protein: 7.3g

134. Charred Shishito Peppers

Cooking Time: 5 minutes • Servings: 4

INGREDIENTS

- 20Shishito peppers
- 1teaspoon vegetable oil
- Sea salt to taste
- 1lemon, juiced

DIRECTIONS

1. Preheat your air fryer to 390°Fahrenheit. Toss Shishito peppers with salt and oil adding to the air basket. Air fry for 5-minutes and transfer peppers to bowl. Squeeze lemon juice over peppers and season with coarse sea salt. Serve as finger food.

NUTRITION: Calories: 243, Total Fat: 8.4g, Carbs: 6.3g, Protein: 6.2g

135. Samosas

Cooking Time: 20 minutes • Servings: 4

INGREDIENTS

- 2cups all-purpose flour
- ½ teaspoon cumin seeds
- 2tablespoons olive oil
- 1teaspoon turmeric
- 1teaspoon chili powder
- 1teaspoon ginger-garlic paste
- 2teaspoons garam masala powder
- ½ cup green peas
- 2russet potatoes, peeled and cubed
- 1teaspoon carom seeds
- 2teaspoons ghee butter

DIRECTIONS

1. Prepare the crust in a bowl, combining the carom seeds, flour, water as needed to make a dough. Knead dough and chill in the fridge for 30-minutes. Prepare the filling: in a saucepan, cover the potatoes with water and bring to a boil. Add peas and continue to boil until vegetables are tender. Drain and mash well. Add the garam masala, ginger-garlic paste, chili powder, and turmeric to potato mixture. Season with salt and mix well.
2. In a small pan sautė oil over medium heat. Add the cumin seeds and toast they are sizzling and aromatic. Add the cumin to potato mixture, mix well, then set aside. Retrieve the dough out of the fridge, roll it out on the counter, and cut into several squares about 4-inches across. Place a spoonful of filling in each square and fold samosa to a triangle-like shape, carefully sealing edges. Preheat your air fryer to 350°Fahrenheit. Brush the samosas with oil, place them into air fryer, cook them until they are golden brown for about 20-minutes and serve warm or cold.

NUTRITION: Calories: 253, Total Fat: 11.3g, Carbs: 8.6g, Protein: 7.2g

136. Baked Tomatoes with Feta & Pesto

Cooking Time: 14 minutes • Servings: 4

INGREDIENTS

- Pesto:
- ½ cup fresh parsley and basil, chopped
- ½ cup Parmesan cheese, grated
- Pinch of salt
- 1tablespoon olive oil
- 1clove garlic, toasted
- 3tablespoons pine nuts, toasted
- Tomatoes & Feta:
- 2Heirloom tomatoes, cut into ½ inch slices
- 8-ounces feta cheese, cut into ½ inch slices
- 1tablespoon olive oil
- Pinch of salt
- ½ cup red onion, sliced paper-thin

DIRECTIONS

1. 1. Prepare the pesto by combining all the pesto ingredients excluding olive oil and salt into a food processor. Run the food processor on slow until thick paste forms. Season with salt to taste. Toss tomatoes, feta, and red onion with the olive oil. Briefly, preheat your air fryer to 350°Fahrenheit. Arrange tomato mixture in food

tray and cook for 14- minutes. Portion the tomato mixture onto individual serving plates and top with some pesto and serve!

NUTRITION: Calories: 246, Total Fat: 10.4g, Carbs: 8.6g, Protein: 8.4g

137. Cumin, Chili & Squash

Cooking Time: 20 minutes Servings: 4

INGREDIENTS

- 1medium butternut squash
- 1bunch coriander
- 2/3 cup Greek yogurt
- ¼ cup pine nuts
- 1tablespoon olive oil
- 1pinch chili flakes
- 2teaspoons cumin seeds
- Salt and pepper to taste

DIRECTIONS

1. Slice the squash into small chunks. Mix with the spices and oil in a baking pan. Roast the squash in your air fryer at 380°Fahrenheit for 20-minutes. Toast the pine nuts and serve with Greek yogurt and sprinkle coriander on top.

NUTRITION: Calories: 252, Total Fat: 10.3g, Carbs: 7.6g, Protein: 8.7g

138. Pineapple Sticks with Yogurt Dip

Cooking Time: 10 minutes • Servings: 2

INGREDIENTS

- ¼ cup dried coconut
- ½ pineapple
- Yogurt Dip:
- 1cup vanilla yogurt
- 1sprig of fresh mint

DIRECTIONS

1. Preheat your air fryer to 390°Fahrenheit. Cut the pineapple into sticks. Dip pineapple sticks into the dried coconut. Place the sticks covered with desiccated coconut into air fryer basket and cook for 10-minutes. Prepare the yogurt dip. Dice the mint leaves and combine with vanilla yogurt and stir. Serve pineapple sticks with yogurt dip and enjoy!

NUTRITION: Calories: 246, Total Fat: 8.4g, Carbs: 7.2g, Protein: 6.3g

139. Low-Carb Zucchini Roll-Ups

Cooking Time: 5 minutes Servings: 4

INGREDIENTS

- 3zucchinis, sliced thin, lengthwise
- Sea salt to taste
- 1cup goat cheese
- ¼ teaspoon black pepper
- 1tablespoon olive oil

DIRECTIONS

1. preheat air fryer to 390°fahrenheit. brush each zucchini strip with olive oil. mix sea salt and black pepper with goat cheese. spoon the goat cheese into the middle of each strip of zucchini and roll it up and fasten with a toothpick. place into air fryer and cook for 5-minutes.

NUTRITION: Calories: 243, Total Fat: 8.7g, Carbs: 6.4g, Protein: 6.5g

140. Zucchini Fries & Roasted Garlic Aioli

Cooking Time: 12 minutes • Servings: 4

INGREDIENTS

- Roasted Garlic Aioli:
- ½ cup mayonnaise
- Sea salt and pepper to taste
- 1teaspoon roasted garlic, pureed
- 2tablespoons olive oil
- ½ lemon, juiced
- Zucchini Fries:
- Sea salt and pepper to taste
- ½ cup almond flour
- 2eggs, beaten
- 1cup breadcrumbs
- 1large zucchini, cut into ½-inch sticks
- 1tablespoon olive oil
- Cooking spray

DIRECTIONS

1. Take three bowls and line them up on the counter. In the first, combine flour, salt, and pepper. Place eggs in the second bowl. Place breadcrumbs combined with salt and pepper in the third bowl. Take zucchini sticks and dip first into flour, then in the eggs, and then into crumbs. Preheat your air fryer to 400°Fahrenheit.
2. Cover sticks with cooking spray and layer in the basket. There should be two layers, pointing in opposite directions. Halfway through the 12- minute cook time rotate and turn the fries and spray with more cooking spray. Prepare the roasted garlic aioli in a medium bowl by mixing mayonnaise, pureed roasted garlic, olive oil and lemon juice. Stir in some pepper and salt. Serve the fries with the roasted garlic aioli and enjoy!

NUTRITION: Calories: 246, Total Fat: 9.3g, Carbs: 8.1g, Protein: 7.4g

141. Zucchini, Carrots & Yellow Squash

Cooking Time: 35 minutes • Servings: 4

INGREDIENTS

- ½ lb carrots, diced
- 1lime, cut into wedges
- ½ teaspoon ground white pepper
- 1lb. zucchini, trim stem and root ends, cut into ¾ inch semicircles
- 1lb. yellow squash, with roots and stems, trimmed
- 6teaspoons olive oil, divided
- 1teaspoon sea salt
- 1tablespoon tarragon leaves, chopped

DIRECTIONS

1. In a bowl add carrots and cover with 2 teaspoons of oil and stir. Put the carrots in fryer basket and set to 400°Fahrenheit and cook for 5-minutes. Place the zucchini and yellow squash into a bowl. Cover with the remaining 4 teaspoons of olive oil. Season with pepper and salt. When air fryer timer goes off, stir in zucchini and yellow squash with carrots. Cook for 30-minutes. Stir from time to time. Garnish with lime wedges and tarragon leaves.

NUTRITION: Calories: 256, Total Fat: 9.4g, Carbs: 8.6g, Protein: 7.4g

142. Roast Butternut Pumpkin with Nuts & Balsamic Vinaigrette

Cooking Time: 20 minutes • Servings: 4

INGREDIENTS

- 1butternut pumpkin, cut into 1-inch slices
- Sprigs of thyme for garnishing
- 2½ tablespoons toasted pine nuts
- Sea salt and pepper to taste
- 1½ tablespoons olive oil
- Vinaigrette:
- 6tablespoons olive oil
- 1tablespoon Dijon mustard
- Sea salt and black pepper to taste
- 2tablespoons balsamic vinegar

DIRECTIONS

1. Preheat air fryer to 390°Fahrenheit for 5-minutes. Cover the slices of pumpkin with olive oil and

season with thyme, salt, and pepper. Set the air fryer to cook for 20-minutes, and place seasoned pumpkin slices into air fryer. Prepare the vinaigrette by combining all the vinaigrette ingredients in a bowl. Serve pumpkin covered with vinaigrette, sprinkle top with toasted pine nuts and sprigs of thyme.

NUTRITION: Calories: 257, Total Fat: 11.3g, Carbs: 10.6g, Protein: 8.3g

143. Crispy Black-Eyed Peas

Cooking Time: 10 minutes • Servings: 6

INGREDIENTS

- 15-ounces black-eyed peas
- 1/8 teaspoon chipotle chili powder
- ¼ teaspoon salt
- ½ teaspoon chili powder
- 1/8 teaspoon black pepper

DIRECTIONS

1. Rinse the beans well with running water then set aside. In a large bowl, mix the spices until well combined. Add the peas to spices and mix. Place the peas in the wire basket and cook for 10-minutes at 360°Fahrenheit. Serve and enjoy!

NUTRITION: Calories: 262, Total Fat: 9.4g, Carbs: 8.6g, Protein: 9.2g

144. Lemony Green Beans

Cooking Time: 12 minutes • Servings: 4

INGREDIENTS

- 1lb. green beans washed and destemmed
- Sea salt and black pepper to taste
- 1lemon
- ¼ teaspoon extra virgin olive oil

DIRECTIONS

1. Preheat your air fryer to 400°Fahrenheit. Place the green beans in the air fryer basket. Squeeze lemon over beans and season with salt and pepper. Cover ingredients with oil and toss well. Cook green beans for 12- minutes and serve!

NUTRITION: Calories: 263, Total Fat: 9.2g, Carbs: 8.6g, Protein: 8.7g

145. Roasted Orange Cauliflower

Cooking Time: 20 minutes • Servings: 2

INGREDIENTS

- 1head cauliflower
- ½ lemon, juiced

- ½ tablespoon olive oil
- 1teaspoon curry powder
- Sea salt and black pepper to taste

DIRECTIONS

1. Prepare your cauliflower by washing and removing the leaves and core. Slice it into florets of comparable size. Grease your air fryer with oil and preheat it for 2- minutes at 390°Fahrenheit. Combine fresh lemon juice and curry powder, add the cauliflower florets and stir. Use salt and pepper as seasoning and stir again. Cook for 20-minutes and serve warm.

146. Eggplant Parmesan Panini

Cooking Time: 25 minutes • Servings: 2

INGREDIENTS

- 1medium eggplant, cut into ½ inch slices
- ½ cup mayonnaise
- 2tablespoons milk
- Black pepper to taste
- ½ teaspoon garlic powder
- ½ teaspoon onion powder
- 1tablespoon dried parsley
- ½ teaspoon Italian seasoning
- ½ cup breadcrumbs
- Sea salt to taste
- Fresh basil, chopped for garnishing
- ¾ cup tomato sauce
- 2tablespoons parmesan, grated cheese
- 2cups grated mozzarella cheese
- 2tablespoons olive oil
- 4slices artisan Italian bread
- Cooking spray

DIRECTIONS

1. Cover both sides of eggplant with salt. Place them between sheets of paper towels. Set aside for 30-minutes to get rid of excess moisture. In a mixing bowl, combine Italian seasoning, breadcrumbs, parsley, onion powder, garlic powder and season with salt and pepper. In another small bowl, whisk mayonnaise and milk until smooth.
2. Preheat your air fryer to 400°Fahrenheit. Remove the excess salt from eggplant slices. Cover both sides of eggplant with mayonnaise mixture. Press the eggplant slices into the breadcrumb mixture. Use cooking spray on both sides of eggplant slices. Air fry slices in batches for 15-minutes, turning over when halfway done. Each bread slice must be greased with olive oil. On a cutting board, place two

slices of bread with oiled sides down. Layer mozzarella cheese and grated parmesan cheese. Place eggplant on cheese. Cover with tomato sauce and add remaining mozzarella and parmesan cheeses. Garnish with chopped fresh basil. Put the second slice of bread oiled side up on top. Take preheated Panini press and place sandwiches on it. Close the lid and cook for 10-minutes. Slice panini into halves and serve.

NUTRITION: Calories: 267, Total Fat: 11.3g, Carbs: 8.7g, Protein: 8.5g

147. Spinach Samosa

Cooking Time: 15 minutes • Servings: 2

INGREDIENTS

- 1½ cups of almond flour
- ½ teaspoon baking soda
- 1teaspoon garam masala
- 1teaspoon coriander, chopped
- ¼ cup green peas
- ½ teaspoon sesame seeds
- ¼ cup potatoes, boiled, small chunks
- 2tablespoons olive oil
- ¾ cup boiled and blended spinach puree
- Salt and chili powder to taste

DIRECTIONS

1. In a bowl, mix baking soda, salt, and flour to make the dough. Add 1-tablespoon of oil. Add the spinach puree and mix until the dough is smooth. Place in fridge for twenty-minutes. In the pan add one tablespoon of oil, then add potatoes, peas and cook for 5-minutes. Add the sesame seeds, garam masala, coriander, and stir. Knead the dough and make the small ball using a rolling pin. Form balls, make into cone shapes, which are then filled with stuffing that is not yet fully cooked. Make sure flour sheets are well sealed. Preheat air fryer to 390°Fahrenheit. Place samosa in air fryer basket and cook for 10-minutes.

NUTRITION: Calories: 254, Total Fat: 12.2g, Carbs: 9.3g, Protein: 10.2g

148. Avocado Fries

Cooking Time: 10 minutes • Servings: 4

INGREDIENTS

- 1-ounce aquafina
- 1avocado, sliced

- ½ teaspoon salt
- ½ cup panko breadcrumbs

DIRECTIONS

1. Toss the panko breadcrumbs and salt together in a bowl. Pour Aquafina into another bowl. Dredge the avocado slices in Aquafina and then panko breadcrumbs. Arrange the slices in single layer in air fryer basket. Air fry at 390°Fahrenheit for 10-minutes.

NUTRITION: Calories: 263, Total Fat: 7.4g, Carbs: 6.5g, Protein: 8.2g

149. Honey Roasted Carrots

Cooking Time: 12 minutes • Servings: 2

INGREDIENTS

- 1tablespoon honey
- Salt and pepper to taste
- 3cups of baby carrots
- 1tablespoon olive oil

DIRECTIONS

1. In a mixing bowl, combine carrots, honey, and olive oil. Season with salt and pepper. Cook in air fryer at 390°Fahrenheit for 12-minutes.

NUTRITION: Calories: 257, Total Fat: 11.6g, Carbs: 8.7g, Protein: 7.3g

150. Crispy & Crunchy Baby Corn

Cooking Time: 10 minutes • Servings: 4

INGREDIENTS

- 1cup almond flour
- 1teaspoon garlic powder
- ¼ teaspoon chili powder
- 4baby corns, boiled
- Salt to taste
- ½ teaspoon carom seeds
- Pinch of baking soda

DIRECTIONS

1. In a bowl, add flour, chili powder, garlic powder, baking soda, carom seed, and salt. Mix well. Pour a little water into the batter to make a nice batter. Dip boiled baby corn into the batter to coat. Preheat your air fryer to 350°Fahrenheit. Line the air fryer basket with foil and place the baby corns on foil. Cook baby corns for 10-minutes.

NUTRITION: Calories: 243, Total Fat: 9.6g, Carbs: 8.2g, Protein: 10.3g

151. Tasty Tofu

Cooking Time: 12 minutes Servings: 4

INGREDIENTS

- ¼ cup cornmeal
- 15-ounces extra firm tofu, drained, cubed
- Salt and pepper to taste
- 1teaspoon chili flakes
- ¾ cup cornstarch

DIRECTIONS

1. Line the air fryer basket with aluminum foil and brush with oil. Preheat your air fryer to 370°Fahrenheit. Mix all ingredients in a bowl. Place in air fryer and cook for 12-minutes.

NUTRITION: Calories: 246, Total Fat: 11.2g, Carbs: 8.7g, Protein: 7.6g

152. Crispy Herb Cauliflower Florets

Cooking Time: 20 minutes • Servings: 2

INGREDIENTS

- 1egg, beaten
- 2tablespoons parmesan cheese, grated
- 2cups cauliflower florets, boiled
- ¼ cup almond flour
- 1tablespoon olive oil
- Salt to taste
- ½ tablespoon mixed herbs
- ½ teaspoon chili powder
- ½ teaspoon garlic powder
- ½ cup breadcrumbs

DIRECTIONS

1. In a bowl, combine garlic powder, breadcrumbs, chili powder, mixed herbs, salt, and cheese. Add olive oil to the breadcrumb mixture and mix well. Place flour in a bowl and place the egg in another bowl. Dip the cauliflower florets into the beaten egg, then in flour, and coat with breadcrumbs. Preheat your air fryer to 350°Fahrenheit. Place the coated cauliflower florets inside air fryer basket and cook for 20-minutes.

Nutrition: Calories: 253, Total Fat: 11.3g, Carbs: 9,5g, Protein: 8.5g

153. Roasted Corn

Cooking Time: 10 minutes • Servings: 8

INGREDIENTS

- 4ears of corn
- Salt and pepper to taste
- 3teaspoons vegetable oil

DIRECTIONS

1. Remove the husks from corn, wash and pat them dry. Cut if needed to fit into air fryer basket. Drizzle with vegetable oil and season with salt and pepper. Cook at 400°Fahrenheit for 10-minutes.

NUTRITION: Calories: 256, Total Fat: 9.4g, Carbs: 8.7g, Protein: 9.2g

154. Spicy Nuts

Cooking Time: 4 minutes • Servings: 8

INGREDIENTS

- 2cups mixed nuts
- 1teaspoon chipotle chili powder
- 1teaspoon salt
- 1teaspoon pepper
- 1tablespoon butter, melted
- 1easpoon ground cumin

DIRECTIONS

1. In a bowl, add all ingredients and toss to coat. Preheat your air fryer to 350°Fahrenheit for 5-minutes. Add mixed nuts into air fryer basket and roast for 4-minutes.

NUTRITION: Calories: 252, Total Fat: 8.6g, Carbs: 7.2g, Protein: 8.4g

155. Tawa Veggies

Cooking Time: 25 minutes • Servings: 4

INGREDIENTS

- ¼ cup okra
- 2teaspoons garam masala
- 1teaspoon red chili powder
- 1teaspoon amchur powder
- ¼ cup taro root
- ¼ cup potato
- ¼ cup eggplant
- Salt to taste
- Olive oil for brushing

DIRECTIONS

1. Cut potato and taro root into fries and soak in salt water for 10 minutes. Cut okra and eggplant into four pieces. Rinse potatoes and taro root and pat dry. Add the spices to potatoes, taro roots, okra, and eggplant. Brush pan with oil and preheat to 390°Fahrenheit and cook for 10-minutes. Lower the heat to 355°Fahrenheit and cook for an additional 15-minutes.

NUTRITION: Calories: 264, Total Fat: 11.3g, Carbs: 10.4g, Protein: 8.7g

156. Mediterranean Veggie Mix

Cooking Time: 20 minutes • Servings: 4

INGREDIENTS

- 1large zucchini, sliced
- 1green pepper, sliced
- 1large parsnip, peeled and cubed
- Salt and black pepper to taste
- 2tablespoons honey
- 2cloves garlic, crushed
- 1teaspoon mixed herbs
- 1teaspoon mustard
- 6tablespoons olive oil, divided
- 4cherry tomatoes
- 1medium carrot, peeled and cubed

DIRECTIONS

1. Add the zucchini, green pepper, parsnip, cherry tomatoes, carrot to bottom of air fryer.
2. Cover ingredients with 3 tablespoons of oil and adjust the time to 15-minutes.
3. Cook at 360°Fahrenheit. Prepare your marinade by combining remaining ingredients in air fryer safe baking dish.
4. Combine marinade and vegetables in baking dish and stir well.
5. Sprinkle with salt and pepper. Cook it at 390°Fahrenheit for 5-minutes.

NUTRITION: Calories: 262, Total Fat: 11.3g, Carbs: 9.5g, Protein: 7.4g

CHAPTER 4

SEAFOOD

157. Salmon Fish Sticks

Preparation time: 10 minutes • Cooking time: 10 minutes • Servings: 4

INGREDIENTS

- 1pound salmon filets
- ¼ cup mayonnaise
- 2Tbsp mustard
- ½ tsp salt
- ½ tsp ground black pepper
- 1½ cups ground pork rinds
- 2Tbsp whole milk

DIRECTIONS:

1. Preheat your air fryer to 400 degrees F and line your air fryer tray with foil and spray with cooking grease.
2. Dry the salmon filets by patting with a paper towel. Cut the fish into strips about 1 inch wide and two inches long.
3. In a small bowl, combine the mustard, mayo and milk and stir together well.
4. In a separate bowl, combine the ground pork rinds, salt and pepper.
5. Dip the fish strips into the mayonnaise mix and then into the pork rind mix, coating the fish completely. Place it on the prepared tray when done and repeat with the remaining fish sticks.
6. Place the tray in the air fryer and bake the fish for 5 minutes, flip and bake for another minutes Servings while hot!

NUTRITION: Calories 282, Total Fat 18g, Saturated Fat 5g, Total Carbs 1g, Net Carbs 0g, Protein 27g, Sugar 0g, Fiber 1g, Sodium 664mg, Potassium 68g

158. Cajun Salmon Fish Sticks

Preparation time: 10 minutes • Cooking time: 10 minutes • Servings: 4

INGREDIENTS

- 1pound salmon
- ¼ cup mayonnaise
- 2Tbsp mustard
- ½ tsp salt
- 1tsp Cajun seasoning
- 1½ cups ground pork rinds
- 2Tbsp whole milk

DIRECTIONS:

1. Preheat your air fryer to 400 degrees F and line your air fryer tray with foil and spray with cooking grease.

2. Dry the salmon filets by patting with a paper towel. Cut the fish into strips about 1 inch wide and two inches long.
3. In a small bowl, combine the mustard, mayo and milk and stir together well.
4. In a separate bowl, combine the ground pork rinds, Cajun seasoning, and salt.
5. Dip the fish strips into the mayonnaise mix and then into the pork rind mix, coating the fish completely. Place it on the prepared tray when done and repeat with the remaining fish sticks.
6. Place the tray in the air fryer and bake the fish for 5 minutes, flip and bake for another minutes Servings while hot!

NUTRITION: Calories 288, Total Fat 18g, Saturated Fat 5g, Total Carbs 1g, Net Carbs 0g, Protein 27g, Sugar 0g, Fiber 1g, Sodium 676mg, Potassium 68g

159. Bacon Wrapped Fish Sticks

Preparation time: 10 minutes • Cooking time: 18 minutes • Servings: 4

INGREDIENTS

- 1pound cod
- ¼ cup mayonnaise
- 2Tbsp mustard
- ½ tsp salt
- ½ tsp ground black pepper
- 1½ cups ground pork rinds
- 2Tbsp whole milk
- ½ pound bacon, uncooked, strips

DIRECTIONS:

1. Preheat your air fryer to 400 degrees F and line your air fryer tray with foil and spray with cooking grease.
2. Dry the cod filets by patting with a paper towel. Cut the fish into strips about 1 inch wide and two inches long.
3. In a small bowl, combine the mustard, mayo and milk and stir together well.
4. In a separate bowl, combine the ground pork rinds, salt and pepper.
5. Dip the fish strips into the mayonnaise mix and then into the pork rind mix, coating the fish completely. Place it on the prepared tray when done and repeat with the remaining fish sticks.
6. Wrap each fish stick in the bacon and place back onto the tray.
7. Place the tray in the air fryer and bake the fish for 10 minutes, flip and bake for another 8 minutes or until the bacon is brown and crispy. Serve while hot!

NUTRITION: Calories 310, Total Fat 24g, Saturated Fat 5g, Total Carbs 1g, Net Carbs 0g, Protein 34g, Sugar 0g, Fiber 1g, Sodium 899mg, Potassium 112g

160. Keto Tuna Melt Cups

Preparation time: 10 minutes • Cooking time: 20 minutes • Servings: 7

INGREDIENTS

- 5oz canned tuna, drained
- 2eggs
- ¼ cup sour cream
- ¼ cup mayonnaise
- ¾ cup shredded cheddar cheese
- ¾ cup pepper jack cheese
- ¼ tsp salt
- ¼ tsp ground black pepper
- 1Tbsp parsley, chopped

DIRECTIONS:

1. Preheat your air fryer to 325 degrees F and grease a muffin tin or individual muffin cups-whichever option fits in your air fryer better.
2. In a large bowl, combine the tuna, mayonnaise, sour cream, both kinds of grated cheese, parsley, salt and pepper.
3. Scoop the mix into the prepared muffin tin, filling each cup to the top.
4. Bake in the air fryer for 20 minutes or until the tops are golden brown.
5. Place on a slice of keto bread, serve with keto crackers or enjoy plain with a spoon!

NUTRITION: Calories 160, Total Fat 13g, Saturated Fat 3, Total Carbs 1g, Net Carbs 1g, Protein 9g, Sugar 1g, Fiber 0g, Sodium 321mg, Potassium 197g

161. Garlic Shrimp Bacon Bake

Preparation time: 10 minutes • Cooking time: 8 minutes • Servings: 4

INGREDIENTS

- ¼ cup butter
- 2Tbsp minced garlic
- 1pound shrimp, peeled and cleaned
- ¼ tsp ground black pepper
- ½ cup cooked, chopped bacon
- 1/3 cup heavy cream
- ¼ cup parmesan cheese

DIRECTIONS:

1. Preheat your air fryer to 400 degrees F and grease an 8x8 inch baking pan.

2. Add the butter and shrimp to the pan and place in the air fryer for 3 minutes. Remove the pan from the air fryer.
3. Add the remaining ingredients to the pan and return to the air fryer to cook for another 5 minutes. The mix should be bubbling and the shrimp should be pink.
4. Serve with zucchini noodles or enjoy plain.

NUTRITION: Calories 350, Total Fat 27g, Saturated Fat 15g, Total Carbs 3g, Net Carbs 3g, Protein 36g, Sugar 0g, Fiber 0g, Sodium 924mg, Potassium 16g

162. Gruyere Shrimp Bacon Bake

Preparation time: 10 minutes • Cooking time: 10 minutes • Servings: 4

INGREDIENTS

- ¼ cup butter
- 2Tbsp minced garlic
- 1pound shrimp, peeled and cleaned
- ¼ tsp ground black pepper
- ½ cup cooked, chopped bacon
- 1/3 cup heavy cream
- ¼ cup parmesan cheese
- ½ cup gruyere cheese, grated

DIRECTIONS:

1. Preheat your air fryer to 400 degrees F and grease an 8x8 inch baking pan.
2. Add the butter and shrimp to the pan and place in the air fryer for 3 minutes. Remove the pan from the air fryer.
3. Add the remaining ingredients to the pan and return to the air fryer to cook for another 5 minutes. The mix should be bubbling and the shrimp should be pink.
4. Sprinkle the gruyere over the shrimp and return to the air fryer for another 2 minutes to brown the top of the cheese.
5. Serve with zucchini noodles or enjoy plain.

NUTRITION: Calories 410, Total Fat 32g, Saturated Fat 18g, Total Carbs 4g, Net Carbs 3g, Protein 38g, Sugar 0g, Fiber 0g, Sodium 988mg, Potassium 24g

163. Cajun Shrimp Bacon Bake

Preparation time: 10 minutes • Cooking time: 10 minutes • Servings: 4

INGREDIENTS

- ¼ cup butter
- 2Tbsp minced garlic
- 1pound shrimp, peeled and

cleaned

- ½ tsp Cajun seasoning
- ½ cup cooked, chopped bacon
- 1/3 cup heavy cream
- ¼ cup parmesan cheese

DIRECTIONS:

1. Preheat your air fryer to 400 degrees F and grease an 8x8 inch baking pan.
2. Add the butter and shrimp to the pan and place in the air fryer for 3 minutes. Remove the pan from the air fryer.
3. Add the remaining ingredients to the pan and return to the air fryer to cook for another 5 minutes. The mix should be bubbling and the shrimp should be pink.
4. Serve with zucchini noodles or enjoy plain.

NUTRITION: Calories 352, Total Fat 27g, Saturated Fat 15g, Total Carbs 3g, Net Carbs 3g, Protein 36g, Sugar 0g, Fiber 0g, Sodium 930mg, Potassium 18g

164. Garlic Shrimp Prosciutto Bake

Preparation time: 10 minutes • Cooking time: 10 minutes • Servings: 4

INGREDIENTS

- ¼ cup butter
- 2Tbsp minced garlic
- 1pound shrimp, peeled and cleaned
- ¼ tsp ground black pepper
- 2oz thinly sliced, shredded prosciutto
- 1/3 cup heavy cream
- ¼ cup parmesan cheese

DIRECTIONS:

1. Preheat your air fryer to 400 degrees F and grease an 8x8 inch baking pan.
2. Add the butter and shrimp to the pan and place in the air fryer for 3 minutes. Remove the pan from the air fryer.
3. Add the remaining ingredients to the pan and return to the air fryer to cook for another 5 minutes. The mix should be bubbling and the shrimp should be pink.
4. Serve with zucchini noodles or enjoy plain.

NUTRITION: Calories 358, Total Fat 27g, Saturated Fat 15g, Total Carbs 3g, Net Carbs 3g, Protein 36g, Sugar 0g, Fiber 0g, Sodium 1026mg, Potassium 16g

165. Garlic Shrimp Tuna Bake

Preparation time: 10 minutes • Cooking time: 10 minutes • Servings: 4

INGREDIENTS

- ¼ cup butter

- 2Tbsp minced garlic
- 1pound shrimp, peeled and cleaned
- ¼ tsp ground black pepper
- 1tin canned tuna, drained well
- 1/3 cup heavy cream
- ¼ cup parmesan cheese

DIRECTIONS:

1. Preheat your air fryer to 400 degrees F and grease an 8x8 inch baking pan.
2. Add the butter and shrimp to the pan and place in the air fryer for 3 minutes. Remove the pan from the air fryer.
3. Add the remaining ingredients to the pan and return to the air fryer to cook for another 5 minutes. The mix should be bubbling and the shrimp should be pink.
4. Serve with zucchini noodles or enjoy plain.

NUTRITION: Calories 376, Total Fat 30g, Saturated Fat 15g, Total Carbs 3g, Net Carbs 3g, Protein 43g, Sugar 0g, Fiber 0g, Sodium 924mg, Potassium 16g

166. Jalapeno Tuna Melt Cups

Preparation time: 10 minutes • Cooking time: 20 minutes • Servings: 7

INGREDIENTS

- 5oz canned tuna, drained
- 2eggs
- ¼ cup sour cream
- ¼ cup mayonnaise
- ¾ cup shredded cheddar cheese
- ¾ cup pepper jack cheese
- ¼ tsp salt
- ¼ tsp ground black pepper
- 1Tbsp parsley, chopped
- ½ cup jalapeno slices

DIRECTIONS:

1. Preheat your air fryer to 325 degrees F and grease a muffin tin or individual muffin cups- whichever option fits in your air fryer better.
2. In a large bowl, combine the tuna, mayonnaise, sour cream, both kinds of grated cheese, parsley, jalapeno slices, salt, and pepper.
3. Scoop the mix into the prepared muffin tin, filling each cup to the top.
4. Bake in the air fryer for 20 minutes or until the tops are golden brown.
5. Place on a slice of keto bread, serve with keto crackers or enjoy plain with a spoon!

NUTRITION: Calories 167, Total Fat 13g, Saturated Fat 3, Total Carbs 2g, Net Carbs 1g, Protein 9g, Sugar 2g, Fiber 0g, Sodium 321mg, Potassium 197g

167. Herbed Tuna Melt Cups

Preparation time: 10 minutes Cooking time: 20 minutes Servings: 7

INGREDIENTS

- 5oz canned tuna, drained
- 2eggs
- ¼ cup sour cream
- ¼ cup mayonnaise
- ¾ cup shredded cheddar cheese
- ¾ cup pepper jack cheese
- ¼ tsp salt
- ¼ tsp ground black pepper
- 1Tbsp parsley, chopped
- 1tsp fresh chopped rosemary
- 1tsp fresh chopped basil

DIRECTIONS:

1. Preheat your air fryer to 325 degrees F and grease a muffin tin or individual muffin cups- whichever option fits in your air fryer better.
2. In a large bowl, combine the tuna, mayonnaise, sour cream, both kinds of grated cheese, parsley, rosemary, basil, salt, and pepper.
3. Scoop the mix into the prepared muffin tin, filling each cup to the top.
4. Bake in the air fryer for 20 minutes or until the tops are golden brown.
5. Place on a slice of keto bread, serve with keto crackers or enjoy plain with a spoon!

NUTRITION: Calories 163, Total Fat 13g, Saturated Fat 3, Total Carbs 1g, Net Carbs 1g, Protein 9g, Sugar 1g, Fiber 0g, Sodium 325mg, Potassium 197g

168. Cajun Tuna Melt Cups

Preparation time: 10 minutes • Cooking time: 20 minutes • Servings: 7

INGREDIENTS

- 5oz canned tuna, drained
-
- 2eggs
- ¼ cup sour cream
- ¼ cup mayonnaise
- ¾ cup shredded cheddar cheese
- ¾ cup pepper jack cheese
- ¼ tsp salt
- ½ tsp Cajun seasoning
- 1Tbsp parsley, chopped

DIRECTIONS:

1. Preheat your air fryer to 325 degrees F and grease a muffin tin or individual muffin cups- whichever option fits in your air fryer better.
2. In a large bowl, combine the tuna, mayonnaise, sour

cream, both kinds of grated cheese, parsley, Cajun seasoning, salt, and pepper.
3. Scoop the mix into the prepared muffin tin, filling each cup to the top.
4. Bake in the air fryer for 20 minutes or until the tops are golden brown.
5. Place on a slice of keto bread, serve with keto crackers or enjoy plain with a spoon!

NUTRITION: Calories 161, Total Fat 13g, Saturated Fat 3, Total Carbs 1g, Net Carbs 1g, Protein 9g, Sugar 1g, Fiber 0g, Sodium 321mg, Potassium 197g

169. Cheddar Tuna Melt Cups

Preparation time: 10 minutes • Cooking time: 20 minutes • Servings: 7

INGREDIENTS

- 5oz canned tuna, drained
- 2eggs
- ¼ cup sour cream
- ¼ cup mayonnaise
- 1½ cups shredded cheddar cheese
- ¼ tsp salt
- ¼ tsp ground black pepper
- 1Tbsp parsley, chopped

DIRECTIONS

1. Preheat your air fryer to 325 degrees F and grease a muffin tin or individual muffin cups-whichever option fits in your air fryer better.
2. In a large bowl, combine the tuna, mayonnaise, sour cream, cheese, parsley, salt and pepper.
3. Scoop the mix into the prepared muffin tin, filling each cup to the top.
4. Bake in the air fryer for 20 minutes or until the tops are golden brown.
5. Place on a slice of keto bread, serve with keto crackers or enjoy plain with a spoon!

NUTRITION: Calories 160, Total Fat 13g, Saturated Fat 3, Total Carbs 1g, Net Carbs 1g, Protein 9g, Sugar 1g, Fiber 0g, Sodium 321mg, Potassium 197g

170. Sesame Tuna Melt Cups

Preparation time: 10 minutes • Cooking time: 20 minutes • Servings: 7

INGREDIENTS

- 5oz canned tuna, drained
- 2eggs
- ¼ cup sour cream

- ¼ cup mayonnaise
- 1Tbsp sesame seeds
- 1Tbsp coconut aminos
- ¾ cup shredded cheddar cheese
- ¾ cup pepper jack cheese
- ¼ tsp salt
- ¼ tsp ground black pepper
- 1Tbsp parsley, chopped

DIRECTIONS:

1. Preheat your air fryer to 325 degrees F and grease a muffin tin or individual muffin cups- whichever option fits in your air fryer better.
2. In a large bowl, combine the tuna, mayonnaise, sour cream, sesame seeds, coconut aminos, both kinds of grated cheese, parsley, salt and pepper.
3. Scoop the mix into the prepared muffin tin, filling each cup to the top.
4. Bake in the air fryer for 20 minutes or until the tops are golden brown.
5. Place on a slice of keto bread, serve with keto crackers or enjoy plain with a spoon!

NUTRITION: Calories 172, Total Fat 16g, Saturated Fat 3, Total Carbs 4g, Net Carbs 2g, Protein 9g, Sugar 1g, Fiber 2g, Sodium 327mg, Potassium 202g

171. sian Style Crunchy Flounder

Preparation time: 10 minutes • Cooking time: 10 minutes • Servings: 4

INGREDIENTS

- 1pound flounder filets
- ½ cup pork rinds, crushed
- ¼ tsp black pepper
- ½ tsp salt
- ¼ tsp garlic powder
- 2tsp fresh minced garlic
- 1Tbsp melted butter
- 1Tbsp coconut aminos

DIRECTIONS:

1. Preheat your air fryer to 450 degrees F and line your air fryer tray with foil.
2. Place the flounder filets on the foil lined tray.
3. In a small bowl or food processor, combine the remaining ingredients and mix well.
4. Press the pork rind mix onto the salmon filets, coating the whole top evenly and packing the crust into the fish filets.
5. Bake the filets in the preheated oven for 10 minutes. The top crust should be nicely browned.
6. Serve while hot.

NUTRITION: Calories 323, Total Fat 21g, Saturated Fat 10g, Total Carbs 2g, Net Carbs 1g, Protein 40g, Sugar 0g, Fiber 1g, Sodium 482mg, Potassium 199g

172. Prosciutto Wrapped Cod

Preparation time: 5 minutes • Cooking time: 15 minutes • Servings: 2

INGREDIENTS

- 1pound cod fillets
- ¼ tsp salt
- ¼ tsp ground black pepper
- 2oz prosciutto de parma, very thinly sliced
- 2Tbsp olive oil
- 1tsp minced garlic
- 4cups baby spinach
- 2tsp lemon juice

DIRECTIONS:

1. Preheat your air fryer to 325 degrees F and line your air fryer tray with foil.
2. Dry the cod fillets by patting with a paper towel the sprinkle with salt and pepper.
3. Wrap the filets in the prosciutto, enclosing them as fully as possible.
4. Place the wrapped filets on the prepared tray.
5. Toss the spinach with the olive oil, garlic and lemon juice and place on the tray as well, around the wrapped cod.
6. Place in the air fryer and bake for 12 minutes. The spinach should be nicely wilted and the fish 145 degrees F internally.
7. Serve hot!

NUTRITION: Calories 416, Total Fat 19g, Saturated Fat 3g, Total Carbs 11g, Net Carbs 9g, Protein 49g, Sugar 3g, Fiber 2g, Sodium 482mg, Potassium 582g

173. Prosciutto Wrapped Salmon

Preparation time: 5 minutes • Cooking time: 16 minutes • Servings: 2

INGREDIENTS

- 1pound salmon fillets
- ¼ tsp salt
- ¼ tsp ground black pepper
- 2oz prosciutto de parma, very thinly sliced
- 2Tbsp olive oil
- 1tsp minced garlic
- 4cups baby spinach
- 2tsp lemon juice

DIRECTIONS:

1. Preheat your air fryer to 325 degrees F and line your air fryer tray with foil.
2. Dry the salmon fillets by patting with a paper towel the sprinkle with salt and pepper.
3. Wrap the filets in the prosciutto, enclosing them as fully as possible.
4. Place the wrapped filets on the prepared tray.
5. Toss the spinach with the olive oil, garlic and lemon juice and place on the tray as well, around the wrapped salmon.
6. Place in the air fryer and bake for 12 minutes. The spinach should be nicely wilted and the fish 145 degrees F internally.
7. Serve hot!

NUTRITION: Calories 464, Total Fat 22g, Saturated Fat 5g, Total Carbs 11g, Net Carbs 9g, Protein 49g, Sugar 3g, Fiber 2g, Sodium 482mg, Potassium 582g

174. Fast Seared Scallops

Preparation time: 5 minutes • Cooking time: 5 minutes • Servings: 4

INGREDIENTS

- 1pound jumbo scallops
- 2Tbsp butter
- ¼ tsp salt
- ¼ tsp ground black pepper

DIRECTIONS:

1. Preheat your air fryer to 400 degrees F and line your air fryer tray with foil.
2. Place the butter on the air fryer tray and place inside the air fryer for one minute to melt.
3. Remove the tray and add the scallops and seasonings, toss together and return to the air fryer for 5 minutes. The bottom of the scallops should be golden brown.
4. Serve hot.

NUTRITION: Calories 160, Total Fat 9g, Saturated Fat 4g, Total Carbs 3g, Net Carbs 2g, Protein 13g, Sugar 0g, Fiber 1g, Sodium 640mg, Potassium 232g

175. Lemon Scallops

Preparation time: 5 minutes • Cooking time: 5 minutes • Servings: 4

INGREDIENTS

- 1pound jumbo scallops
- 2Tbsp butter
- 1tsp lemon zest
- ¼ tsp salt
- ¼ tsp ground black pepper

DIRECTIONS:

1. Preheat your air fryer to 400 degrees F and line your air fryer tray with foil.

2. Place the butter on the air fryer tray and place inside the air fryer for one minute to melt.
3. Remove the tray and add the scallops and seasonings, toss together and return to the air fryer for 5 minutes. The bottom of the scallops should be golden brown.
4. Serve hot.

NUTRITION: Calories 163, Total Fat 9g, Saturated Fat 4g, Total Carbs 3g, Net Carbs 2g, Protein 13g, Sugar 0g, Fiber 1g, Sodium 640mg, Potassium 232g

176. Dijon Baked Salmon

Preparation time: 5 minutes • Cooking time: 18 minutes • Servings: 5

INGREDIENTS

- 1½ pounds salmon
- ¼ cup parsley, freshly chopped
- ¼ cup Dijon mustard
- 1Tbsp olive oil
- 1Tbsp fresh squeezed lemon juice
- 1Tbsp minced garlic
- ¼ tsp salt
- ¼ tsp ground black pepper

DIRECTIONS:

1. Preheat your air fryer to 375 degrees F line your air fryer tray with a piece of parchment paper.
2. Place the salmon on the parchment lined tray.
3. In a small bowl, mix together the remaining ingredients and then spread over the top of the salmon.
4. Place the salmon in the air fryer and bake for 18 minutes. Slice and serve hot!

NUTRITION: Calories 250, Total Fat 13g, Saturated Fat 2g, Total Carbs 2g, Net Carbs 1g, Protein 31g, Sugar 0g, Fiber 1g, Sodium 371mg, Potassium 42g

177. Garlic Dijon Baked Salmon

Preparation time: 5 minutes • Cooking time: 18 minutes • Servings: 5

INGREDIENTS

- 1½ pounds salmon
- ¼ cup parsley, freshly chopped
- ¼ cup Dijon mustard
- 1Tbsp olive oil
- 1Tbsp fresh squeezed lemon juice
- 3Tbsp minced garlic
- ¼ tsp salt
- ¼ tsp ground black pepper

DIRECTIONS:

1. Preheat your air fryer to 375 degrees F line your air fryer tray with a piece of parchment paper.

2. Place the salmon on the parchment lined tray.
3. In a small bowl, mix together the remaining ingredients and then spread over the top of the salmon.
4. Place the salmon in the air fryer and bake for 18 minutes. Slice and serve hot!

NUTRITION: Calories 272, Total Fat 13g, Saturated Fat 2g, Total Carbs 3g, Net Carbs 1g, Protein 31g, Sugar 1g, Fiber 1g, Sodium 371mg, Potassium 42g

178. Crispy Salmon Fillets

.

Preparation Time: 20 minutes • Servings: 4

INGREDIENTS

- 4salmon fillets, skinless
- ½ cup coconut flakes
- 1tbsp. parmesan; grated
- 1tsp. mustard
- Cooking spray
- A pinch of salt and black pepper

DIRECTIONS

1. Take a bowl and mix the parmesan with the other ingredients except the fish and cooking spray and stir well.
2. Coat the fish in this mix, grease it with cooking spray and arrange in the air fryer's basket.
3. Cook at 400°F for 15 minutes, divide between plates and serve with a side salad

NUTRITION: Calories: 240; Fat: 13g; Fiber: 3g; Carbs: 6g; Protein: 15g

179. Tilapia and Tomato

Preparation Time: 25 minutes • Servings: 4

INGREDIENTS

- 4tilapia fillets; boneless and halved
- ¼ cup tomato paste
- 1cup tomatoes; cubed
- 1cup roasted peppers; chopped.
- 2tbsp. olive oil
- 1tbsp. lemon juice
- 1tsp. oregano; dried
- 1tsp. garlic powder
- Salt and black pepper to taste.

DIRECTIONS

1. In a baking dish that fits your air fryer, mix the fish with all the other ingredients, toss.

2. Introduce in your air fryer and cook at 380°F for 20 minutes. Divide into bowls and serve

NUTRITION: Calories: 250; Fat: 9g; Fiber: 2g; Carbs: 5g; Protein: 14g

180. Cod and Spring Onions Sauce

Preparation Time: 20 minutes • Servings: 2

INGREDIENTS

- 2cod fillets; boneless
- 3tbsp. ghee; melted
- 1bunch spring onions; chopped.
- Salt and black pepper to taste.

DIRECTIONS

1. In a pan that fits the air fryer, combine all the ingredients, toss gently, introduce in the air fryer and cook at 360°F for 15 minutes
2. Divide the fish and sauce between plates and serve.

NUTRITION: Calories: 240; Fat: 12g; Fiber: 2g; Carbs: 5g; Protein: 11g

181. Sesame Crusted Tuna Steak

Preparation Time: 13 minutes • Servings: 2

INGREDIENTS

- 2(6-oz.tuna) steaks
- 1tbsp. coconut oil; melted
- 2tsp. black sesame seeds
- ½ tsp. garlic powder.
- 2tsp. white sesame seeds

DIRECTIONS

1. Brush each tuna steak with coconut oil and sprinkle with garlic powder
2. Take a large bowl, mix sesame seeds and then press each tuna steak into them, covering the steak as completely as possible. Place tuna steaks into the air fryer basket
3. Adjust the temperature to 400 Degrees F and set the timer for 8 minutes. Flip the steaks halfway through the cooking time. Steaks will be well-done at 145 Degrees F internal temperature. Serve warm.

NUTRITION: Calories: 280; Protein: 42.7g; Fiber: 0.8g; Fat: 10.0g; Carbs: 2.0g

182. Mustard Crusted Cod

Preparation Time: 24 minutes Servings: 4

INGREDIENTS

- 4cod fillets; boneless
- 1cup parmesan; grated
- 1tbsp. mustard
- Salt and black pepper to taste.

DIRECTIONS

1. Take a bowl and mix the parmesan with salt, pepper and the mustard and stir
2. Spread this over the cod, arrange the fish in the air fryer's basket and cook at 370°F for 7 minutes on each side.
3. Divide between plates and serve with a side salad

NUTRITION: Calories: 270; Fat: 14g; Fiber: 3g; Carbs: 5g; Protein: 12g

183. Italian Style Shrimp

Preparation Time: 15 minutes • Servings: 4

INGREDIENTS

- 2lb. shrimp; peeled and deveined
- 8garlic cloves, crushed
- ¼ cup chicken stock
- 1tsp. red pepper flakes, crushed
- 1tbsp. Italian seasoning
- A drizzle of olive oil
- Salt and black pepper to taste.

DIRECTIONS

1. Grease a pan that fits your air fryer with the oil, add the shrimp and the rest of the ingredients, toss.
2. Introduce the pan in the fryer and cook at 390°F for 10 minutes.
3. Divide into bowls and serve.

NUTRITION: Calories: 261; Fat: 12g; Fiber: 6g; Carbs: 7g; Protein: 12g

184. Rosemary Tomatoes and Shrimp

Preparation Time: 17 minutes • Servings: 4

INGREDIENTS

- 1lb. shrimp; peeled and deveined
- 4garlic cloves; minced
- 1cup cherry tomatoes; halved
- 2tbsp. ghee; melted
- 1tbsp. rosemary; chopped.
- Salt and black pepper to taste.

DIRECTIONS

1. In a pan that fits the air fryer, mix all the ingredients, toss.
2. Put the pan in the fryer and cook at 380°F for 12 minutes. Divide into bowls and serve hot

NUTRITION: Calories: 220; Fat: 14g; Fiber: 2g; Carbs: 6g; Protein: 15g

185. Shrimp and Lemon Vinaigrette

Preparation Time: 17 minutes • Servings: 4

INGREDIENTS

- 1½ lb. shrimp; peeled and deveined
- Zest of ½ lemon; grated
- Juice of ½ lemon
- 2tbsp. parsley; chopped.
- 2tbsp. olive oil
- 2tbsp. mustard
- A pinch of salt and black pepper

DIRECTIONS

1. Take a bowl and mix all the ingredients and toss well.
2. Put the shrimp in your air fryer's basket and reserve the lemon vinaigrette
3. Cook at 350°F for 12 minutes, flipping the shrimp halfway, divide between plates and serve with reserved vinaigrette drizzled on top.

NUTRITION: Calories: 202; Fat: 8g; Fiber: 2g; Carbs: 5g; Protein: 14g

186. Shrimp and Chives

Preparation Time: 17 minutes • Servings: 4

INGREDIENTS

- 1lb. shrimp; peeled and deveined
- ¼ cup coconut cream
- 1tbsp. parsley; chopped.
- 1tbsp. ghee; melted
- 1tbsp. chives; chopped.
- A pinch of red pepper flakes
- A pinch of salt and black pepper

DIRECTIONS

1. In a pan that fits the fryer, combine all the ingredients except the parsley, put the pan in the fryer and cook at 360°F for 12 minutes
2. Divide the mix into bowls, sprinkle the parsley on top and serve.

NUTRITION: Calories: 195; Fat: 11g; Fiber: 2g; Carbs: 4g; Protein: 11g

187. Tilapia and Capers

Preparation Time: 25 minutes • Servings: 4

INGREDIENTS

- 4tilapia fillets; boneless
- 2tbsp. lemon juice
- 2tbsp. capers
- 3tbsp. ghee; melted
- 1tsp. garlic powder
- ½ tsp. smoked paprika
- ½ tsp. oregano; dried
- A pinch of salt and black pepper

DIRECTIONS

1. Take a bowl and mix all the ingredients except the fish and toss.
2. Arrange the fish in a pan that fits the air fryer, pour the capers mix all over, put the pan in the air fryer and cook 360°F for 20 minutes, shaking halfway
3. Divide between plates and serve hot.

NUTRITION: Calories: 224; Fat: 10g; Fiber: 0g; Carbs: 2g; Protein: 18g

188. Pesto Almond Salmon

Preparation Time: 17 minutes • Servings: 2

INGREDIENTS

- 2(1 ½-inch-thicksalmon fillets (about 4 oz. each
- ¼ cup sliced almonds, roughly chopped
- ¼ cup pesto
- 2tbsp. unsalted butter; melted.

DIRECTIONS

1. In a small bowl, mix pesto and almonds. Set aside. Place fillets into a 6-inch round baking dish
2. Brush each fillet with butter and place half of the pesto mixture on the top of each fillet. Place dish into the air fryer basket. Adjust the temperature to 390 Degrees F and set the timer for 12 minutes
3. Salmon will easily flake when fully cooked and reach an internal temperature of at least 145 Degrees F. Serve warm.

NUTRITION: Calories: 433; Protein: 23.3g; Fiber: 2.4g; Fat: 34.0g; Carbs: 6.1g

189. Glazed Cod Fillets

Preparation Time: 19 minutes • Servings: 4

INGREDIENTS

- 4cod fillets; boneless
- 1/3 cup stevia
- 2tbsp. coconut aminos
- A pinch of salt and black pepper

DIRECTIONS

1. In a pan that fits the air fryer, combine all the ingredients and toss gently.
2. Introduce the pan in the fryer and cook at 350°F for 14 minutes, flipping the fish halfway.
3. Divide everything between plates and serve

NUTRITION: Calories: 267; Fat: 18g; Fiber: 2g; Carbs: 5g; Protein: 20g

190. Lemongrass Sea Bass

Preparation Time: 20 minutes • Servings: 4

INGREDIENTS

- 4sea bass fillets; boneless
- 1-inch ginger; grated
- 4lemongrass; chopped.
- 4small chilies; minced
- 1cup veggie stock
- 1bunch coriander; chopped.
- 4garlic cloves; minced
- Juice of 1 lime
- 1tbsp. black peppercorns, crushed
- A pinch of salt and black pepper

DIRECTIONS

1. In a blender, combine all the ingredients except the fish and pulse well.
2. Pour the mix in a pan that fits the air fryer, add the fish, toss, introduce in the fryer and cook at 380°F for 15 minutes. Divide between plates and serve

NUTRITION: Calories: 271; Fat: 12g; Fiber: 4g; Carbs: 6g; Protein: 12g

191. Baked Black Sea Bass

Preparation Time: 25 minutes • Servings: 4

INGREDIENTS

- 1lb. broccoli florets
- 4black sea bass fillets; boneless
- 4tbsp. butter; melted
- ½ tsp. red pepper flakes, crushed
- 1tsp. lemon zest; grated
- A pinch of salt and black pepper

DIRECTIONS

1. In a pan that fits your air fryer, mix the broccoli with the other ingredients except the fish and half of the butter, toss,
2. Put the pan in the fryer and cook at 380°F for 8 minutes.
3. Add the fish greased with the rest of the butter, cook at 380°F for 12 minutes more, divide between plates and serve.

NUTRITION: Calories: 251; Fat: 15g; Fiber: 4g; Carbs: 6g; Protein: 12g

192. Roasted Red Snapper

Preparation Time: 20 minutes • Servings: 4

INGREDIENTS

- 4red snapper fillets; boneless
- 2garlic cloves; minced
- 1tbsp. hot chili paste
- 2tbsp. olive oil
- 2tbsp. coconut aminos
- 2tbsp. lime juice
- A pinch of salt and black pepper

DIRECTIONS

1. Take a bowl and mix all the ingredients except the fish and whisk well
2. Rub the fish with this mix, place it in your air fryer's basket and cook at 380°F for 15 minutes
3. Serve with a side salad.

NUTRITION: Calories: 220; Fat: 13g; Fiber: 4g; Carbs: 6g; Protein: 11g

193. Tuna Kabobs

Preparation Time: 17 minutes • Servings: 4

INGREDIENTS

- 1lb. tuna steaks; boneless and cubed
- 4green onions; chopped.
- 1chili pepper; minced
- 2tbsp. lime juice
- A drizzle of olive oil
- Salt and black pepper to taste.

DIRECTIONS

1. In a bowl mix all the ingredients and toss them.
2. Thread the tuna cubes on skewers, arrange them in your air fryer's basket and cook at 370°F for 12 minutes.
3. Divide between plates and serve with a side salad

NUTRITION: Calories: 226; Fat: 12g; Fiber: 2g; Carbs: 4g; Protein: 15g

194. Catfish Fillet and Avocado

Preparation Time: 20 minutes • Servings: 4

INGREDIENTS

- 4catfish fillets
- 1avocado; peeled and cubed
- ½ cup spring onions; chopped.
- 2tbsp. cilantro; chopped.
- 2tbsp. lemon juice
- 2tsp. olive oil
- 2tsp. oregano; dried
- 2tsp. cumin, ground
- 2tsp. sweet paprika
- A pinch of salt and black pepper

DIRECTIONS

1. Take a bowl and mix all the ingredients except the fish and toss.
2. Arrange this in a baking pan that fits the air fryer, top with the fish, introduce the pan in the machine and cook at 360°F for 15 minutes, flipping the fish halfway
3. Divide between plates and serve

NUTRITION: Calories: 280; Fat: 14g; Fiber: 3g; Carbs: 5g; Protein: 14g

195. Shrimp and Okra

Preparation Time: 15 minutes • Servings: 4

INGREDIENTS

- 1lb. shrimp; peeled and deveined
- 1½ cups okra
- ½ cup chicken stock
- 2tbsp. coconut aminos
- 3tbsp. balsamic vinegar
- 1tbsp. parsley; chopped.
- A pinch of salt and black pepper

DIRECTIONS

1. In a pan that fits your air fryer, mix all the ingredients, toss, introduce in the fryer and cook at 380°F for 10 minutes. Divide into bowls and serve.

NUTRITION: Calories: 251; Fat: 10g; Fiber: 3g; Carbs: 4g; Protein: 8g

196. Chives Salmon

Preparation Time: 17 minutes • Servings: 4

INGREDIENTS

- 4salmon fillets; boneless
- ¼ cup chives; chopped.

- 4cilantro springs; chopped.
- 3tbsp. olive oil
- Juice of ½ lemon
- Salt and black pepper to taste.

DIRECTIONS

1. Take a bowl and mix the salmon with all the other ingredients and toss
2. Put the fillets in your air fryer's basket and cook at 370°F for 12 minutes, flipping the fish halfway.
3. Divide everything between plates and serve with a side salad

NUTRITION: Calories: 240; Fat: 12g; Fiber: 5g; Carbs: 6g; Protein: 14g

197. Basil Swordfish Fillets

Preparation Time: 17 minutes • Servings: 4

INGREDIENTS

- 4swordfish fillets; boneless
- 2tbsp. butter; melted
- 1tbsp. olive oil
- 2tsp. basil; dried
- ¾ tsp. sweet paprika
- Juice of 1 lemon

DIRECTIONS

1. Take a bowl and mix the oil with the other ingredients except the fish fillets and whisk
2. Brush the fish with this mix, place it in your air fryer's basket and cook for 6 minutes on each side
3. Divide between plates and serve with a side salad.

NUTRITION: Calories: 216; Fat: 11g; Fiber: 3g; Carbs: 6g; Protein: 12g

198. Shrimp and Pesto

Preparation Time: 17 minutes • Servings: 4

INGREDIENTS

- 1½ lb. shrimp; peeled and deveined
- 1/3 cup pine nuts
- ½ cup olive oil
- ½ cup basil leaves
- ¼ cup parmesan; grated
- ½ cup parsley leaves
- 2tbsp. lemon juice
- ¼ tsp. lemon zest; grated
- A pinch of salt and black pepper

DIRECTIONS

1. In a blender, combine all the ingredients except the shrimp and pulse well. Take a bowl and mix the shrimp with the pesto and toss
2. Put the shrimp in your air fryer's basket and cook at 360°F for 12 minutes, flipping the shrimp halfway.
3. Divide the shrimp into bowls and serve.

NUTRITION: Calories: 240; Fat: 10g; Fiber: 1g; Carbs: 4g; Protein: 12g

CHAPTER 5

POULTRY

199. Almond Chicken

Preparation time: 10 - 20Minutes • Cooking time: 15 – 30 • Servings: 6

INGREDIENTS

- 500 g chicken breast
- 130g crushed almonds
- ½ onion
- 1tbsp grated fresh ginger
- 60 g of soy sauce
- Water (sufficient quantity

DIRECTION:

1. Pour the almonds into the basket.
2. Roast the almonds for 5 minutes at 1500C.
3. Remove the almonds and pour the chopped onion and ginger, the oil into the tank and brown for about 2 minutes.
4. Add lightly floured chicken, salt, pepper and cook for additional 13 minutes.
5. Pour the soy sauce, a ladle of hot water, the roasted almonds and simmer for additional 5 minutes.

NUTRITION: Calories 458 Fat 34g Carbohydrates 22g Sugars 7.3g Protein 20g Cholesterol 24mg

200. Mushroom Chicken

Preparation time: 10-20Minutes • Cooking time: 15-30 • Servings: 6

INGREDIENTS:

- 500 g chicken breast
- Mushroom 300g
- 100 g of fresh cream
- 1shallot

DIRECTION:

1. Cut the chicken into pieces and sliced mushrooms. Spray the basket and chopped shallot into the basket. Set the temperature to 1500C and lightly brown for 5 minutes.
2. Add the mushrooms and cook for additional 6 minutes.
3. Finally pour the chicken, salt, pepper, and simmer for another 10 minutes.
4. Then add the fresh cream and cook for 5 min. until the sauce has thickened.

NUTRITION: Calories 220 Fat 14g Carbohydrates 11g Sugar 4g Protein 12g Cholesterol 50mg

201. Pepper Chicken

Preparation time: 10-20 • Cooking time: 45-60 • Servings: 6

INGREDIENTS

- 1kg of chicken pieces
- 500 g of red and yellow peppers
- salt to taste
- 50g onion

DIRECTION:

1. Pour the chopped onion into the bowl with the chopped peppers and chicken. Add salt and pepper.
2. Set the temperature to 1500C.
3. Cook everything for about 50 minutes, mixing 3 to 4 times during cooking, both meat and peppers.

NUTRITION: Calories 281 Fat 12g Carbohydrates 21g Sugars 3.4g Protein 23g Cholesterol 102mg

202. Stuffed Chicken and Baked Potatoes

Preparation time: 10-20Minutes • Cooking time: 45-60 • Servings: 4

INGREDIENTS

- 800 g boneless chicken
- 300 g minced meat
- 150 g sausage
- 80 g French toast
- 1tbsp chopped parsley

DIRECTION:

1. Bone the chicken (or bone directly by the butcher).
2. Prepare the filling:
3. Put in a food processor the meat, the sausage, the French toast bathed in milk to soften it, the parsley, the eggs, the grated cheese, the salt, the pepper and mix until obtaining a homogeneous and compact mixture.
4. Fill the boneless chicken and tie it well with a kitchen rope so that the filling does not come out.
5. Place the chicken inside the bowl, add the chopped potatoes, oil, salt, and pepper.
6. Set the air fryer to 1600C. Cook everything for 60 minutes over mix the potatoes 2-3 times to cook evenly and turn the chicken about once in the middle of cooking.

NUTRITION: Calories 223.8 Fat 6.5 g Carbohydrate 19.8 g Sugars 1.9 g Protein21.2 g Cholesterol 48.8 mg

203. Tandoori Chicken

Preparation time: more than 30Minutes • Cooking time: 15 – 30 • Servings: 4

INGREDIENTS

- 600 g chicken pieces
- 125 g whole yogurt

- 1tbsp curry
- 3tsp of spices for roasted meats

DIRECTION:

1. Place all ingredients in a bowl, flame well and let stand for 1 hour in the refrigerator.
2. Place the pieces of meat in the basket and set the temperature to 1600C
3. Cook the meat for 30 minutes, turning it 1-2 times to brown the chicken on both sides.

NUTRITION: Calories 263 Fat 12g Carbohydrates 6.1g Sugars 3.7g Protein 31g Cholesterol 135mg

204. Crispy Chicken Fillets in Brine in Pickle Juice

Preparation time: 10 minutes • Cooking time: 12 minutes • Servings: 4

INGREDIENTS

- 12chicken offers (1 ¼ pounds in total
- 1¼ cups pickled dill juice
- 1large egg
- 1large egg white
- ½ tsp kosher salt
- Freshly ground black pepper
- ½ cup seasoned breadcrumbs, regular or gluten free
- ½ cup seasoned breadcrumbs, regular or gluten free
- Olive oil spray

DIRECTION:

1. Place the chicken in a shallow bowl and cover with the pickle juice (enough to cover completely). Cover and marine for 8 hours in the refrigerator.
2. Drain the chicken and dry it completely with a paper towel (discard the marinade). In a medium bowl, beat the whole egg, egg white, salt, and pepper. In a shallow arch, combine the breadcrumbs.
3. Dip the chicken in the egg mixture, piece by piece, then in the breadcrumbs, pressing lightly. Remove excess breadcrumbs and place it on a work surface. Spray generously both sides of the chicken with oil.
4. Preheat the fryer to 400°F.
5. Working in batches, place a single layer of chicken in the fryer basket. Cook 10 to 12 minutes, turning halfway through cooking, until cooked, crispy and golden brown. (For a toaster-style air fryer, the temperature stays the same; cook for about 10 minutes.

NUTRITION: Calories: 244kcal Carbohydrates 10g Protein: 37g Fat: 6g Cholesterol 150mg Sugar 1g

205. Turkey and Rosemary Butter

Preparation Time: 29 minutes Servings: 4

INGREDIENTS

- 1turkey breast, skinless; boneless and cut into 4 pieces
- 2tbsp. rosemary; chopped
- 2tbsp. butter; melted
- Juice of 1 lemon
- A pinch of salt and black pepper

DIRECTIONS

1. Take a bowl and mix the butter with the rosemary, lemon juice, salt and pepper and whisk really well.
2. Brush the turkey pieces with the rosemary butter, put them your air fryer's basket, cook at 380°F for 12 minutes on each side. Divide between plates and serve with a side salad

NUTRITION: Calories: 236; Fat: 12g; Fiber: 4g; Carbs: 6g; Protein: 13g

206. Spiced Chicken Breasts

Preparation Time: 25 minutes • Servings: 4

INGREDIENTS

- 4chicken breasts, skinless and boneless
- 1tbsp. parsley; chopped
- 1tsp. smoked paprika
- 1tsp. garlic powder
- 1tsp. chili powder
- A drizzle of olive oil
- A pinch of salt and black pepper

DIRECTIONS

1. Season chicken with salt and pepper and rub it with the oil and all the other ingredients except the parsley
2. Put the chicken breasts in your air fryer's basket and cook at 350°F for 10 minutes on each side
3. Divide between plates, sprinkle the parsley on top and serve

NUTRITION: Calories: 222; Fat: 11g; Fiber: 4g; Carbs: 6g; Protein: 12g

207. Chicken and Pepperoni Pizza Bake

Preparation Time: 25 minutes • Servings: 4

INGREDIENTS

- 20slices pepperoni
- 2cups cubed cooked chicken
- 1cup shredded mozzarella

cheese

- ¼ cup grated Parmesan cheese.
- 1cup low-carb, sugar-free pizza sauce

DIRECTIONS

1. In a 4-cup round baking dish add chicken, pepperoni and pizza sauce. Stir so meat is completely covered with sauce.
2. Top with mozzarella and grated Parmesan. Place dish into the air fryer basket. Adjust the temperature to 375 Degrees F and set the timer for 15 minutes
3. Dish will be brown and bubbling when cooked. Serve immediately.

NUTRITION: Calories: 353; Protein: 34.4g; Fiber: 1.0g; Fat: 17.4g; Carbs: 7.5g

208. Ginger Chicken Breasts

Preparation Time: 25 minutes • Servings: 4

INGREDIENTS

- 4chicken breasts, skinless; boneless and halved
- ¼ cup chicken stock
- 2tbsp. stevia
- 1tbsp. ginger, grated
- 4tbsp. coconut aminos
- 1tsp. olive oil
- Salt and black pepper to taste.

DIRECTIONS

1. In a pan that fits the air fryer, combine the chicken with the ginger and all the ingredients and toss.
2. Put the pan in your air fryer and cook at 4380°F for 20, shaking the fryer halfway
3. Divide between plates and serve with a
4. side salad.

NUTRITION: Calories: 256; Fat: 12g; Fiber: 4g; Carbs: 6g; Protein: 14g

209. Creamy Chicken Wings

Preparation Time: 35 minutes • Servings: 4

INGREDIENTS

- 2lb. chicken wings
- ¼ cup parmesan, grated
- ½ cup heavy cream
- 3garlic cloves; minced
- 3tbsp. butter; melted
- ½ tsp. oregano; dried
- ½ tsp. basil; dried
- Salt and black pepper to taste.

DIRECTIONS

1. In a baking dish that fits your air fryer, mix the chicken wings with all the ingredients except the parmesan and toss
2. Put the dish to your air fryer and cook at 380°F for 30 minutes. Sprinkle the cheese on top, leave the mix aside for 10 minutes, divide between plates and serve

NUTRITION: Calories: 270; Fat: 12g; Fiber: 3g; Carbs: 6g; Protein: 17g

210. Jalapeño Popper Hasselback Chicken

Preparation Time: 40 minutes • Servings: 2

INGREDIENTS

- 4slices sugar-free bacon; cooked and crumbles
- 2(6-oz.boneless, skinless chicken breasts
- 2oz. full-fat cream cheese; softened.
- ¼ cup sliced pickled jalapeños
- ½ cup shredded sharp Cheddar cheese, divided.

DIRECTIONS

1. Take a medium bowl, place cooked bacon, then fold in cream cheese, half of the Cheddar and the jalapeño slices.
2. Use a sharp knife to make slits in each of the chicken breasts about ¾of the way across the chicken, being careful not to cut all the way through.
3. Depending on the size of the chicken breast, you'll likely have 6–8 slits per breast
4. Spoon the cream cheese mixture into the slits of the chicken.
5. Sprinkle remaining shredded cheese over chicken breasts and place into the air fryer basket.
6. Adjust the temperature to 350 Degrees F and set the timer for 20 minutes
7. Servings warm.

NUTRITION: Calories: 501; Protein: 53.8g; Fiber: 0.2g; Fat: 25.3g; Carbs: 1.6g

211. Thyme Duck Legs

Preparation Time: 35 minutes • Servings: 4

INGREDIENTS

- 4duck legs
- 2tbsp. olive oil
- 4tsp. thyme; dried
- 3tsp. fennel seeds, crushed
- A pinch of salt and black pepper

DIRECTIONS

1. Take a bowl and mix the duck legs with all the other ingredients and toss well.
2. Put the duck legs in your air fryer's basket and cook at 380°F for 15 minutes on each side. Divide between plates and serve

NUTRITION: Calories: 274; Fat: 11g; Fiber: 4g; Carbs: 6g; Protein: 14g

212. Chicken Enchiladas

Preparation Time: 30 minutes • Servings: 4

INGREDIENTS

- ½ lb. medium-sliced deli chicken
- 1medium avocado; peeled, pitted and sliced
- 1cup shredded medium Cheddar cheese.
- ½ cup shredded Monterey jack cheese
- ⅓ cup low-carb enchilada sauce, divided.
- ½ cup full-fat sour cream.
- 1½ cups shredded cooked chicken

DIRECTIONS

1. Take a large bowl, mix shredded chicken and half of the enchilada sauce. Lay slices of deli chicken on a work surface and spoon 2 tbsp. shredded chicken mixture onto each slice
2. Sprinkle 2 tbsp. of Cheddar onto each roll. Gently roll closed
3. In a 4-cup round baking dish, place each roll, seam side down. Pour remaining sauce over rolls and top with Monterey jack. Place dish into the air fryer basket. Adjust the temperature to 370 Degrees F and set the timer for 10 minutes.
4. Enchiladas will be golden on top and bubbling when cooked. Serve warm with sour cream and sliced avocado.

NUTRITION: Calories: 416; Protein: 34.2g; Fiber: 2.3g; Fat: 25.2g; Carbs: 6.5g

213. Crispy Chicken Tenders

Preparation Time: 25 minutes • Servings: 4

INGREDIENTS

- 9oz. coconut flakes
- 4chicken breasts, skinless; boneless and cut into tenders
- 1/3 cup almond flour
- 2eggs, whisked

- A pinch of salt and black pepper

DIRECTIONS

1. Season the chicken tenders with salt and pepper, dredge them in almond flour, then dip in eggs and roll in coconut flakes.
2. Put the chicken tenders in your air fryer's basket and cook at 400°F for 10 minutes on each side.
3. Divide between plates and serve with a side salad.

NUTRITION: Calories: 250; Fat: 12g; Fiber: 4g; Carbs: 6g; Protein: 15g

214. Chicken Cheese Sticks

Preparation Time: 13 minutes • Servings: 2

INGREDIENTS

- 1cup shredded cooked chicken
- 1large egg.
- ¼ cup crumbled feta
- 1cup shredded mozzarella cheese
- ¼ cup buffalo sauce

DIRECTIONS

1. Take a large bowl, mix all ingredients except the feta. Cut a piece of parchment to fit your air fryer basket and press the mixture into a ½-inch-thick circle
2. Sprinkle the mixture with feta and place into the air fryer basket. Adjust the temperature to 400 Degrees F and set the timer for 8 minutes
3. After 5 minutes, flip over the cheese mixture. Allow to cool 5 minutes before cutting into sticks. Serve warm.

NUTRITION: Calories: 369; Protein: 35.7g; Fiber: 0.0g; Fat: 21.5g; Carbs: 2.2g

215. Marinated Drumsticks

Preparation Time: 40 minutes • Servings: 4

INGREDIENTS

- 2lb. chicken drumsticks
- 1½ cups tomato sauce
- 1tbsp. coconut aminos
- 1tsp. onion powder
- ½ tsp. chili powder
- A pinch of salt and black pepper

DIRECTIONS

1. In bowl, mix the chicken drumsticks with all the other ingredients, toss and keep in the fridge for 10 minutes.
2. Drain the drumsticks, put them in your air fryer's basket and cook at 380°F for 15 minutes on each side. Divide everything between plates and serve

NUTRITION: Calories: 254; Fat: 14g; Fiber: 4g; Carbs: 6g; Protein: 15g

216. Mustard Turkey Bites

Preparation Time: 25 minutes • Servings: 4

INGREDIENTS

- 1big turkey breast, skinless; boneless and cubed
- 4garlic cloves; minced
- 1tbsp. mustard
- 1½ tbsp. olive oil
- Salt and black pepper to taste.

DIRECTIONS

1. Take a bowl and mix the chicken with the garlic and the other ingredients and toss.
2. Put the turkey in your air fryer's basket, cook at 360°F for 20 minutes, divide between plates and serve with a side salad

NUTRITION: Calories: 240; Fat: 12g; Fiber: 4g; Carbs: 6g; Protein: 15g

217. Lemon Pepper Drumsticks

Preparation Time: 30 minutes • Servings: 8 drumsticks

INGREDIENTS

- 8chicken drumsticks
- 1tbsp. lemon pepper seasoning
- 4tbsp. salted butter; melted.
- 2tsp. baking powder.
- ½ tsp. garlic powder.

DIRECTIONS

1. Sprinkle baking powder and garlic powder over drumsticks and rub into chicken skin. Place drumsticks into the air fryer basket.
2. Adjust the temperature to 375 Degrees F and set the timer for 25 minutes
3. Use tongs to turn drumsticks halfway through the cooking time. When skin is golden and internal temperature is at least 165 Degrees F, remove from fryer
4. Take a large bowl, mix butter and lemon pepper seasoning. Add drumsticks to the bowl and toss until coated. Serve warm.

NUTRITION: Calories: 532; Protein: 48.3g; Fiber: 0.0g; Fat: 32.3g; Carbs: 1.2g

218. Chives Chicken Tenders

Preparation Time: 25 minutes • Servings: 4

INGREDIENTS

- 1lb. chicken tenders, boneless, skinless
- 1tbsp. chives; chopped
- A drizzle of olive oil
- Juice of 1 lemon
- A pinch of salt and black pepper

DIRECTIONS

1. Take a bowl and mix the chicken tenders with all ingredients except the chives, toss, put the meat in your air fryer's basket and cook at 370°F for 10 minutes on each side
2. Divide between plates and serve with chives sprinkled on top.

NUTRITION: Calories: 230; Fat: 13g; Fiber: 4g; Carbs: 6g; Protein: 16g

219. Cinnamon Duck Breasts

Preparation Time: 25 minutes • Servings: 2

INGREDIENTS

- 2duck breasts; boneless and skin scored
- 4tbsp. stevia
- 3tbsp. balsamic vinegar
- ¼ tsp. cinnamon powder
- A pinch of salt and black pepper

DIRECTIONS

1. Take a bowl and mix the duck breasts with the rest of the ingredients and rub well.
2. Put the duck breasts in your air fryer's basket and cook at 380°F for 10 minutes on each side. Divide everything between plates and serve

NUTRITION: Calories: 294; Fat: 12g; Fiber: 4g; Carbs: 6g; Protein: 15g

220. Cheddar Turkey Bites

Preparation Time: 25 minutes • Servings: 4

INGREDIENTS:

- 1big turkey breast, skinless; boneless and cubed
- 1tbsp. olive oil
- ¼ cup cheddar cheese, grated
- ¼ tsp. garlic powder
- Salt and black pepper to taste.

DIRECTIONS

1. Rub the turkey cubes with the oil, season with salt, pepper and garlic powder and dredge

in cheddar cheese.

2. Put the turkey bits in your air fryer's basket and cook at 380°F for 20 minutes. Divide between plates and serve with a side salad

NUTRITION: Calories: 240; Fat: 11g; Fiber: 2g; Carbs: 5g; Protein: 12g

221. Crispy Chicken Wings

Preparation Time: 35 minutes • Servings: 4

INGREDIENTS

- 2lb. chicken wings
- ¼ cup olive oil
- Zest of 1 lemon, grated
- 2garlic cloves; minced
- Juice of 2 lemons
- A pinch of salt and black pepper

DIRECTIONS

1. Take a bowl and mix the chicken wings with the rest of the ingredients and toss well
2. Put the chicken wings in your air fryer's basket and cook at 400°F for 30 minutes, shaking halfway. Divide between plates and serve with a side salad

NUTRITION: Calories: 263; Fat: 14g; Fiber: 4g; Carbs: 6g; Protein: 15g

222. Mozzarella Chicken Breasts

Preparation Time: 29 minutes • Servings: 6

INGREDIENTS

- 1lb. mozzarella; sliced
- 2tomatoes; sliced
- 2cups baby spinach
- 6chicken breasts, skinless; boneless and halved
- 2tbsp. olive oil
- 1tbsp. basil; chopped
- 1tsp. Italian seasoning
- A pinch of salt and black pepper

DIRECTIONS

1. Make slits in each chicken breast halves, season with salt, pepper and Italian seasoning and stuff with mozzarella, spinach and tomatoes.
2. Drizzle the oil over stuffed chicken, put it in your air fryer's basket and cook at 370°F for 12 minutes on each side. Divide between plates and serve with basil sprinkled on top.

NUTRITION: Calories: 285; Fat: 12g; Fiber: 4g; Carbs: 7g; Protein: 15g

223. Smoked Chicken Wings

Preparation Time: 35 minutes • Servings: 4

INGREDIENTS

- 2lb. chicken wings
- 1tbsp. olive oil
- 1tbsp. lime juice
- 1tsp. red pepper flakes, crushed
- 2tsp. smoked paprika
- Salt and black pepper to taste.

DIRECTIONS:

1. Take a bowl and mix the chicken wings with all the other ingredients and toss well
2. Put the chicken wings in your air fryer's basket and cook at 380°F for 15 minutes on each side. Divide between plates and serve with a side salad.

NUTRITION: Calories: 280; Fat: 13g; Fiber: 3g; Carbs: 6g; Protein: 14g

224. Mediterranean Chicken

Preparation Time: 40 minutes • Servings: 4

INGREDIENTS

- 1lb. chicken thighs; boneless and skinless
- ½ lb. asparagus, trimmed and halved
-
- 1zucchini; halved lengthwise and sliced into half-moons
- 3garlic cloves; minced
- Juice of 1 lemon
- 2tbsp. olive oil
- 1tsp. oregano; dried
- A pinch of salt and black pepper

DIRECTIONS

1. Take a bowl and mix the chicken with all the ingredients except the asparagus and the zucchinis, toss and leave aside for 15 minutes
2. Add the zucchinis and the asparagus, toss, put everything into a pan that fits the air fryer and cook at 380°F for 25 minutes. Divide everything between plates and serve.

NUTRITION: Calories: 280; Fat: 11g; Fiber: 4g; Carbs: 6g; Protein: 17g

225. Lemon-Oregano Chicken BBQ

Servings: 6 • Cooking Time: 40 minutes

INGREDIENTS

- 1tablespoon grated lemon zest
- 2tablespoons fresh lemon juice
- 2tablespoons oregano, chopped

- 3pounds chicken breasts
- 4cloves of garlic, minced
- Salt and pepper to taste

DIRECTIONS:

1. Preheat the air fryer to 3900F.
2. Place the grill pan accessory in the air fryer.
3. Season the chicken with oregano, garlic, lemon zest, lemon juice, salt and pepper.
4. Grill for 40 minutes and flip every 10 minutes to cook evenly.

NUTRITION: Calories: 388; Carbs: 1.9g; Protein: 47.5g; Fat: 21.2g

226. Chicken BBQ Recipe from Peru

Servings: 4 • Cooking Time: 40 minutes

INGREDIENTS

- ½ teaspoon dried oregano
- 1teaspoon paprika
- 1/3 cup soy sauce
- 2½ pounds chicken, quartered
- 2tablespoons fresh lime juice
- 2teaspoons ground cumin
- 5 cloves of garlic, minced

DIRECTIONS:

1. Place all Ingredients in a Ziploc bag and shake to mix everything.
2. Allow to marinate for at least 2 hours in the fridge.
3. Preheat the air fryer to 3900F.
4. Place the grill pan accessory in the air fryer.
5. Grill the chicken for 40 minutes making sure to flip the chicken every 10 minutes for even grilling.

NUTRITION: Calories: 377; Carbs: 7.9g; Protein: 59.7g; Fat: 11.8g

227. Turmeric and Lemongrass Chicken Roast

Servings: 6 • Cooking Time: 40 minutes

INGREDIENTS

- 1teaspoon turmeric
- 2lemongrass stalks
- 2tablespoons fish sauce
- 3cloves of garlic, minced
- 3pounds whole chicken
- 3shallots, chopped
- Salt and pepper to taste

DIRECTIONS:

1. Place all Ingredients in a Ziploc bag and allow to marinate for at least 2 hours in the fridge.
2. Preheat the air fryer to 3900F.
3. Place the grill pan accessory in the air fryer.
4. Grill the chicken for 40 minutes making sure to flip every 10 minutes for even grilling.

NUTRITION: Calories: 495; Carbs: 49.1g; Protein: 38.5g; Fat: 16.1g

228. Roast Chicken Recipe from Africa

Servings: 6 • Cooking Time: 45 minutes

INGREDIENTS

- ¼ cup fresh lemon juice
- ½ cup piri piri sauce
- 1large shallots, quartered
- 1-inch fresh ginger, peeled and sliced thinly
- 3cloves of garlic, minced
- 3pounds chicken breasts
- Salt and pepper to taste

DIRECTIONS:

1. Preheat the air fryer to 3900F.
2. Place the grill pan accessory in the air fryer.
3. On a large foil, place the chicken top with the rest of the Ingredients.
4. Fold the foil and crimp the edges.
5. Grill for 45 minutes.

NUTRITION: Calories: 395; Carbs: 3.4g; Protein: 47.9g; Fat: 21.1g

229. Shishito Pepper Rubbed Wings

Servings: 6 • Cooking Time: 30 minutes

INGREDIENTS

- 1½ cups shishito peppers, pureed
- 2tablespoons sesame oil
- 3pounds chicken wings
- Salt and pepper to taste

DIRECTIONS:

1. Place all Ingredients in a Ziploc bowl and allow to marinate for at least 2 hours in the fridge.
2. Preheat the air fryer to 3900F.
3. Place the grill pan accessory in the air fryer.
4. Grill for at least 30 minutes flipping the chicken every 5 minutes and basting with the remaining sauce.

NUTRITION: Calories: 321; Carbs: 1.7g; Protein: 50.2g; Fat: 12.6g

230. Grilled Chicken Recipe from Korea

Servings: 4 • Cooking Time: 30 minutes

INGREDIENTS

- ½ cup gochujang
- ½ teaspoon fresh ground black pepper
- 1scallion, sliced thinly
- 1teaspoon salt
- 2pounds chicken wings

DIRECTIONS:

1. Place in a Ziploc bag the chicken wings, salt, pepper, and gochujang sauce.
2. Allow to marinate in the fridge for at least 2 hours.
3. Preheat the air fryer to 3900F.
4. Place the grill pan accessory in the air fryer.
5. Grill the chicken wings for 30 minutes making sure to flip the chicken every 10 minutes.
6. Top with scallions and serve with more gochujang.

NUTRITION: Calories: 278; Carbs: 0.8g; Protein: 50.1g; Fat: 8.2g

231. Lemon-Parsley Chicken Packets

Servings: 4 • Cooking Time: 45 minutes

INGREDIENTS

- ¼ cup smoked paprika
- ½ cup parsley leaves
- ½ teaspoon liquid smoke seasoning
- 1½ tablespoon cayenne pepper
- 2pounds chicken thighs
- 4lemons, halved
- Salt and pepper to taste

DIRECTIONS:

1. Preheat the air fryer to 3900F.
2. Place the grill pan accessory in the air fryer.
3. In a large foil, place the chicken and season with paprika, liquid smoke seasoning, salt, pepper, and cayenne pepper.
4. Top with lemon and parsley.
5. Place on the grill and cook for 45 minutes.

NUTRITION: Calories: 551; Carbs: 10.4g; Protein: 39.2g; Fat: 39.1g

232. Grilled Chicken Wings with Curry- Yogurt Sauce

Servings: 4 • Cooking Time: 35 minutes

INGREDIENTS

- ½ cup plain yogurt
- 1tablespoons curry powder
- 2pounds chicken wings
- Salt and pepper to taste

DIRECTIONS:

1. Season the chicken wings with yogurt, curry powder, salt and pepper. Toss to combine everything.
2. Allow to marinate in the fridge for at least 2 hours.
3. Preheat the air fryer to 3900F.
4. Place the grill pan accessory in the air fryer.
5. Grill the chicken for 35 minutes and make sure to flip the chicken halfway through the cooking time.

NUTRITION: Calories: 301; Carbs: 3.3g; Protein: 51.3g; Fat: 9.2g

233. Tomato, Eggplant 'n Chicken Skewers

Servings: 4 • Cooking Time: 25 minutes

INGREDIENTS

- ¼ teaspoon cayenne pepper
- ¼ teaspoon ground cardamom
- 1½ teaspoon ground turmeric
- 1can coconut milk
- 1cup cherry tomatoes
- 1medium eggplant, cut into cubes
- 1onion, cut into wedges
- 1-inch ginger, grated
- 2pounds boneless chicken breasts, cut into cubes
- 2tablespoons fresh lime juice
- 2tablespoons tomato paste
- 3teaspoons lime zest
- 4cloves of garlic, minced
- Salt and pepper to taste

DIRECTIONS:

1. Place in a bowl the garlic, ginger, coconut milk, lime zest, lime juice, tomato paste, salt, pepper, turmeric, cayenne pepper, cardamom, and chicken breasts. Allow to marinate in the fridge for at least for 2 hours.
2. Preheat the air fryer to 3900F.
3. Place the grill pan accessory in the air fryer.
4. Skewer the chicken cubes with eggplant, onion, and cherry tomatoes on bamboo skewers.
5. Place on the grill pan and cook for 25 minutes making sure to flip the chicken every 5 minutes for even cooking.

NUTRITION: Calories: 485; Carbs:19.7 g; Protein: 55.2g; Fat: 20.6g

234. Garam Masala 'n Yogurt Marinated Chicken

Servings: 3 • Cooking Time: 40 minutes

INGREDIENTS

- ½ cup whole milk yogurt
- ½ teaspoon ground cumin
- 1½ pounds skinless chicken thighs
- 1½ teaspoon garam masala
- 1tablespoon ground coriander
- 1tablespoon smoked paprika
- 1-inch ginger, peeled and chopped
- 2tablespoons prepared mustard
- 3tablespoons fresh lime juice
- 4cloves of garlic, minced
- 7dried chilies, seeds removed and broken into pieces
- Salt and pepper to taste

DIRECTIONS:

1. Place all ingredients in a Ziploc bag and give a good shake to combine everything.
2. Allow to marinate for at least 2 hours in the fridge.
3. Preheat the air fryer to 3900F.
4. Place the grill pan accessory in the air fryer.
5. Grill for at least 40 minutes.
6. Make sure to flip the chicken every 10 minutes.

NUTRITION: Calories: 589; Carbs: 25.5g; Protein:54.6 g; Fat: 29.8g

235. Grilled Chicken Pesto

Servings: 8 • Cooking Time: 30 minutes

INGREDIENTS

- 1¾ cup commercial pesto
- 8chicken thighs
- Salt and pepper to taste

DIRECTIONS:

1. Place all Ingredients in the Ziploc bag and allow to marinate in the fridge for at least 2 hours.
2. Preheat the air fryer to 3900F.
3. Place the grill pan accessory in the air fryer.
4. Grill the chicken for at least 30 minutes.
5. Make sure to flip the chicken every 10 minutes for even grilling.

NUTRITION: Calories: 477; Carbs: 3.8g; Protein: 32.6g; Fat: 36.8g

236. Quick 'n Easy Garlic Herb Wings

Servings: 4 • Cooking Time: 35 minutes

INGREDIENTS

- ¼ cup chopped rosemary
- 2pounds chicken wings
- 6medium garlic cloves , grated
- salt and pepper to taste

DIRECTIONS:

1. Season the chicken with garlic, rosemary, salt and pepper.
2. Preheat the air fryer to 3900F.
3. Place the grill pan accessory in the air fryer.
4. Grill for 35 minutes and make sure to flip the chicken every 10 minutes.

NUTRITION: Calories: 287; Carbs: 2.9g; Protein: 50.4g; Fat: 8.2g

237. Lemon-Aleppo Chicken

Servings: 4 • Cooking Time: 1 hour

INGREDIENTS

- ¼ cup Aleppo-style pepper
- ¼ cup fresh lemon juice
- ¼ cup oregano
- 1cup green olives, pitted and cracked
- 14 cup chopped rosemary
- 2pounds whole chicken, backbones removed and butterflied
- 6cloves of garlic, minced
- Salt and pepper to taste

DIRECTIONS:

1. Place the chicken breast side up and slice through the breasts. Using your palms, press against the breastbone to flatten the breasts or you may remove the bones altogether.
2. Once the bones have been removed, season the chicken with salt, pepper, garlic, pepper, rosemary, lemon juice, and oregano.
3. Allow to marinate in the fridge for at least 12 hours.
4. Preheat the air fryer to 3900F.
5. Place the grill pan accessory in the air fryer.
6. Place the chicken on the grill pan and place the olives around the chicken.
7. Grill for 1 hour and make sure to flip the chicken every 10 minutes for even grilling.

NUTRITION: Calories: 502; Carbs:50.4 g; Protein:37.6 g; Fat: 16.6g

238. Drunken Chicken Jerk Spiced

Servings: 8 • Cooking Time: 60 minutes

INGREDIENTS

- ¾ ground cloves
- ¾ malt vinegar
- ¾ soy sauce
- 1½ teaspoons ground nutmeg
- 2½ teaspoons ground allspice
- 2tablespoons rum
- 2tablespoon salt
- 4habanero chilies
- 5cloves of garlic, minced
- 8pieces chicken legs

DIRECTIONS:

1. Place all Ingredients in a Ziploc bag and give a good shake. Allow to marinate in the fridge for at least 2 hours.
2. Preheat the air fryer to 3900F.
3. Place the grill pan accessory in the air fryer.
4. Grill the chicken for 60 minutes and flip the chicken every 10 minutes for even grilling.

NUTRITION: Calories: 193; Carbs: 1.2g; Protein:28.7 g; Fat: 8.1g

239. Honey, Lime, And Garlic Chicken BBQ

Servings: 4 • Cooking Time: 40 minutes

INGREDIENTS

- ¼ cup lime juice, freshly squeezed
- ½ cup cilantro, chopped finely
- ½ cup honey
- 1tablespoon olive oil
- 2cloves of garlic, minced
- 2pounds boneless chicken breasts
- 2tablespoons soy sauce
- Salt and pepper to taste

DIRECTIONS:

1. Place all Ingredients in a Ziploc bag and give a good shake. Allow to marinate in the fridge for at least 2 hours.
2. Preheat the air fryer to 3900F.
3. Place the grill pan accessory in the air fryer.
4. Grill the chicken for 40 minutes making sure to flip the chicken every 10 minutes to grill evenly on all sides.

NUTRITION: Calories: 458; Carbs: 38.9g; Protein:52.5 g; Fat: 10.2g

240. Chicken in Packets Southwest Style

Servings: 4 • Cooking Time: 40 minutes

INGREDIENTS

- 1can black beans, rinsed and drained
- 1cup cilantro, chopped
- 1cup commercial salsa
- 1cup corn kernels, frozen
- 1cup Mexican cheese blend, shredded
- 4chicken breasts
- 4lime wedges
- 4teaspoons taco seasoning
- Salt and pepper to taste

DIRECTIONS:

1. Preheat the air fryer to 3900F.
2. Place the grill pan accessory in the air fryer.
3. On a big aluminum foil, place the chicken breasts and season with salt and pepper to taste.
4. Add the corn, commercial salsa beans, and taco seasoning.
5. Close the foil and crimp the edges.
6. Place on the grill pan and cook for 40 minutes.
7. Before serving, top with cheese, cilantro and lime wedges.

NUTRITION: Calories: 837; Carbs: 47.5g; Protein: 80.1g; Fat: 36.2g

241. Cheese Stuffed Chicken

Servings: 4 • Cooking Time: 30 minutes

INGREDIENTS

- 1tablespoon creole seasoning
- 1tablespoon olive oil
- 1teaspoon garlic powder
- 1teaspoon onion powder
- 4chicken breasts, butterflied and pounded
- 4slices Colby cheese
- 4slices pepper jack cheese

DIRECTIONS:

1. Preheat the air fryer to 3900F.
2. Place the grill pan accessory in the air fryer.
3. Create the dry rub by mixing in a bowl the creole seasoning, garlic powder, and onion powder. Season with salt and pepper if desired.
4. Rub the seasoning on to the chicken.
5. Place the chicken on a working surface and place a slice each of pepper jack and Colby cheese.
6. Fold the chicken and secure the edges with toothpicks.
7. Brush chicken with olive oil.
8. Grill for 30 minutes and make sure to flip the meat every 10 minutes.

NUTRITION: Calories: 727; Carbs:5.4 g; Protein: 73.1g; Fat: 45.9g

242. Cilantro-Lime 'n Liquid Smoke Chicken Grill

Servings: 4 • Cooking Time: 40 minutes

INGREDIENTS

- 1½ teaspoon honey
- 1tablespoon lime zest
- 1teaspoon liquid smoke
- 1/3 cup chopped cilantro
- 1/3 cup fresh lime juice
- 2tablespoons olive oil
- 3cloves of garlic, minced
- 4chicken breasts, halved
- Salt and pepper to taste

DIRECTIONS:

1. Place all Ingredients in a bowl and allow to marinate in the fridge for at least 2 hours.
2. Preheat the air fryer to 3900F.
3. Place the grill pan accessory in the air fryer.
4. Grill in the chicken for 40 minutes and make sure to flip the chicken every 10 minutes for even grilling.

NUTRITION: Calories: 571; Carbs: 6.1g; Protein: 60.9g; Fat: 33.6g

243. Chicken BBQ on Kale Salad

Servings: 4 • Cooking Time: 30 minutes

INGREDIENTS

- ¼ cup Greek yogurt
- ¼ cup parmesan cheese, grated
- ½ cup cherry tomatoes, halved
- ½ teaspoon Worcestershire sauce
- 1clove of garlic, minced
- 1large bunch Tuscan kale, cleaned and torn
- 3tablespoons extra virgin olive oil
- 4large chicken breasts, pounded
- Juice from 2 lemons, divided
- Salt and pepper to taste

DIRECTIONS:

1. Place all Ingredients in a bowl except for the kale and tomatoes. Allow to marinate in the fridge for at least 2 hours.
2. Preheat the air fryer to 3900F.
3. Place the grill pan accessory in the air fryer.
4. Grill the chicken for 30 minutes.
5. Once cooked, slice the chicken and toss together with the kale and tomatoes.

NUTRITION: Calories: 500; Carbs: 5.9g; Protein: 82.3g; Fat: 16.3g

244. Sriracha-vinegar Marinated Chicken

Servings: 4 • Cooking Time: 40 minutes

INGREDIENTS

- ¼ cup Thai fish sauce
- ¼ cups sriracha sauce
- ½ cup rice vinegar
- 1tablespoons sugar
- 2garlic cloves, minced
- 2pounds chicken breasts
- Juice from 1 lime, freshly squeezed
- Salt and pepper to taste

DIRECTIONS:

1. Place all Ingredients in a Ziploc bag except for the corn. Allow to marinate in the fridge for at least 2 hours.
2. Preheat the air fryer to 3900F.
3. Place the grill pan accessory in the air fryer.
4. Grill the chicken for 40 minutes and make sure to flip the chicken to grill evenly.
5. Meanwhile, place the marinade in a saucepan and heat over medium flame until it thickens.
6. Brush the chicken with the glaze and serve with cucumbers if desired.

NUTRITION: Calories: 427; Carbs: 6.7g; Protein: 49.1g; Fat: 22.6g

245. Chicken BBQ Recipe from Italy

Servings: 2 • Cooking Time: 40 minutes

INGREDIENTS

- 1tablespoon fresh Italian parsley
- 1tablespoon minced garlic
- 1-pound boneless chicken breasts
- 2tablespoons tomato paste
- Salt and pepper to taste

DIRECTIONS:

1. Place all Ingredients in a Ziploc bag except for the corn. Allow to marinate in the fridge for at least 2 hours.
2. Preheat the air fryer to 3900F.
3. Place the grill pan accessory in the air fryer.
4. Grill the chicken for 40 minutes.

NUTRITION: Calories: 292; Carbs: 6.6g; Protein: 52.6g; Fat: 6.1g

246. Chili, Lime & Corn Chicken BBQ

Servings: 4 • Cooking Time: 40 minutes

INGREDIENTS

- ½ teaspoon cumin
- 1tablespoon lime juice
- 1teaspoon chili powder
- 2chicken breasts
- 2chicken thighs
- 2cups barbecue sauce
- 2teaspoon grated lime zest
- 4ears of corn, cleaned
- Salt and pepper to taste

DIRECTIONS:

1. Place all Ingredients in a Ziploc bag except for the corn. Allow to marinate in the fridge for at least 2 hours.

2. Preheat the air fryer to 3900F.
3. Place the grill pan accessory in the air fryer.
4. Grill the chicken and corn for 40 minutes.
5. Meanwhile, pour the marinade in a saucepan over medium heat until it thickens.
6. Before serving, brush the chicken and corn with the glaze.

NUTRITION: Calories per serving:849 ; Carbs: 87.7g; Protein: 52.3g; Fat: 32.1g

247. Honey-Balsamic Orange Chicken

Servings: 3 • Cooking Time: 40 minutes

INGREDIENTS

- ½ cup balsamic vinegar
- ½ cup honey
- 1½ pounds boneless chicken breasts, pounded
- 1tablespoon orange zest
- 1teaspoon fresh oregano, chopped
- 2tablespoons extra virgin olive oil
- Salt and pepper to taste

DIRECTIONS:

1. Put the chicken in a Ziploc bag and pour over the rest of the Ingredients. Shake to combine everything. Allow to marinate in the fridge for at least 2 hours.
2. Preheat the air fryer to 3900F.
3. Place the grill pan accessory in the air fryer.
4. Grill the chicken for 40 minutes.

NUTRITION: Calories: 521; Carbs: 56.1g; Protein: 51.8g; Fat: 9.9g

248. Salsa Verde Over Grilled Chicken

Servings: 2 • Cooking Time: 40 minutes

INGREDIENTS

- ½ red onion, chopped
- ½ teaspoon chili powder
- 1jalapeno thinly sliced
- 1jar salsa verde, divided
- 1-pound boneless skinless chicken breasts
- 2cloves of garlic, minced
- 2tablespoons chopped cilantro
- 2tablespoons extra virgin olive oil
- 4slices Monterey Jack cheese
- Juice from ½ lime
- Lime wedges for serving

DIRECTIONS:

1. In a Ziploc bag, add half of the salsa verde, olive oil, lime juice, garlic, chili powder and chicken. Allow to marinate in the fridge for at least 2 hours.

2. Preheat the air fryer to 3900F.
3. Place the grill pan accessory in the air fryer.
4. Grill the chicken for 40 minutes.
5. Flip the chicken every 10 minutes to cook evenly.
6. Serve the chicken with the cheese, jalapeno, red onion, cilantro, and lime wedges.

NUTRITION: Calories: 541; Carbs: 4.5g; Protein: 65.3g; Fat: 29.1g

249. Chicken Grill Recipe from California

Servings: 4 • Cooking Time: 40 minutes

INGREDIENTS

- ¾ cup balsamic vinegar
- 1teaspoon garlic powder
- 2tablespoons extra virgin olive oil
- 2tablespoons honey
- 2teaspoons Italian seasoning
- 4boneless chicken breasts
- 4slices mozzarella
- 4slices of avocado
- 4slices tomato
- Balsamic vinegar for drizzling
- Salt and pepper to taste

DIRECTIONS:

1. In a Ziploc bag, mix together the balsamic vinegar, garlic powder, honey, olive oil, Italian seasoning, salt, pepper, and chicken.
2. Allow to marinate in the fridge for at least 2 hours.
3. Preheat the air fryer to 3900F.
4. Place the grill pan accessory in the air fryer.
5. Put the chicken on the grill and cook for 40 minutes.
6. Flip the chicken every 10 minutes to grill all sides evenly.
7. Serve the chicken with mozzarella, avocado, and tomato. Drizzle with balsamic vinegar.

NUTRITION: Calories: 853; Carbs: 43.2g; Protein:69.4 g; Fat: 44.7g

250. Grilled Thighs with Honey Balsamic Sauce

Servings: 8 • Cooking Time: 40 minutes

INGREDIENTS

- 1/3 cup honey
- 2tablespoons balsamic vinegar
- 2tablespoons butter
- 3cloves of garlic, minced

- 8bone-in chicken thighs
- Chopped chives for garnish
- Lemon wedges for garnish
- Salt and pepper to taste

DIRECTIONS:

1. In a mixing bowl, season the chicken with salt and pepper to taste.
2. Add the butter, balsamic vinegar, honey, and garlic.
3. Allow to marinate for 2 hours in the fridge.
4. Preheat the air fryer to 3900F.
5. Place the grill pan accessory in the air fryer.
6. Put the chicken on the grill pan and cook for 40 minutes. Flip the chicken every 10 minutes to grill evenly.
7. Meanwhile, place the remaining marinade in a saucepan and allow to simmer until thickened.
8. Once cooked, brush the chicken with the sauce and garnish with chives and lemon wedges.

NUTRITION: Calories: 524; Carbs: 32.4g; Protein: 25.1g; Fat: 32.7g

251. Chicken Roast with Pineapple Salsa

Servings: 2 • Cooking Time: 45 minutes

INGREDIENTS

- ¼ cup extra virgin olive oil
- ¼ cup freshly chopped cilantro
- 1avocado, diced
- 1-pound boneless chicken breasts
- 2cups canned pineapples
- 2teaspoons honey
- Juice from 1 lime
- Salt and pepper to taste

DIRECTIONS:

1. Preheat the air fryer to 3900F.
2. Place the grill pan accessory in the air fryer.
3. Season the chicken breasts with lime juice, olive oil, honey, salt, and pepper.
4. Place on the grill pan and cook for 45 minutes.
5. Flip the chicken every 10 minutes to grill all sides evenly.
6. Once the chicken is cooked, serve with pineapples, cilantro, and avocado.

NUTRITION: Calories: 744; Carbs: 57.4g; Protein: 54.7g; Fat: 32.8g

252. Sweet Lime 'n Chili Chicken Barbecue

Servings: 2 • Cooking Time: 40 minutes

INGREDIENTS

- ¼ cup soy sauce
- 1cup sweet chili sauce
- 1-pound chicken breasts
- Juice from 2 limes, freshly squeezed

DIRECTIONS:

1. In a Ziploc bag, combine all Ingredients and give a good shake. Allow to marinate for at least 2 hours in the fridge.
2. Preheat the air fryer to 3900F.
3. Place the grill pan accessory in the air fryer.
4. Place chicken on the grill and cook for 30 to 40 minutes. Make sure to flip the chicken every 10 minutes to cook evenly.
5. Meanwhile, use the remaining marinade and put it in a saucepan. Simmer until the sauce thickens.
6. Once the chicken is cooked, brush with the thickened marinade.

NUTRITION: Calories: 563; Carbs: 39.2g; Protein: 43.6g; Fat: 25.7g

253. Sticky-Sweet Chicken BBQ

Servings: 2 • Cooking Time: 40 minutes

INGREDIENTS

- ½ cup balsamic vinegar
- ½ cup soy sauce
- 1-pound chicken drumsticks
- 2cloves of garlic, minced
- 2green onion, sliced thinly
- 2tablespoons sesame seeds
- 3tablespoons honey

DIRECTIONS:

1. In a Ziploc bag, combine the soy sauce, balsamic vinegar, honey, garlic, and chicken. Allow to marinate in the fridge for at least 30 minutes.
2. Preheat the air fryer to 3300F.
3. Place the grill pan accessory in the air fryer.
4. Place on the grill and cook for 30 to 40 minutes. Make sure to flip the chicken every 10 minutes to cook evenly.
5. Meanwhile, use the remaining marinade and put it in a saucepan. Simmer until the sauce thickens.
6. Once the chicken is cooked, brush with the thickened marinade and garnish with sesame seeds and green onions.

NUTRITION: Calories: 594; Carbs: 43.7g; Protein: 48.7g; Fat: 24.9g

CHAPTER 6

MEAT

254. Mediterranean Lamb Meatballs

Preparation time: 10 minutes • Cooking time: 40 minutes • Servings: 4

INGREDIENTS

- 454g ground lamb
- 3cloves garlic, minced
- 5g of salt
- 1g black pepper
- 2g of mint, freshly chopped
- 2g ground cumin
- 3ml hot sauce
- 1g chili powder
- 1scallion, chopped
- 8g parsley, finely chopped
- 15 ml of fresh lemon juice
- 2g lemon zest
- 10 ml of olive oil

DIRECTION:

1. Mix the lamb, garlic, salt, pepper, mint, cumin, hot sauce, chili powder, chives, parsley, lemon juice and lemon zest until well combined.
2. Create balls with the lamb mixture and cool for 30 minutes.
3. Select Preheat in the air fryer and press Start/Pause.
4. Cover the meatballs with olive oil and place them in the preheated fryer.
5. Select Steak, set the time to 10 minutes and press Start/Pause.

NUTRITION: Calories: 282, Fat: 23.41, Carbohydrates: 0g Protein: 16.59 Sugar: 0g Cholesterol: 73gm

255. Pork Rind

Preparation time: 10 minutes • Cooking time: 1h • Serve: 4

INGREDIENTS

- 1kg of pork rinds
- Salt
- ½ tsp black pepper coffee

DIRECTION:

1. Preheat the air fryer. Set the time of 5 minutes and the temperature to 2000C.
2. Cut the bacon into cubes - 1 finger wide.

3. Season with salt and a pinch of pepper.
4. Place in the basket of the air fryer. Set the time of 45 minutes and press the power button.
5. Shake the basket every 10 minutes so that the pork rinds stay golden brown equally.
6. Once they are ready, drain a little on the paper towel so they stay dry. Transfer to a plate and serve.

NUTRITION: Calories: 172 Fat: 10.02g Carbohydrates: 0g Protein: 19.62g Sugar: 0g Cholesterol: 30 mg

256. Pork Trinoza Wrapped in Ham

Preparation time: 10 minutes Cooking time: 20 minutes Servings: 4

INGREDIENTS

- 400g of very thin sliced pork fillets c / n
- 2boiled and chopped eggs
- 100g chopped Serrano ham
- 1beaten egg
- Breadcrumbs

DIRECTION:

1. Make a roll with the pork fillets. Introduce half cooked egg and Serrano ham. So that the roll does not lose its shape, fasten with a string or chopsticks.
2. Pass the rolls through beaten egg and then through the breadcrumbs until it forms a good layer.
3. Preheat the air fryer a few minutes at 180° C.
4. Insert the rolls in the basket and set the timer for about 8 minutes at 180o C.
5. Serve right away.

NUTRITION: Calories: 250 Fat: 14.20g Carbohydrates: 35g Protein: 27.60g Sugar: 0g Cholesterol: 0g

257. Homemade Flamingos

Preparation time: 10 minutes • Cooking time: 20 minutes • Servings: 6

INGREDIENTS

- 6pieces of Serrano ham, thinly sliced
- 454g pork, halved, with butter and crushed
- 6g of salt
- 1g black pepper
- 227g fresh spinach leaves, divided
- 4slices of mozzarella cheese, divided
- 18g sun-dried tomatoes, divided
- 10ml of olive oil, divided

DIRECTION:

1. Place 3 pieces of ham on baking paper, slightly overlapping each other. Place 1 half of the pork in the ham. Repeat with the other half.
2. Season the inside of the pork rolls with salt and pepper.
3. Place half of the spinach, cheese, and sun-dried tomatoes on top of the pork loin, leaving a 13 mm border on all sides.
4. Roll the fillet around the filling well and tie with a kitchen cord to keep it closed.
5. Repeat the process for the other pork steak and place them in the fridge.
6. Select Preheat in the air fryer and press Start/Pause.
7. Brush 5 ml of olive oil on each wrapped steak and place them in the preheated air fryer.
8. Select Steak. Set the timer to 9 minutes and press Start/Pause.
9. Allow it to cool for 10 minutes before cutting.

NUTRITION: Calories: 424 Fat: 15.15g Carbohydrates: 37.47g Protein: 31.84g Sugar: 3.37g Cholesterol: 157mg

258. North Carolina Style Pork Chops

Preparation time: 5 minutes • Cooking time: 10 minutes • Servings: 2

INGREDIENTS

- 2boneless pork chops
- 15ml of vegetable oil
- 25g dark brown sugar, packaged
- 6g of Hungarian paprika
- 2g ground mustard
- 2g freshly ground black pepper
- 3g onion powder
- 3g garlic powder
- Salt and pepper to taste

DIRECTION:

1. Preheat the air fryer a few minutes at 1800C.
2. Cover the pork chops with oil.
3. Put all the spices and season the pork chops abundantly, almost as if you were making them breaded.
4. Place the pork chops in the preheated air fryer.
5. Select Steak, set the time to 10 minutes.
6. Remove the pork chops when it has finished cooking. Let it stand for 5 minutes and serve.

NUTRITION: Calories: 118 Fat: 6.85g Carbohydrates: 0 Protein: 13.12g Sugar: 0g Cholesterol: 39mg

259. Beef with Sesame and Ginger

Preparation time: 10 minutes • Cooking time: 23 minutes • Servings: 4-6

INGREDIENTS

- ½ cup tamari or soy sauce
- 3tbsp olive oil

- 2tbsp toasted sesame oil
- 1tbsp brown sugar
- 1tbsp ground fresh ginger
- 3cloves garlic, minced
- 1to 1½ pounds skirt steak, boneless sirloin, or low loin

DIRECTION:

1. Put together the tamari sauce, oils, brown sugar, ginger, and garlic in small bowl. Add beef to a quarter-size plastic bag and pour the marinade into the bag. Press on the bag as much air as possible and seal it.
2. Refrigerate for 1 to 1½ hours, turning half the time. Remove the meat from the marinade and discard the marinade. Dry the meat with paper towels. Cook at a temperature of 350°F for 20 to 23 minutes, turning halfway through cooking.

NUTRITION: Calories: 381 Fat: 5g Carbohydrates: 9.6g Protein: 38g Sugar: 1.8g Cholesterol: 0mg

260. Katsu Pork

Preparation time: 10 minutes • Cooking time: 14 minutes • Servings: 2

INGREDIENTS

- 170g pork chops, boneless
- 56g of breadcrumbs
- 3g garlic powder
- 2g onion powder
- 6g of salt
- 1g white pepper
- 60g all-purpose flour
- 2eggs, shakes
- Nonstick Spray Oil

DIRECTION:

1. Place the pork chops in an airtight bag or cover them with a plastic wrap.
2. Crush the pork with a meat roller or hammer until it is 13 mm thick.
3. Combine the crumbs and seasonings in a bowl. Leave aside.
4. Pass each pork chop through the flour, then soak them in the beaten eggs and finally pass them through the crumb mixture.
5. Preheat the air fryer set the temperature to 180°C.
6. Spray pork chops on each side with cooking oil and place them in the preheated air fryer.
7. Cook the pork chops at 180°C for 4 minutes.
8. Remove them from the air fryer when finished and let them sit for 5 minutes.
9. Cut them into pieces and serve them.

NUTRITION: Calories: 820 Fat: 24.75g Carbohydrates: 117g Protein: 33.75g Sugar: 0g Cholesterol: 120mg

261. Pork on A Blanket

Preparation time: 5 minutes • Cooking time: 10 minutes • Servings: 4

INGREDIENTS

- ½ puff pastry sheet, defrosted
- 16thick smoked sausages
- 15ml of milk

DIRECTION:

1. Preheat la air fryer to 200°C and set the timer to 5 minutes.
2. Cut the puff pastry into 64 x 38 mm strips.
3. Place a cocktail sausage at the end of the puff pastry and roll around the sausage, sealing the dough with some water.
4. Brush the top (with the seam facing downof the sausages wrapped in milk and place them in the preheated air fryer.
5. Cook at 200°C for 10 minutes or until golden brown.

NUTRITION: Calories: 242 Fat: 14g Carbohydrates: 0g Protein: 27g Sugar: 0g Cholesterol: 80mg

262. Lamb Shawarma

Preparation time: 12 minutes • Cooking time: 8 minutes • Servings: 2

INGREDIENTS

- 340g ground lamb
- 2g cumin
- 2g of paprika
- 3g garlic powder
- 2g onion powder
- 1g of cinnamon
- 1g turmeric
- 1g fennel seeds
- 1g ground coriander seed
- 3g salt
- 4bamboo skewers (229 mm

DIRECTION:

1. Put all the ingredients in a bowl and mix well.
2. Stir 85g of meat into each skewer, then place them in the fridge for 10 minutes.
3. Preheat in the air fryer to 200°C.
4. Place the skewers in the preheated air fryer, select Steak. Adjust to 8 minutes.
5. Serve with lemon yogurt dressing or alone.

NUTRITION: Calories: 562 Fat: 11.19g Carbohydrates: 76.89g Protein: 35.84g Sugar: 7.45g Cholesterol: 69mg

263. Stuffed Cabbage and Pork Loin Rolls

Preparation time: 5 minutes • Cooking time: 25 minutes Servings: 4

INGREDIENTS

- 500g of white cabbage
- 1onion

- 8pork tenderloin steaks
- 2carrots
- 4tbsp soy sauce
- 50g of olive oil
- Salt
- 8sheets of rice

DIRECTION:

1. Put the chopped cabbage in the Thermomix glass together with the onion and the chopped carrot.
2. Select 5 seconds, speed Add the extra virgin olive oil. Select 5 minutes, varoma temperature, left turn, spoon speed.
3. Cut the tenderloin steaks into thin strips. Add the meat to the Thermomix glass. Select 5 minutes, varoma temperature, left turn, spoon speed. Without beaker
4. Add the soy sauce. Select 5 minutes, varoma temperature, left turn, spoon speed. Rectify salt. Let it cold down.
5. Hydrate the rice slices. Extend and distribute the filling between them.
6. Make the rolls, folding so that the edges are completely closed. Place the rolls in the air fryer and paint with the oil.
7. Select 10 minutes, 1800C.

NUTRITION: Calories: 120 Fat: 3.41g Carbohydrates: 0g Protein: 20.99g Sugar: 0g Cholesterol: 65mg

264. Pork Head Chops with Vegetables

Preparation time: 5 minutes • Cooking time: 20 minutes • Servings: 2-4

INGREDIENTS

- 4pork head chops
- 2red tomatoes
- 1large green pepper
- 4mushrooms
- 1onion
- 4slices of cheese
- Salt
- Ground pepper
- Extra virgin olive oil

DIRECTION:

1. Put the four chops on a plate and salt and pepper.
2. Put two of the chops in the air fryer basket.
3. Place tomato slices, cheese slices, pepper slices, onion slices and mushroom slices. Add some threads of oil.
4. Take the air fryer and select 1800C, 15 minutes.
5. Check that the meat is well made and take out.
6. Repeat the same operation with the other two pork chops.

NUTRITION: Calories: 106 Fat: 5g Carbohydrates: 2g Protein: 11g Sugar: 0g Cholesterol: 0mg

265. Provencal Ribs

Preparation time: 10 minutes • Cooking time: 1h 20 minutes • Servings: 4

INGREDIENTS

- 500g of pork ribs
- Provencal herbs
- Salt
- Ground pepper
- Oil

DIRECTION:

1. Put the ribs in a bowl and add some oil, Provencal herbs, salt, and ground pepper.
2. Stir well and leave in the fridge for at least 1 hour.
3. Put the ribs in the basket of the air fryer and select 2000C, 20 minutes.
4. From time to time shake the basket and remove the ribs.

NUTRITION: Calories: 296 Fat: 22.63g Carbohydrates: 0g Protein: 21.71g Sugar: 0g Cholesterol: 90mg

266. Beef Scallops

Preparation time: 15 minutes • Cooking time: 20 minutes • Servings: 4

INGREDIENTS

- 16veal scallops
- Salt
- Ground pepper
- Garlic powder
- 2eggs
- Breadcrumbs
- Extra virgin olive oil

DIRECTION:

1. Put the beef scallops well spread and salt and pepper. Add some garlic powder.
2. In a bowl, beat the eggs.
3. In another bowl put the breadcrumbs.
4. Pass the Beef scallops for beaten egg and then for the breadcrumbs.
5. Spray with extra virgin olive oil on both sides.
6. Put a batch in the basket of the air fryer. Do not pile the scallops too much.
7. Select 1800C, 15 minutes. From time to time shake the basket so that the scallops move.
8. When finishing that batch, put the next one and so on until you finish with everyone, usually 4 or 5 scallops enter per batch.

NUTRITION: Calories: 330 Fat: 16.27g Carbohydrates: 0g Protein: 43g Sugar: 0g Cholesterol: 163mg

267. Potatoes with Loin and Cheese

Preparation time: 10 minutes • Cooking time: 30 minutes • Servings: 4

INGREDIENTS

- 1kg of potatoes
- 1large onion

- 1piece of roasted loin
- Extra virgin olive oil
- Salt
- Ground pepper
- Grated cheese

DIRECTION:

1. Peel the potatoes, cut the cane, wash, and dry.
2. Put salt and add some threads of oil, we bind well.
3. Pass the potatoes to the basket of the air fryer and select 1800C, 20 minutes.
4. Meanwhile, in a pan, put some extra virgin olive oil and add the peeled onion and cut into julienne.
5. When the onion is transparent, add the chopped loin.
6. Sauté well and pepper.
7. Put the potatoes on a baking sheet.
8. Add the onion with the loin.
9. Cover with a layer of grated cheese.
10. Bake a little until the cheese takes heat and melts.

NUTRITION: Calories: 332 Fat: 7g Carbohydrates: 41g Protein: 23g Sugar: 0g Cholesterol: 0mg

268. Potatoes with Loin and Cheese

Preparation time: 10 minutes • Cooking time: 30 minutes • Servings: 4

INGREDIENTS

- 1kg of potatoes
- 1large onion
- 1piece of roasted loin
- Extra virgin olive oil
- Salt
- Ground pepper
- Grated cheese

DIRECTION:

1. Peel the potatoes, cut the cane, wash, and dry.
2. Put salt and add some threads of oil, bind well.
3. Pass the potatoes to the basket of the air fryer and select 1800C, 20 minutes.
4. Meanwhile, in a pan, put some extra virgin olive oil and add the peeled onion and cut into julienne.
5. When the onion is transparent, add the chopped loin.
6. Sauté well and pepper.
7. Put the potatoes on a baking sheet.
8. Add the onion with the loin.
9. Cover with a layer of grated cheese.
10. Bake a little until the cheese takes heat and melts.

NUTRITION: Calories: 332 Fat: 7g Carbohydrates: 41g Protein: 23g Sugar: 0g Cholesterol: 0mg

269. Russian Steaks with Nuts and Cheese

Preparation time: 5 minutes • Cooking time: 20 minutes • Servings: 4

INGREDIENTS

- 800g of minced pork
- 200g of cream cheese
- 50g peeled walnuts

- 1onion
- Salt
- Ground pepper
- 1egg
- Breadcrumbs
- Extra virgin olive oil

DIRECTION:

1. Put the onion cut into quarters in the Thermomix glass and select 5 seconds speed
2. Add the minced meat, cheese, egg, salt, and pepper.
3. Select 10 seconds, speed 5, turn left.
4. Add the chopped and peeled walnuts and select 4 seconds, turn left, speed
5. Pass the dough to a bowl.
6. Make Russian steaks and go through breadcrumbs.
7. Paint the Russian fillets with extra virgin olive oil on both sides with a brush.
8. Put in the basket of the air fryer, without stacking the Russian fillets.
9. Select 1800C, 15 minutes.

NUTRITION: Calories: 36 Fat: 20g Carbohydrates: 6g Protein: 46g Sugar: 0g Cholesterol: 63mg

270. Potatoes with Bacon, Onion and Cheese

Preparation time: 10 minutes • Cooking time: 15 minutes • Servings: 4

INGREDIENTS

- 200g potatoes
- 150g bacon
- 1onion
- Slices of cheese
- Extra virgin olive oil
- Salt

DIRECTION:

1. Peel the potatoes, cut into thin slices, and wash them well.
2. Drain and dry the potatoes, put salt and a few strands of extra virgin olive oil.
3. Stir well and place in the basket of the air fryer.
4. Cut the onion into julienne, put a little oil, and stir, place on the potatoes.
5. Finally, put the sliced bacon on the onion.
6. Take the basket to the air fryer and select 20 minutes, 1800C.
7. From time to time, remove the basket.
8. Take all the contents of the basket to a source and when it is still hot, place the slices of cheese on top.
9. You can let the heat of the potatoes melt the cheese or you can gratin a few minutes in the oven.

NUTRITION: Calories: 125 Fat: 2g Carbohydrates: 24g Protein: 5g Sugar: 0.1g Cholesterol: 40mg

271. Pork Liver

Preparation time: 5 minutes • Cooking time: 15 minutes • Servings: 4

INGREDIENTS

- 500g of pork liver cut into steaks
- Breadcrumbs

- Salt
- Ground pepper
- 1lemon
- Extra virgin olive oil

DIRECTION:

1. Put the steaks on a plate or bowl.
2. Add the lemon juice, salt, and ground pepper.
3. Leave a few minutes to macerate the pork liver fillets.
4. Drain well and go through breadcrumbs, it is not necessary to pass the fillets through beaten egg because the liver is very moist, the breadcrumbs are perfectly glued.
5. Spray with extra virgin olive oil. If you don't have a sprayer, paint with a silicone brush.
6. Put the pork liver fillets in the air fryer basket.
7. Program 1800C, 10 minutes.
8. Take out if you see them golden to your liking and put another batch.
9. You should not pile the pork liver fillets, which are well extended so that the empanada is crispy on all sides.

NUTRITION: Calories: 134 Fat: 3.65g Carbohydrates: 2.47g Protein: 21.39g

272. Marinated Loin Potatoes

Preparation time: 10 minutes • Cooking time: 1h. • Serve: 2

INGREDIENTS

- 2medium potatoes
- 4fillets of marinated loin
- A little extra virgin olive oil
- Salt

DIRECTION:

1. Peel the potatoes and cut. Cut with match-sized mandolin, potatoes with a cane but very thin.
2. Wash and immerse in water 30 minutes.
3. Drain and dry well.
4. Add a little oil and stir so that the oil permeates well in all the potatoes.
5. Go to the basket of the air fryer and distribute well.
6. Select 1600C, 10 minutes.
7. Take out the basket, shake so that the potatoes take off. Let the potato tender. If it is not, leave 5 more minutes.
8. Place the steaks on top of the potatoes.
9. Select 1600C, 10 minutes and 180 degrees 5 minutes again.

NUTRITION: Calories: 136 Fat: 5.1g Carbohydrates: 1.9g Protein: 20.7g Sugar: 0.4g Cholesterol: 65mg

273. Pork Fritters

Preparation time: 5 minutes • Cooking time: 20 minutes • Servings: 2-4

INGREDIENTS

- Pork fillets cut into pieces
- 264g flour
- ½ tsp salt
- ½ tsp ground paprika
- A pinch of cayenne pepper
- 500 ml of sparkling water
- Flour to cover
- Nonstick cooking spray

DIRECTION:

1. Coat the pork pieces with flour, shaking off the excess.
2. Mix the flour, seasonings and carbonated water creating a dough in a medium container. Beat until smooth.
3. Preheat the air fryer to 360°F (182°C).
4. Introduce previously sprinkled pork into the dough.
5. Spray the basket of the air fryer with nonstick cooking spray
6. Place the battered pork pieces in the air fryer basket in a single layer.
7. Cook the pork for 10 to 12 minutes, turning it in the middle of the process.
8. Pork fritters will be ready when the breaded has a brown-gold color and the pork is fully cooked.

NUTRITION: Calories: 412 Fat: 18.30g Carbohydrates: 59.5g Protein: 3.10g Sugar: 35.11g Cholesterol: 11mg

274. Pork Tenderloin

Preparation time: 10 minutes • Cooking time: 45 minutes • Servings: 2-4

INGREDIENTS

- 2large eggs
- ¼ cup milk
- 2cups seasoned breadcrumbs
- Salt and pepper to taste
- Nonstick cooking spray

DIRECTION:

1. Slice the tenderloin into ½ inch slices.
2. Place the slices between two plastic sheets and tap them until each piece is ¼ inch thick.
3. In a large container, mix the eggs and milk.
4. In a separate container or dish, pour the breadcrumbs.
5. Introduce each piece of pork in the mixture of eggs and milk, letting the excess drain.

6. Then introduce the pork in the breadcrumbs, covering each side.
7. Place the covered pork on a wire rack for 30 minutes to make sure the cover adheres.
8. Preheat the air fryer to 400°F (204 °C).
9. Spray the basket of the air fryer with nonstick cooking spray. Place the covered sirloin in the basket in a single layer.
10. Cook the sirloin for 10 minutes, then take it out, turn it over and sprinkle with more nonstick spray.
11. Cook for 5-minutes more or until both sides are crispy and golden brown.

NUTRITION: Calories: 158 Fat: 7.12g Carbohydrates: 0g Protein: 22.05g Sugar: 0g Cholesterol: 67mg

275. Cheesy Beef Paseíllo

Preparation time: 10 minutes • Cooking time: 20 minutes • Servings: 15

INGREDIENTS

- 1-2 tbsp olive oil
- 2pounds lean ground beef
- ½ chopped onion
- 2cloves garlic, minced
- ½ tbsp Adobo seasoning
- 2tsp dried oregano
- 1packet of optional seasoning
- 2tbsp chopped cilantro
- ¼ cup grated cheese
- 15dough disks
- 15slices of yellow cheese

DIRECTION:

1. In a large skillet over medium-high heat, heat the oil. Once the oil has warmed, add the meat, onions, and Adobo seasoning.
2. Brown veal, about 6-7 minutes. Drain the ground beef. Add the remaining seasonings and cilantro. Cook an additional minute. Add grated cheese, if desired. Melt the cheese.
3. On each dough disk, add a slice of cheese to the center and add 3-4 tablespoons of meat mixture over the slice of cheese. Fold over the dough disk, and with a fork, fold the edges and set it aside.
4. Preheat the air fryer to 3700C for 3 minutes.
5. Once three minutes have passed, spray the air fryer pan with cooking spray and add 3-4 cupcakes to the basket. Close the basket and set to 3700C and cook for 7 minutes. After 7 minutes, verify it. Cook up to 3 additional minutes, or the desired level of sharpness, if desired.
6. Repeat until finished.

NUTRITION: Calories: 225 Fat: 5g Carbohydrates: 10g Protein: 10g Sugar: 0g Cholesterol: 25mg

276. Beef Patty

Preparation time: 20 minutes • Cooking time: 30 minutes • Servings: 4

INGREDIENTS

- Prepared dough
- 300g beef
- 1large onion
- 1red pepper
- 2hard-boiled eggs
- Salt
- Pepper to taste.
- 1tsp oil

DIRECTION:

1. Remove the dough from the refrigerator 10 minutes before.
2. In a pan, place oil, 1 onion, 1 pepper, garlic, seasoning. Add ground beef until cooked well. Season with salt and pepper to taste.
3. Let the filling cool
4. Place the filling in each circle of the dough and seal with egg white at the edges.
5. Butter a refractory mold and accommodate the patty.
6. Preheat the oven to 190°C for 10 minutes by pressing the Convection button
7. Place the refractory on the metal rack and bring to the preheated oven for 30 minutes at 190°C.

NUTRITION: Calories: 263 Fat: 17.25g Carbohydrates: 20.22g Protein: 6.65g Sugar: 0.96g Cholesterol: 59mg

277. Roasted Pork

Preparation time: 5 minutes • Cooking time: 30 minutes • Servings: 2-4

INGREDIENTS

- 500-2000g Pork meat (To roast
- Salt
- Oil

DIRECTION:

1. Join the cuts in an orderly manner.
2. Place the meat on the plate
3. Varnish with a little oil.
4. Place the roasts with the fat side down.
5. Cook in air fryer at 1800C for 30 minutes.
6. Turn when you hear the beep.
7. Remove from the oven. Drain excess juice.
8. Let stand for 10 minutes on aluminum foil before serving.

NUTRITION: Calories: 820 Fat: 24.75g Carbohydrates: 117g Protein: 33.75g Sugar: 0g Cholesterol: 120mg

278. Fried Pork Chops

Preparation time: 5 minutes • Cooking time: 35 minutes • Servings: 2

INGREDIENTS

- 3cloves of ground garlic
- 2tbsp olive oil
- 1tbsp of marinade
- 4thawed pork chops

DIRECTION:

1. Mix the cloves of ground garlic, marinade, and oil. Then apply this mixture on the chops.
2. Put the chops in the air fryer at 3600C for 35 minutes.

NUTRITION: Calories: 118 Fat: 6.85g Carbohydrates: 0 Protein: 13.12gSugar: 0g Cholesterol: 39mg

279. Crispy Pork Chops

Preparation time: 5 minutes • Cooking time: 12 minutes • Servings: 4

INGREDIENTS

- Olive oil spray
- 6(3/4-inch thick central cut boneless pork chops, trimmed fat (5 oz each
- Kosher salt
- 1large egg, beaten
- ½ cup panko crumbs (check labels for GF
- 1/3 cup crushed corn crumbs
- 2tbsp grated Parmesan cheese (skip for vegetarians
- 1¼ tsp sweet paprika
- ½ tsp garlic powder
- ½ tsp onion powder
- ¼ tsp chili powder
- 1/8 tsp black pepper

DIRECTION:

1. Preheat the fryer with air at 4000F for 12 minutes and lightly spray the basket with oil.
2. Season the pork chops on both sides with ½ teaspoon of kosher salt.
3. Put the panko, corn crumbs, Parmesan cheese, ¾ teaspoon kosher salt, paprika, garlic powder, onion powder, chili powder and black pepper in a large, shallow bowl.
4. Place the beaten egg in another. Dip the pork in the egg, then the crumb mixture.
5. When the fryer is ready, place 3 of the chops in the prepared basket and sprinkle the top with oil.
6. Cook 12 minutes turning in half, sprinkling both sides with oil. Set aside and repeat with the rest.

NUTRITION: Calories: 378 Fat: 13g Carbohydrates: 8g Protein: 33g Sugar: 1 g Cholesterol: 121 mg

280. Pork Bondiola Chop

Preparation time: 5 minutes • Cooking time: 20 minutes • Servings: 4

INGREDIENTS

- 1kg bondiola in pieces
- Breadcrumbs
- 2eggs
- Seasoning to taste

DIRECTION:

1. Cut the bondiola into small pieces, seasonings to taste.
2. Beat the eggs.
3. Pass the bondiola seasoned by beaten egg and then by breadcrumbs.
4. Then place in the air fryer for 20 minutes, halfway around turn and ready snacks of bondiola.

NUTRITION: Calories: 265 Fat: 20.36g Carbohydrates: 0g Protein: 19.14g Sugar: 0g Cholesterol: 146mg

281. Pork Taquitos

Preparation time: 10 minutes • Cooking time: 15 minutes • Servings: 6

INGREDIENTS

- 3cups shredded pork loin (previously cooked
- Lemon juice
- 10templates
- 2cups mozzarella cheese
- Cooking spray (oil
- Sauce to taste
- Sour cream to taste

DIRECTION:

1. Preheat the fryer to 380 degrees F. Meanwhile, soften the templates in the microwave for 10 seconds.
2. On the other hand, in a bowl add the pork with a pinch of lemon.
3. Then, add the shredded pork and cheese to the template. Roll up the template and close.
4. Once ready, add spray on them and take to the air fryer for 10 minutes.

NUTRITION: Calories: 133 Fat: 4g Carbohydrates: 22g Protein: 5g Sugar: 0g Cholesterol: 0mg

282. Pork Knuckle

Preparation time: 15 minutes • Cooking time: 50 minutes • Servings: 2

INGREDIENTS

- Knuckle:
- 3potatoes
- 1head of garlic

- Water
- Extra virgin olive oil
- Salt
- Peppercorns
- 1bay leaf
- Vinaigrette
- Mustard and beer (to accompany
- For the sauerkraut:
- 1cabbage
- 100g of butter
- 1glass of white wine
- 5tbsp vinegar
- a pinch of cumin
- Some coriander seeds
- Peppercorns
- Juniper berries

DIRECTION:

1. Cook the knuckle in a quick pot with the potatoes and a little salt.
2. Add some pepper balls, a bay leaf, and a garlic head.
3. Cover with water and cook for 40 minutes.
4. When it starts to boil, lower the heat to medium heat.
5. For sauerkraut, chop the cabbage into quarters and cut into strips with the mandolin.
6. Put the cabbage in a bowl, water with a glass of white wine and a dash of vinegar and mix everything well.
7. Crush some juniper berries with a knife, add them and sprinkle with pepper, coriander, and cumin.
8. Mix the whole well, wet with a glass of water and let stand for 3 days or more.
9. Cook the cabbage for 15 minutes in a pot, drain and sauté over medium heat for 8 minutes.
10. Season and water with a dash of olive oil.
11. Pass the knuckle in the air fryer basket, dip extra virgin olive oil at 250°C for 10 minutes
12. Servings the knuckle with potatoes and sauerkraut.

NUTRITION: Calories: 333 Fat: 22g Carbohydrates: 0g Protein: 28g Sugar: 0g Cholesterol: 84mg

CHAPTER 7

VEGETABLES

283. Bugnes Lyonnaises

Preparation: 30 minutes; Rest: 2 hours; • Cook: 15 minutes

INGREDIENTS

- 250 g flour
- ½ packet of yeast
- 50g of powdered sugar
- 50g butter
- 2eggs
- 1tsp rum
- 1pinch of salt
- Frying oil

DIRECTION:

1. Soften the butter; beat the eggs with a fork.
2. Place the flour in a bowl; add the salt, the butter, the beaten eggs, the aroma.
3. Mix until you have a consistent paste. Form a ball and let stand at least 2 hours in the fridge.
4. Heat the fryer oil at 1500C for 15 minutes.
5. Stretch the dough to a thickness of 5 mm. Cut into strips of 10 cm by 4 cm and make an incision in the center of 5 cm.
6. Pass a corner of the strip in the incision to tie a knot or leave it as is.
7. Dip the bugnes in the fryer, flip them 1 time and drain once cooked on absorbent paper.
8. Sprinkle with icing sugar or icing sugar and serve hot.

NUTRITION: Calories 140 Carbohydrate 6 g Fat 13 g Protein 1 g Sodium 29 mg Sugar 1 g

284. Green salad with roasted pepper

Preparation time: 5 minutes • Cooking time: 10 minutes • Servings: 2

INGREDIENTS

- 1red pepper
- 1tbsp lemon juice
- 3tbsp yogurt
- 2tbsp olive oil
- Freshly ground black pepper
- 1romaine lettuce, cut into large strips
- 50g arugula leaves

DIRECTION:

1. Preheat the Air Fryer to 200°C.
2. Place the pepper in the basket and insert it into the Air Fryer. Set the timer for 10 minutes and roast the pepper until the skin is slightly

burned.

3. Then cut the pepper into quarters and remove the seeds and skin. Cut the pepper into strips.
4. Prepare vinaigrette in a bowl with 2 tablespoons of pepper juice, lemon juice, yogurt, and olive oil. Add pepper and salt according to your taste.
5. Mix the lettuce and arugula leaves in the vinaigrette and garnish the salad with the pepper strips.

NUTRITION: Calories 47.3 Fat 0.4 g Carbohydrate 10.8 g Sugars 2.0 g Protein1.8 g Cholesterol 0.0 mg

285. Fat Free Crispy Fries

Preparation time: about 15 minutes • Cooking time: 10 to 35 minutes • Servings: 4

INGREDIENTS

- 500g of special fries
- 1tbsp olive oil
- 1freezer bag
- Salt + pepper

DIRECTION:

1. Peel the potatoes, cut them with a potato chip cutter, rinse them with clean water and dry them well with a cloth.
2. It is important to cut all the potatoes evenly; otherwise you may have some overcooked and not enough fries.
3. Place the sliced fries in a freezer bag, add 1 tablespoon of oil, close the bag, and stir everything.
4. Place the French fries in the basket, close it, and close the lid of the fryer and set to 230°C to 35 minutes.
5. At the end of cooking, remove the basket with the tongs and remove the fries. Add salt and pepper.

NUTRITION: Calories 118 Fat 7g Carbohydrates 27 Sugars 1g Protein 2 Cholesterol 0mg

286. Marinated Potatoes with Chimichurri Sauce

Preparation time: 20 minutes • Cooking time: 45 minutes • Servings: 4

INGREDIENTS

- 1kg to 1.2kg of potatoes
- 2tablespoons chimichurri sauce

DIRECTION:

1. Depending on the taste, you can peel the potatoes, but the real potatoes are prepared with the skin.
2. Wash the potatoes before cutting them.
3. Cut them in quarters to get the

shape of the potatoes and place them in a freezer bag.

4. Add the sauce and use the solid closure of the sachet to keep it closed.
5. Mix everything by handling the bag in all directions. Potatoes should be well impregnated with the preparation.
6. Pour all the preparation in the air fryer without oil.
7. Set the air fryer at 1800C for 45 minutes and serve immediately after the end of cooking.

NUTRITION: Calories 367 Fat 18.4 g Carbohydrate 45 g Sugars 2.0 g Protein 5.7 g Cholesterol 0mg

287. Homemade Gluten Free Spicy Chips

Preparation time: 25 minutes • Cooking time: 30 minutes • Servings: 1

INGREDIENTS

- 500g of potatoes to choose from among those with firm meat
- 1tbsp vegetable oil
- 1pinch of salt
- 1mixture of texmex spices

DIRECTION:

1. Peel the potatoes and cut them into slices approximately 2 millimeters thick. Preferably use a mandolin for a very fine and regular cut.
2. Rinse the potatoes to get rid of their starch and let them stand for 15 minutes in a bowl of cold water.
3. Drain the potatoes and dry them with a paper towel by simply sliding them. Avoid rubbing them as they could break.
4. Pour the potatoes in the fryer and cover them with the necessary tablespoon of oil.
5. Set the air fryer at 1500C for 30 minutes.
6. Be sure to stir the fries with a wooden utensil every ten minutes to make sure they cook perfectly.
7. Wait 5 minutes before the end of cooking to add salt and spices.

NUTRITION: Calories 150 Cal 17% Carbohydrates 15g Fat 32g Protein 1g Sugars 3g Cholesterol 0mg

288. Funghetto Eggplant (Golden Neapolitan)

Preparation time: 0-10 minutes • Cooking time: 15-30 minutes • Servings:

INGREDIENTS

- 600g Eggplant
- 100g Broth
- 1Garlic clove

- Salt
- Pepper
- 3spoons Olive oil
- Parsley

DIRECTION:

1. Wash the eggplants, dry them, and cut them into 1.5 cm cubes.
2. Place the mixing blade in the tank
3. Pour oil and peeled garlic, close the lid.
4. Set the air fryer to 1500C to brown for about 2 min.
5. Add eggplant, broth, salt and pepper and simmer for another 23 min.
6. Finally, before serving, sprinkle with chopped fresh parsley.

NUTRITION: Calories 142 Fat 12.9g Carbohydrate 5.20g Protein 1.9g Sugars 0g Cholesterol 0.1mg

289. Fried Bananas

Preparation time: 0-10 minutes • Cooking time: 0 – 15 minutes • Servings: 3

INGREDIENTS

- 3Bananas
- 2Eggs
- Breadcrumbs
- Flour at discretion
- Salt
- 1tsp Oil

DIRECTION:

1. Peel the bananas and cut them into sections of approximately 2 to 3 cm.
2. Pass them first in the flour, then in the egg beaten with salt and then in the breadcrumbs.
3. Heat the air fryer at 1800C for 10 minutes. Then, place the breaded bananas.
4. Cook the bananas for 8 to 10 minutes, turning them 2 to 3 times during cooking to match the Dorado.
5. Serve warm.

NUTRITION: Calories 262.4 Fat 12.1 g Carbohydrate 33.9 g Sugars20.7 g Protein1.3 g Cholesterol 30.5 mg

290. Sautéed air mushrooms and parsley

Preparation time: 10 – 20 minutes • Cooking time: 15 – 30 minutes • Servings: 6

INGREDIENTS:

- 600 g mushrooms
- 1clove garlic
- 1tsp olive oil
- Parsley
- Leave at discretion
- Black pepper at discretion

DIRECTION:

1. Clean the mushrooms well and chop them.
2. Place the garlic and oil inside the basket close. Set the temperature to 1500C.
3. Brown for 2 minutes.
4. Add the mushrooms and cook for another 15 minutes.
5. Add (at discretion) salt and pepper, parsley, and finish cooking for another 3 minutes.

NUTRITION: Calories 130 Fat 7g Carbohydrates 17g Sugars 4g Protein 4g Cholesterol 0mg

291. Cauliflowers au gratin

Preparation time: 20-30 minutes Cooking time: 15-30 minutes Servings: 6

INGREDIENTS:

- 800g cauliflower
- 4slices of cheese
- ½ liter of Béchamel
- Parmesan to taste

DIRECTION:

1. Separately, cook the cauliflowers in water. Meanwhile, prepare ½ liter of bechamel (dose: 500 ml of milk, 50 g of flour, 50 g of butter, salt, and nutmeg).
2. Pour some bechamel into the basket. Arrange the cauliflower flowers, covered with the slices of cheese and cover with the béchamel sauce. Sprinkle with Parmesan cheese.
3. Set the air fryer to 1500C. Simmer for about 20 minutes or according to the degree of gratin desired.

NUTRITION: Calories 285 Fat 19g Carbohydrates 17g Sugars 2.5g Protein 14g Cholesterol 55mg

292. Peach Clafoutis

Preparation time: 20 – 30 minutes • Cooking time: 30 – 45 minutes • Servings: 10

INGREDIENTS

- 300g flour
- 150g butter
-
- 150g of sugar
- 4eggs
- 1sachet of baking powder
- 500g peaches in syrup
- 1lemon
- 3-4 tbsp milk
- Icing sugar at discretion

DIRECTION:

1. Melt the butter in the microwave; Work the butter, sugar, and eggs in a bowl.
2. Add flour, baking powder, grated lemon peel and milk. Work everything with an electric mixer until you get a smooth and homogeneous mixture.
3. Butter and flour the tank and pour the mixture inside, smearing well.
4. Place a whole peach in the center and place the others (cut into quarters) next to each other following the circumference of the mold.
5. Set the air fryer on the lower heating temperature.
6. Bake the cake for 45 minutes.
7. Let cool and remove it from the tank; sprinkle with icing sugar.

NUTRITION: Calories 148 Carbohydrates 14g Fat 8g Sugars 6 g Protein 4g Cholesterol 102mg

293. Cauliflower Steak

Preparation Time: 12 minutes • Servings: 4

INGREDIENTS

- 1medium head cauliflower
- ¼ cup blue cheese crumbles
- ¼ cup hot sauce
- ¼ cup full-fat ranch dressing
- 2tbsp. salted butter; melted.

DIRECTIONS

1. Remove cauliflower leaves. Slice the head in ½-inch-thick slices.
2. In a small bowl, mix hot sauce and butter. Brush the mixture over the cauliflower.
3. Place each cauliflower steak into the air fryer, working in batches if necessary. Adjust the temperature to 400 Degrees F and set the timer for 7 minutes
4. When cooked, edges will begin turning dark and caramelized. To serve, sprinkle steaks with crumbled blue cheese. Drizzle with ranch dressing.

NUTRITION: Calories: 122; Protein: 4.9g; Fiber: 3.0g; Fat: 8.4g; Carbs: 7.7g

294. Chocolate Chip Pan Cookie

Preparation Time: 17 minutes • Servings: 4

INGREDIENTS

- ½ cup blanched finely ground almond flour.
- 1large egg.
- ¼ cup powdered erythritol
- 2tbsp. unsalted butter; softened.

- 2tbsp. low-carb, sugar-free chocolate chips
- ½ tsp. unflavored gelatin
- ½ tsp. baking powder.
- ½ tsp. vanilla extract.

DIRECTIONS

1. Take a large bowl, mix almond flour and erythritol. Stir in butter, egg and gelatin until combined.
2. Stir in baking powder and vanilla and then fold in chocolate chips
3. Pour batter into 6-inch round baking pan. Place pan into the air fryer basket.
4. Adjust the temperature to 300 Degrees F and set the timer for 7 minutes
5.
6. When fully cooked, the top will be golden brown and a toothpick inserted in center will come out clean. Let cool at least 10 minutes.

NUTRITION: Calories: 188; Protein: 5.6g; Fiber: 2.0g; Fat: 15.7g; Carbs: 16.8g

295. Mustard Greens and Green Beans

Preparation Time: 22 minutes • Servings: 4

INGREDIENTS

- 1lb. green beans; halved
- ¼ cup tomato puree
- 3garlic cloves; minced
- 1bunch mustard greens, trimmed
- 2tbsp. olive oil
- 1tbsp. balsamic vinegar
- Salt and black pepper to taste.

DIRECTIONS

1. In a pan that fits your air fryer, mix the mustard greens with the rest of the ingredients, toss, put the pan in the fryer and cook at 350°F for 12 minutes
2. Divide everything between plates and serve.

NUTRITION: Calories: 163; Fat: 4g; Fiber: 3g; Carbs: 4g; Protein: 7g

296. Artichoke Spinach Casserole

Preparation Time: 30 minutes • Servings: 4

INGREDIENTS

- ⅓ cup full-fat mayonnaise
- 8oz. full-fat cream cheese; softened.
- ¼ cup diced yellow onion
- ⅓ cup full-fat sour cream.
- ¼ cup chopped pickled jalapeños.
- 2cups fresh spinach; chopped
- 2cups cauliflower florets; chopped
- 1cup artichoke hearts; chopped
- 1tbsp. salted butter; melted.

DIRECTIONS

1. Take a large bowl, mix butter, onion, cream cheese, mayonnaise and sour cream. Fold in jalapeños, spinach, cauliflower and artichokes.
2. Pour the mixture into a 4-cup round baking dish. Cover with foil and place into the air fryer basket
3. Adjust the temperature to 370 Degrees F and set the timer for 15 minutes. In the last 2 minutes of cooking, remove the foil to brown the top. Serve warm.

NUTRITION: Calories: 423; Protein: 6.7g; Fiber: 5.3g; Fat: 36.3g; Carbs: 12.1g

297. Baked Egg and Veggies

Preparation Time: 20 minutes Servings: 2

INGREDIENTS

- 1cup fresh spinach; chopped
- 1small zucchini, sliced lengthwise and quartered
- 1medium Roma tomato; diced
- ½ medium green bell pepper; seeded and diced
- 2large eggs.
- 2tbsp. salted butter
- ¼ tsp. garlic powder.
- ¼ tsp. onion powder.
- ½ tsp. dried basil
- ¼ tsp. dried oregano.

DIRECTIONS

1. Grease two (4-inchramekins with 1 tbsp. butter each.
2. Take a large bowl, toss zucchini, bell pepper, spinach and tomatoes. Divide the mixture in two and place half in each ramekin.
3. Crack an egg on top of each ramekin and sprinkle with onion powder, garlic powder, basil and oregano. Place into the air fryer basket. Adjust the temperature to 330 Degrees F and set the timer for 10 minutes
Servings immediately.

NUTRITION: Calories: 150; Protein: 8.3g; Fiber: 2.2g; Fat: 10.0g; Carbs: 6.6g

298. Mini Cheesecake

Preparation Time: 25 minutes • Servings: 2

INGREDIENTS

- 4oz. full-fat cream cheese; softened.
- ⅛ cup powdered erythritol

- 1large egg.
- ½ cup walnuts
- 2tbsp. granular erythritol.
- 2tbsp. salted butter
- ½ tsp. vanilla extract.

DIRECTIONS

1. Place walnuts, butter and granular erythritol in a food processor. Pulse until ingredients stick together and a dough form
2. Press dough into 4-inch springform pan then place the pan into the air fryer basket.
3. Adjust the temperature to 400 Degrees F and set the timer for 5 minutes. When timer beeps, remove the crust and let cool
4. Take a medium bowl, mix cream cheese with egg, vanilla extract and powdered erythritol until smooth.
5. Spoon mixture on top of baked walnut crust and place into the air fryer basket. Adjust the temperature to 300 Degrees F and set the timer for 10 minutes. Once done, chill for 2 hours before serving

NUTRITION: Calories: 531; Protein: 11.4g; Fiber: 2.3g; Fat: 48.3g; Carbs: 31.4g

299. Savoy Cabbage

Preparation Time: 20 minutes • Servings: 4

INGREDIENTS

- 1Savoy cabbage head, shredded
- 1tbsp. dill; chopped.
- 1½ tbsp. ghee; melted
- ¼ cup coconut cream
- Salt and black pepper to taste.

DIRECTIONS

1. In a pan that fits the air fryer, combine all the ingredients except the coconut cream, toss, put the pan in the air fryer and cook at 390°F for 10 minutes
2. Add the cream, toss, cook for 5 minutes more, divide between plates and serve

NUTRITION: Calories: 173; Fat: 5g; Fiber: 3g; Carbs: 5g; Protein: 8g

300. Spaghetti Squash Alfredo.

Preparation Time: 25 minutes • Servings: 2

INGREDIENTS

- ½ large cooked spaghetti squash
- ¼ cup grated vegetarian Parmesan cheese.

- ½ cup shredded Italian blend cheese
- ½ cup low-carb Alfredo sauce
- 2tbsp. salted butter; melted.
- ¼ tsp. ground peppercorn
- ½ tsp. garlic powder.
- 1tsp. dried parsley.

DIRECTIONS

1. Using a fork, remove the strands of spaghetti squash from the shell. Place into a large bowl with butter and Alfredo sauce. Sprinkle with Parmesan, garlic powder, parsley and peppercorn
2. Pour into a 4-cup round baking dish and top with shredded cheese. Place dish into the air fryer basket. Adjust the temperature to 320 Degrees F and set the timer for 15 minutes.
3. When finished, cheese will be golden and bubbling. Serve immediately

NUTRITION: Calories: 375; Protein: 13.5g; Fiber: 4.0g; Fat: 24.2g; Carbs: 24.1g

301. Vanilla Pound Cake.

Preparation Time: 35 minutes Servings: 6

INGREDIENTS

- ½ cup full-fat sour cream.
- 1oz. full-fat cream cheese; softened.
- 2large eggs.
- ½ cup granular erythritol.
- 1cup blanched finely ground almond flour.
- ¼ cup salted butter; melted.
- 1tsp. baking powder.
- 1tsp. vanilla extract.

DIRECTIONS

1. Take a large bowl, mix almond flour, butter and erythritol.
2. Add in vanilla, baking powder, sour cream and cream cheese and mix until well combined. Add eggs and mix.
3. Pour batter into a 6-inch round baking pan. Place pan into the air fryer basket. Adjust the temperature to 300 Degrees F and set the timer for 25 minutes.
4. When the cake is done, a toothpick inserted in center will come out clean. The center should not feel wet. Allow it to cool completely, or the cake will crumble when moved.

NUTRITION: Calories: 253; Protein: 6.9g; Fiber: 2.0g; Fat: 22.6g; Carbs: 25.2g

302. Pumpkin Spice Pecans

Preparation Time: 11 minutes • Servings: 4

INGREDIENTS

- 1cup whole pecans
- 1large egg. white
- ¼ cup granular erythritol.
- ½ tsp. pumpkin pie spice

- ½ tsp. vanilla extract.
- ½ tsp. ground cinnamon.

DIRECTIONS

1. Toss all ingredients in a large bowl until pecans are coated. Place into the air fryer basket.
2. Adjust the temperature to 300 Degrees F and set the timer for 6 minutes. Toss two to three times during cooking. Allow to cool completely. Store in an airtight container up to 3 days

NUTRITION: Calories: 178; Protein: 3.2g; Fiber: 2.6g; Fat: 17.0g; Carbs: 19.0g

303. Cream Puffs

Preparation Time: 21 minutes
Servings: 8 puffs

INGREDIENTS

- 2oz. full-fat cream cheese.
- 1large egg.
- ¼ cup powdered erythritol
- ½ cup blanched finely ground almond flour.
- ½ cup low-carb vanilla protein powder
- ½ cup granular erythritol.
- 2tbsp. heavy whipping cream.
- 5tbsp. unsalted butter; melted.
- ½ tsp. baking powder.
- ¼ tsp. ground cinnamon.
- ½ tsp. vanilla extract.

DIRECTIONS

1. Mix almond flour, protein powder, granular erythritol, baking powder, egg and butter in a large bowl until a soft dough forms.
2. Place the dough in the freezer for 20 minutes. Wet your hands with water and roll the dough into eight balls.
3. Cut a piece of parchment to fit your air fryer basket. Working in batches as necessary, place the dough balls into the air fryer basket on top of parchment.
4. Adjust the temperature to 380 Degrees F and set the timer for 6 minutes. Flip cream puffs halfway through the cooking time.
5. When the timer beeps, remove the puffs and allow to cool.
6. Take a medium bowl, beat the cream cheese, powdered erythritol, cinnamon, cream and vanilla until fluffy.
7. Place the mixture into a pastry bag or a storage bag with the end snipped. Cut a

small hole in the bottom of each puff and fill with some of the cream mixture. Store in an airtight container up to 2 days in the refrigerator.

NUTRITION: Calories: 178; Protein: 14.9g; Fiber: 1.3g; Fat: 12.1g; Carbs: 22.1g

304. Tomato and Asparagus

Preparation Time: 20 minutes • Servings: 4

INGREDIENTS

- 1lb. asparagus, trimmed
- 1jalapeno pepper; chopped.
- 10cherry tomatoes; halved
- 2green onions; chopped.
- 1tbsp. olive oil
- 2tsp. chili powder
- A pinch of salt and black pepper

DIRECTIONS

1. In a pan that fits your air fryer, mix the asparagus with tomatoes and the rest of the ingredients, toss.
2. Put the pan in the fryer and cook at 390°F for 15 minutes
3. Divide the mix between plates and serve.

NUTRITION: Calories: 173; Fat: 4g; Fiber: 2g; Carbs: 4g; Protein: 6g

305. Peanut Butter Cheesecake Brownies

Preparation Time: 55 minutes• Servings: 6

INGREDIENTS

- ½ cup blanched finely ground almond flour.
- 8oz. full-fat cream cheese; softened.
- ¼ cup unsalted butter; softened.
- 2large eggs, divided.
- 1cup powdered erythritol, divided.
- ¼ cup heavy whipping cream.
- 2tbsp. unsweetened cocoa powder
- ½ tsp. baking powder.
- 2tbsp. no-sugar-added peanut butter
- 1tsp. vanilla extract.

DIRECTIONS

1. Take a large bowl, mix almond flour, ½ cup erythritol, cocoa powder and baking powder. Stir in butter and one egg.
2. Scoop mixture into 6-inch round baking pan. Place pan into the air fryer basket. Adjust the temperature to 300 Degrees F and set the timer for 20 minutes.
3. When fully cooked a toothpick inserted in center

will come out clean. Allow 20 minutes to fully cool and firm up

4. Take a large bowl, beat cream cheese, remaining ½ cup erythritol, heavy cream, vanilla, peanut butter and remaining egg until fluffy.
5. Pour mixture over cooled brownies. Place pan back into the air fryer basket. Adjust the temperature to 300 Degrees F and set the timer for 15 minutes
6. Cheesecake will be slightly browned and mostly firm with a slight jiggle when done.
7. Allow to cool, then refrigerate 2 hours before serving.

NUTRITION: Calories: 347; Protein: 8.3g; Fiber: 2.0g; Fat: 30.9g; Carbs: 29.8g

306. BBQ Pulled Mushrooms

Preparation Time: 17 minutes • Servings: 2

INGREDIENTS:

- 4large portobello mushrooms
- ½ cup low-carb, sugar-free barbecue sauce
- 1tbsp. salted butter; melted.
- 1tsp. paprika
- ¼ tsp. onion powder.
- ¼ tsp. ground black pepper
- 1tsp. chili powder

DIRECTIONS

1. Remove stem and scoop out the underside of each mushroom. Brush the caps with butter and sprinkle with pepper, chili powder, paprika and onion powder.
2. Place mushrooms into the air fryer basket. Adjust the temperature to 400 Degrees F and set the timer for 8 minutes.
3. When the timer beeps, remove mushrooms from the basket and place on a cutting board or work surface. Using two forks, gently pull the mushrooms apart, creating strands.
4. Place mushroom strands into a 4-cup round baking dish with barbecue sauce. Place dish into the air fryer basket.
5. Adjust the temperature to 350 Degrees F and set the timer for 4 minutes. Stir halfway through the cooking time. Serve warm.

NUTRITION: Calories: 108; Protein: 3.3g; Fiber: 2.7g; Fat: 5.9g; Carbs: 10.9g

307. Blackberry Crisp

Preparation Time: 20 minutes • Servings: 4

INGREDIENTS

- 1cup Crunchy Granola
- 2cups blackberries
- ⅓ cup powdered erythritol
- 2tbsp. lemon juice
- ¼ tsp. xanthan gum

DIRECTIONS

1. Take a large bowl, toss blackberries, erythritol, lemon juice and xanthan gum.
2. Pour into 6-inch round baking dish and cover with foil. Place into the air fryer basket.
3. Adjust the temperature to 350 Degrees F and set the timer for 12 minutes.
4. When the timer beeps, remove the foil and stir.
5. Sprinkle granola over mixture and return to the air fryer basket. Adjust the temperature to 320 Degrees F and set the timer for 3 minutes or until top is golden. Serve warm.

NUTRITION: Calories: 496; Protein: 9.2g; Fiber: 12.5g; Fat: 42.1g; Carbs: 44.0g

308. Cheese Zucchini Boats

Preparation Time: 35 minutes Servings: 2

INGREDIENTS

- 2medium zucchini
- ¼ cup full-fat ricotta cheese
- ¼ cup shredded mozzarella cheese
- ¼ cup low-carb, no-sugar-added pasta sauce.
- 2tbsp. grated vegetarian Parmesan cheese
- 1tbsp. avocado oil
- ¼ tsp. garlic powder.
- ½ tsp. dried parsley.
- ¼ tsp. dried oregano.

DIRECTIONS

1. Cut off 1-inch from the top and bottom of each zucchini.
2. Slice zucchini in half lengthwise and use a spoon to scoop out a bit of the inside, making room for filling. Brush with oil and spoon 2 tbsp. pasta sauce into each shell
3. Take a medium bowl, mix ricotta, mozzarella, oregano, garlic powder and parsley
4. Spoon the mixture into each zucchini shell. Place stuffed zucchini shells into the air fryer basket.
5. Adjust the temperature to 350 Degrees F and set the timer for 20 minutes
6. To remove from the fryer basket, use tongs or a spatula and carefully lift out. Top with Parmesan. Serve immediately.

NUTRITION: Calories: 215; Protein: 10.5g; Fiber: 2.7g; Fat: 14.9g; Carbs: 9.3g

309. Green Beans and Lime Sauce

Preparation Time: 13 minutes • Servings: 4

INGREDIENTS

- 1lb. green beans, trimmed
- 2tbsp. ghee; melted

- 1tbsp. lime juice
- 1tsp. chili powder
- A pinch of salt and black pepper

DIRECTIONS

1. Take a bowl and mix the ghee with the rest of the ingredients except the green beans and whisk really well.
2. Mix the green beans with the lime sauce, toss
3. Put them in your air fryer's basket and
   cook at 400°F for 8 minutes
4. Servings right away.

NUTRITION: Calories: 151; Fat: 4g; Fiber: 2g; Carbs: 4g; Protein: 6g

310. Roasted Broccoli Salad

Preparation Time: 17 minutes • Servings: 2

INGREDIENTS

- 3cups fresh broccoli florets.
- ½ medium lemon.
- ¼ cup sliced almonds.
- 2tbsp. salted butter; melted.

DIRECTIONS

1. Place broccoli into a 6-inch round baking dish. Pour butter over broccoli. Add almonds and toss. Place dish into the air fryer basket
2. Adjust the temperature to 380 Degrees F and set the timer for 7 minutes. Stir halfway through the cooking time. When timer beeps, zest lemon onto broccoli and squeeze juice into pan. Toss. Serve warm.

NUTRITION: Calories: 215; Protein: 6.4g; Fiber: 5.0g; Fat: 16.3g; Carbs: 12.1g

311. Quiche Stuffed Peppers

Preparation Time: 20 minutes • Servings: 2

INGREDIENTS

- 2medium green bell peppers
- 3large eggs.
- ½ cup chopped broccoli
- ½ cup shredded medium Cheddar cheese.
- ¼ cup diced yellow onion
- ¼ cup full-fat ricotta cheese

DIRECTIONS

1. Cut the tops off of the peppers and remove the seeds and white membranes with a small knife. Take a medium bowl, whisk eggs

and ricotta

2. Add onion and broccoli. Pour the egg and vegetable mixture evenly into each pepper. Top with Cheddar. Place peppers into a 4-cup round baking dish and place into the air fryer basket. Adjust the temperature to 350 Degrees F and set the timer for 15 minutes
3. Eggs will be mostly firm and peppers tender when fully cooked. Serve immediately.

NUTRITION: Calories: 314; Protein: 21.6g; Fiber: 3.0g; Fat: 18.7g; Carbs: 10.8g

312. Monkey Bread

Preparation
Time: 27 minutes
• Servings: 6

INGREDIENTS:

- ½ cup blanched finely ground almond flour.
- 1oz. full-fat cream cheese; softened.
- 1large egg.
- ¼ cup heavy whipping cream.
- ½ cup low-carb vanilla protein powder
- ¾ cup granular erythritol, divided
- 8tbsp. salted butter; melted and divided
- ½ tsp. vanilla extract.
- ½ tsp. baking powder

DIRECTIONS:

1. Take a large bowl, combine almond flour, protein powder, ½ cup erythritol, baking powder, 5 tbsp. butter, cream cheese and egg. A soft, sticky dough will form.
2. Place the dough in the freezer for 20 minutes. It will be firm enough to roll into balls. Wet your hands with warm water and roll into twelve balls. Place the balls into a 6-inch round baking dish
3. In a medium skillet over medium heat, melt remaining butter with remaining erythritol. Lower the heat and continue stirring until mixture turns golden, then add cream and vanilla. Remove from heat and allow it to thicken for a few minutes while you continue to stir
4. While the mixture cools, place baking dish into the air fryer basket. Adjust the temperature to 320 Degrees F and set the timer for 6 minutes
5. When the timer beeps, flip the monkey bread over onto a plate and slide it back into the baking pan. Cook an additional 4 minutes until all the tops are brown.
6. Pour the caramel sauce over the monkey bread and cook an additional 2 minutes.
7. Let cool completely before serving.

NUTRITION: Calories: 322; Protein: 20.4g; Fiber: 1.7g; Fat: 24.5g; Carbs: 33.7g

313. Broccoli Crust Pizza

Preparation Time: 27 minutes • Servings: 4

INGREDIENTS

- 3cups riced broccoli, steamed and drained well
- ½ cup shredded mozzarella cheese
- ½ cup grated vegetarian Parmesan cheese.
- 1large egg.
- 3tbsp. low-carb Alfredo sauce

DIRECTIONS

1. Take a large bowl, mix broccoli, egg and Parmesan.
2. Cut a piece of parchment to fit your air fryer basket. Press out the pizza mixture to fit on the parchment, working in two batches if necessary. Place into the air fryer basket. Adjust the temperature to 370 Degrees F and set the timer for 5 minutes.
3. When the timer beeps, the crust should be firm enough to flip. If not, add 2 additional minutes. Flip crust.
4. Top with Alfredo sauce and mozzarella. Return to the air fryer basket and cook an additional 7 minutes or until cheese is golden and bubbling. Serve warm.

NUTRITION: Calories: 136; Protein: 9.9g; Fiber: 2.3g; Fat: 7.6g; Carbs:5.7g

314. Cheesy Zoodle Bake

Preparation Time: 18 minutes • Servings: 4

INGREDIENTS

- ½ cup heavy whipping cream.
- 2oz. full-fat cream cheese.
- 1cup shredded sharp Cheddar cheese.
- 2medium zucchini, spiralized
- ¼ cup diced white onion
- 2tbsp. salted butter
- ½ tsp. minced garlic

DIRECTIONS

1. In a large saucepan over medium heat, melt butter. Add onion and sauté until it begins to soften, 1–3 minutes. Add garlic and sauté 30 seconds, then pour in cream and add cream cheese
2. Remove the pan from heat and stir in Cheddar. Add the zucchini and toss in the sauce, then put into a 4-cup round baking dish.
3. Cover the dish with foil and place into the air fryer basket. Adjust the temperature to 370 Degrees F and set the timer for 8 minutes
4. After 6 minutes remove the foil and let the top brown for remaining cooking time. Stir and serve.

NUTRITION: Calories: 337; Protein: 9.6g; Fiber: 1.2g; Fat: 28.4g; Carbs: 5.9g

315. Eggplant Stacks

Preparation Time: 17 minutes • Servings: 4

INGREDIENTS

- 2large tomatoes; cut into ¼-inch slices
- ¼ cup fresh basil, sliced
- 4oz. fresh mozzarella; cut into ½-oz. slices
- 1medium eggplant; cut into ¼-inch slices
- 2tbsp. olive oil

DIRECTIONS

1. In a 6-inch round baking dish, place four slices of eggplant on the bottom. Place a slice of tomato on top of each eggplant round, then mozzarella, then eggplant. Repeat as necessary.
2. Drizzle with olive oil. Cover dish with foil and place dish into the air fryer basket. Adjust the temperature to 350 Degrees F and set the timer for 12 minutes.
3. When done, eggplant will be tender. Garnish with fresh basil to serve.

NUTRITION: Calories: 195; Protein: 8.5g; Fiber: 5.2g; Fat: 12.7g; Carbs: 12.7g

316. Roasted Garlic Zucchini Rolls

Preparation Time: 40 minutes Servings: 4

INGREDIENTS

- 2medium zucchini
- ½ cup full-fat ricotta cheese
- ¼ white onion; peeled.and diced
- 2cups spinach; chopped
- ¼ cup heavy cream
- ½ cup sliced baby portobello mushrooms
- ¾ cup shredded mozzarella cheese, divided.
- 2tbsp. unsalted butter.
- 2tbsp. vegetable broth.
- ½ tsp. finely minced roasted garlic
- ¼ tsp. dried oregano.
- ⅛ tsp. xanthan gum
- ¼ tsp. salt
- ½ tsp. garlic powder.

DIRECTIONS

1. 1Using a mandoline or sharp knife, slice zucchini into long strips lengthwise. Place strips between paper towels to absorb moisture. Set aside
2. 2In a medium saucepan over medium heat, melt butter. Add onion and sauté until fragrant. Add garlic and sauté 30 seconds.
3. 3Pour in heavy cream, broth and xanthan gum. Turn off heat and whisk mixture until it begins to

thicken, about 3 minutes.

4. 4Take a medium bowl, add ricotta, salt, garlic powder and oregano and mix well. Fold in spinach, mushrooms and ½ cup mozzarella
5. 5Pour half of the sauce into a 6-inch round baking pan. To assemble the rolls, place two strips of zucchini on a work surface. Spoon 2 tbsp. of ricotta mixture onto the slices and roll up. Place seam side down on top of sauce. Repeat with remaining ingredients
6. 6Pour remaining sauce over the rolls and sprinkle with remaining mozzarella. Cover with foil and place into the air fryer basket. Adjust the temperature to 350 Degrees F and set the timer for 20 minutes. In the last 5 minutes, remove the foil to brown the cheese. Serve immediately.

NUTRITION: Calories: 245; Protein: 10.5g; Fiber: 1.8g; Fat: 18.9g; Carbs: 7.1g

317. Roasted Veggie Bowl

Preparation Time: 25 minutes • Servings: 2

INGREDIENTS

- ¼ medium white onion; peeled.and sliced ¼-inch thick
- ½ medium green bell pepper; seeded and sliced ¼-inch thick
- 1cup broccoli florets
- 1cup quartered Brussels sprouts
- ½ cup cauliflower florets
- 1tbsp. coconut oil
- ½ tsp. garlic powder.
- ½ tsp. cumin
- 2tsp. chili powder

DIRECTIONS

1. Toss all ingredients together in a large bowl until vegetables are fully coated with oil and seasoning. Pour vegetables into the air fryer basket.
2. Adjust the temperature to 360 Degrees F and set the timer for 15 minutes. Shake two or three times during cooking. Serve warm.

Nutrition: Calories: 121; Protein: 4.3g; Fiber: 5.2g; Fat: 7.1g; Carbs: 13.1g

318. Espresso Mini Cheesecake

Preparation Time: 20 minutes • Servings: 2

INGREDIENTS

- ½ cup walnuts
- 4oz. full-fat cream cheese; softened.
- 1large egg.

- 2tbsp. salted butter
- 2tbsp. granular erythritol.
- 2tbsp. powdered erythritol
- 1tsp. espresso powder
- ½ tsp. vanilla extract.
- 2tsp. unsweetened cocoa powder

DIRECTIONS

1. Place walnuts, butter and granular erythritol in a food processor. Pulse until ingredients stick together and a dough forms.
2. Press dough into 4-inch springform pan and place into the air fryer basket.
3. Adjust the temperature to 400 Degrees F and set the timer for 5 minutes. When timer beeps, remove crust and let cool.
4. Take a medium bowl, mix cream cheese with egg, vanilla extract, powdered erythritol, cocoa powder and espresso powder until smooth.
5. Spoon mixture on top of baked walnut crust and place into the air fryer basket. Adjust the temperature for 300 Degrees F and set the timer for 10 minutes. Once done, chill for 2 hours before serving.

NUTRITION: Calories: 535; Protein: 11.6g; Fiber: 7.2g; Fat: 48.4g; Carbs: 37.1g

CHAPTER 8

SNACKS

319. Pickled Snack

Preparation Time: 25 minutes • Servings: 4

INGREDIENTS

- 4dill pickle spears; sliced in half and quartered
- 1cup avocado mayonnaise
- 8bacon slices; halved

DIRECTIONS:

1. Wrap each pickle spear in a bacon slice, put them in your air fryer's basket and cook at 400°F for 20 minutes.
2. Serve as a snack with the mayonnaise

NUTRITION: Calories: 100; Fat: 4g; Fiber: 2g; Carbs: 3g; Protein: 4g

320. Avocado Bites

Preparation Time: 13 minutes Servings: 4

INGREDIENTS

- 4avocados, peeled, pitted and cut into wedges
- 1½ cups almond meal
- 1egg; whisked
- A pinch of salt and black pepper
- Cooking spray

DIRECTIONS

1. Put the egg in a bowl and the almond meal in another.
2. Season avocado wedges with salt and pepper, coat them in egg and then in meal almond
3. Arrange the avocado bites in your air fryer's basket, grease them with cooking spray and cook at 400°F for 8 minutes Servings as a snack right away

NUTRITION: Calories: 200; Fat: 12g; Fiber: 3g; Carbs: 5g; Protein: 16g

321. Asparagus Wraps

Preparation Time: 20 minutes • Servings: 8

INGREDIENTS

- 16asparagus spears; trimmed
- 16bacon strips
- 1tbsp. lemon juice
- 2tbsp. olive oil
- 1tsp. oregano; chopped.

- 1tsp. thyme; chopped.
- A pinch of salt and black pepper

DIRECTIONS

1. Take a bowl and mix the oil with lemon juice, the herbs, salt and pepper and whisk well.
2. Brush the asparagus spears with this mix and wrap each in a bacon strip
3. Arrange the asparagus wraps in your air fryer's basket and cook at 390°F for 15 minutes.

NUTRITION: Calories: 173; Fat: 4g; Fiber: 2g; Carbs: 3g; Protein: 6g

322. Warm Tomato Salsa

Preparation Time: 13 minutes • Servings: 4

INGREDIENTS

- 2spring onions; chopped.
- 1garlic clove; minced
- 4tomatoes; cubed
- 3chili peppers; minced
- 2tbsp. lime juice
- 2tsp. parsley; chopped.
- 2tsp. cilantro; chopped.
- Cooking spray

DIRECTIONS

1. Grease a pan that fits your air fryer with the cooking spray and mix all the ingredients inside.
2. Introduce the pan in the machine and cook at 360°F for 8 minutes. Divide into bowls and serve

NUTRITION: Calories: 148; Fat: 1g; Fiber: 2g; Carbs: 3g; Protein: 5g

323. Zucchini Chips

Preparation Time: 20 minutes • Servings: 6

INGREDIENTS

- 3zucchinis, thinly sliced
- 1cup almond flour
- 2eggs; whisked
- Salt and black pepper to taste.

DIRECTIONS

1. Take a bowl and mix the eggs with salt and pepper. Put the flour in a second bowl.
2. Dredge the zucchinis in flour and then in eggs
3. Arrange the chips in your air fryer's basket, cook at 350°F for 15 minutes and serve as a snack.

NUTRITION: Calories: 120; Fat: 4g; Fiber: 2g; Carbs: 3g; Protein: 5g

324. Parsley Meatballs

Preparation Time: 25 minutes • Servings: 6

INGREDIENTS

- 1lb. beef meat, ground
- 2tbsp. parsley; chopped.
- 1tsp. onion powder
- 1tsp. garlic powder
- Cooking spray
- A pinch of salt and black pepper

DIRECTIONS

1. Take a bowl and mix all the ingredients except the cooking spray, stir well and shape medium meatballs out of this mix
2. Pace them in your lined air fryer's basket, grease with cooking spray and cook at 360°F for 20 minutes

NUTRITION: Calories: 150; Fat: 4g; Fiber: 3g; Carbs: 4g; Protein: 6g

325. Sweet Pepper Poppers

Preparation Time: 23 minutes • Servings: 16 halves

INGREDIENTS

- 8mini sweet peppers
- 4slices sugar-free bacon; cooked and crumbled
- ¼ cup shredded pepper jack cheese
- 4oz. full-fat cream cheese; softened.

DIRECTIONS:

1. Remove the tops from the peppers and slice each one in half lengthwise. Use a small knife to remove seeds and membranes
2. In a small bowl, mix cream cheese, bacon and pepper jack
3. Place 3 tsp. of the mixture into each sweet pepper and press down smooth. Place into the fryer basket. Adjust the temperature to 400 Degrees F and set the timer for 8 minutes
4. Servings warm.

NUTRITION: Calories: 180; Fat: 5g; Fiber: 2g; Carbs: 5g; Protein: 7g

326. Cheese Chips

Preparation Time: 7 minutes • Servings: 4

INGREDIENTS

- 8oz. cheddar cheese; shredded
- 1tsp. sweet paprika

DIRECTIONS:

1. Divide the cheese in small heaps in a pan that fits the air fryer, sprinkle the paprika on top, introduce the pan in the machine and cook at 400°F for 5 minutes
2. Cool down the chips and serve them.

NUTRITION: Calories: 176; Protein: 7.4g; Fiber: 0.9g; Fat: 13.4g; Carbs: 3.6g

327. Bacon Wrapped Onion Rings.

Preparation Time: 15 minutes • Servings: 4

INGREDIENTS

- 1large onion; peeled.
- 8slices sugar-free bacon.
- 1tbsp. sriracha

DIRECTIONS

1. Slice onion into ¼-inch-thick slices. Brush sriracha over the onion slices. Take two slices of onion and wrap bacon around the rings. Repeat with remaining onion and bacon
2. Place into the air fryer basket. Adjust the temperature to 350 Degrees F and set the timer for 10 minutes.
3. Use tongs to flip the onion rings halfway through the cooking time. When fully cooked, bacon will be crispy. Serve warm

NUTRITION: Calories: 105; Protein: 7.5g; Fiber: 0.6g; Fat: 5.9g; Carbs: 4.3g

328. Zucchini Salsa

Preparation Time: 20 minutes • Servings: 6

INGREDIENTS

- 1½ lb. zucchinis, roughly cubed
- 2tomatoes; cubed
- 2spring onions; chopped.
- 1tbsp. balsamic vinegar
- Salt and black pepper to taste.

DIRECTIONS

1. In a pan that fits your air fryer, mix all the ingredients, toss, introduce the pan in the fryer and cook at 360°F for 15 minutes
2. Divide the salsa into cups and serve cold.

NUTRITION: Calories: 164; Fat: 6g; Fiber: 2g; Carbs: 3g; Protein: 8g

329. Mushroom Platter

Preparation Time: 17 minutes • Servings: 4

INGREDIENTS

- 12oz. Portobello mushrooms; sliced

- 2tbsp. olive oil
- 2tbsp. balsamic vinegar
- ½ tsp. rosemary; dried
- ½ tsp. thyme; dried
- ½ tsp. basil; dried
- ½ tsp. tarragon; dried
- A pinch of salt and black pepper

DIRECTIONS

1. Take a bowl and mix all the ingredients and toss well.
2. Arrange the mushroom slices in your air fryer's basket and cook at 380°F for 12 minutes. Arrange the mushroom slices on a platter and serve

NUTRITION: Calories: 147; Fat: 8g; Fiber: 2g; Carbs: 3g; Protein: 3g

330. Crab Balls

Preparation Time: 25 minutes • Servings: 8

INGREDIENTS

- 16oz. lump crabmeat; chopped.
- 2/3 cup almond meal
- ½ cup coconut cream
- 1egg; whisked
- 2tbsp. chives, mined
- 1tsp. lemon juice
- 1tsp. mustard
- A pinch of salt and black pepper
- Cooking spray

DIRECTIONS

1. Take a bowl and mix all the ingredients except the cooking spray and stir well.
2. Shape medium balls out of this mix, place them in the fryer and cook at 390°F for 20 minutes
3. When cooked, bacon will be crispy and cheese will be soft and melty. To serve; cut into eight slices.
4.

NUTRITION: Calories: 141; Fat: 7 g , Fiber: 2 g, Carbs: 4g; Protein: 9g

331. Bacon Wrapped Brie

Preparation Time: 15 minutes • Servings: 8

INGREDIENTS

- 1.8-oz.round Brie
- 4slices sugar-free bacon.

DIRECTIONS

1. Place two slices of bacon to form an X. Place the third slice of bacon horizontally across the center of the X. Place the fourth slice of bacon vertically

across the
X. It should look like a plus sign (+on top of an X. Place the Brie in the center of the bacon

2. Wrap the bacon around the Brie, securing with a few toothpicks. Cut a piece of parchment to fit your air fryer basket and place the bacon-wrapped Brie on top. Place inside the air fryer basket.
3. Adjust the temperature to 400 Degrees F and set the timer for 10 minutes. When 3 minutes remain on the timer, carefully flip Brie

NUTRITION: Calories: 116; Protein: 7.7g; Fiber 0.0g; Fat: 8.9g; Carbs: 0.2g

332. Shrimp Balls

Preparation Time: 20 minutes • Servings: 4

INGREDIENTS

- 1lb. shrimp, peeled, deveined and minced
- 1egg; whisked
- ½ cup coconut flour
- 1tbsp. avocado oil
- 3tbsp. coconut; shredded
- 1tbsp. cilantro; chopped.

DIRECTIONS

1. Take a bowl and mix all the ingredients, stir well and shape medium balls out of this mix.
2. Place the balls in your lined air fryer's basket, cook at 350°F for 15 minutes and serve

NUTRITION: Calories: 184; Fat: 5g; Fiber: 2g; Carbs: 4g; Protein: 7g

CHAPTER 9

DESSERT

333. Veggie Quesadilla

Preparation Time: 15 minutes • Servings: 2

INGREDIENTS

- 4flatbread dough tortillas
- ⅔ cup shredded pepper jack cheese
- ½ medium avocado; peeled, pitted and mashed
- ½ medium green bell pepper; seeded and chopped
- ¼ cup diced red onion
- ¼ cup chopped white mushrooms
- ¼ cup full-fat sour cream.
- ¼ cup mild salsa
- 1tbsp. coconut oil

DIRECTIONS

1. In a medium skillet over medium heat, warm coconut oil. Add pepper, onion and mushrooms to skillet and sauté until peppers begin to soften, 3–5 minutes
2. Place two tortillas on a work surface and sprinkle each with half of cheese. Top with sautéed veggies, sprinkle with remaining cheese and place remaining two tortillas on top
3. Place quesadillas carefully into the air fryer basket.
4. Adjust the temperature to 400 Degrees F and set the timer for 5 minutes.
5. Flip the quesadillas halfway through the cooking time. Serve warm with avocado, sour cream and salsa.

NUTRITION: Calories: 795; Protein: 34.5g; Fiber: 6.5g; Fat: 61.3g; Carbs: 19.4g

334. Cajun Olives and Peppers

Preparation Time: 16 minutes • Servings: 4

INGREDIENTS

- ½ lb. mixed bell peppers; sliced
- 1cup black olives, pitted and halved
- ½ tbsp. Cajun seasoning
- 1tbsp. olive oil

DIRECTIONS:

1. In a pan that fits the air fryer, combine all the ingredients.

2. Put the pan it in your air fryer and cook at 390°F for 12 minutes. Divide the mix between plates and serve

NUTRITION: Calories: 151; Fat: 3g; Fiber: 2g; Carbs: 4g; Protein: 5g

335. Chili Broccoli

Preparation Time: 20 minutes • Servings: 4

INGREDIENTS:

- 1lb. broccoli florets
- Juice of 1 lime
- 2tbsp. chili sauce
- 2tbsp. olive oil
- A pinch of salt and black pepper

DIRECTIONS

1. Take a bowl and mix the broccoli with the other ingredients and toss well.
2. Put the broccoli in your air fryer's basket and cook at 400°F for 15 minutes
3. Divide between plates and serve.

NUTRITION: Calories: 173; Fat: 6g; Fiber: 2g; Carbs: 6g; Protein: 8g

336. Balsamic Kale

Preparation Time: 14 minutes • Servings: 6

INGREDIENTS

- 2½ lb. kale leaves
- 3garlic cloves; minced
- 2tbsp. olive oil
- 2tbsp. balsamic vinegar
- Salt and black pepper to taste.

DIRECTIONS

1. In a pan that fits the air fryer, combine all the ingredients and toss.
2. Put the pan in your air fryer and cook at 300°F for 12 minutes. Divide between plates and serve

NUTRITION: Calories: 122; Fat: 4g; Fiber: 3g; Carbs: 4g; Protein: 5g

337. Mustard Greens and Green Beans

Preparation Time: 22 minutes • Servings: 4

INGREDIENTS

- 1lb. green beans; halved
-
- ¼ cup tomato puree
- 3garlic cloves; minced
- 1bunch mustard greens, trimmed
- 2tbsp. olive oil
- 1tbsp. balsamic vinegar
- Salt and black pepper to taste.

DIRECTIONS

1. In a pan that fits your air fryer, mix the mustard greens with the rest of the ingredients, toss, put the pan in the fryer and cook at 350°F for 12 minutes
2. Divide everything between plates and serve.

NUTRITION: Calories: 163; Fat: 4g; Fiber: 3g; Carbs: 4g; Protein: 7g

338. Olives and Cilantro Vinaigrette

Preparation Time: 17 minutes • Servings: 4

INGREDIENTS

- 1cup baby spinach
- 2cups black olives, pitted
- 1tbsp. olive oil
- 2tbsp. balsamic vinegar
- A bunch of cilantro; chopped.
- Salt and black pepper to taste.

DIRECTIONS

1. In a pan that fits the air fryer, combine all the ingredients and toss.
2. Put the pan in the air fryer and cook at 370°F for 12 minutes
3. Transfer to bowls and serve.

NUTRITION: Calories: 132; Fat: 4g; Fiber: 2g; Carbs: 4g; Protein: 4g

339. Broccoli and Tomatoes

Preparation Time: 20 minutes • Servings: 4

INGREDIENTS

- 1broccoli head, florets separated
- 2cups cherry tomatoes, quartered
- 1tbsp. cilantro; chopped.
- Juice of 1 lime
- A drizzle of olive oil
- A pinch of salt and black pepper

DIRECTIONS

1. In a pan that fits the air fryer, combine the broccoli with tomatoes and the rest of the ingredients except the cilantro, toss, put the pan in the air fryer and cook at 380°F for 15 minutes
2. Divide between plates and serve with cilantro sprinkled on top.

NUTRITION: Calories: 141; Fat: 3g; Fiber: 2g; Carbs: 4g; Protein: 5g

340. Kale and Mushrooms

Preparation Time: 20 minutes • Servings: 4

INGREDIENTS

- 1lb. brown mushrooms; sliced
- 1lb. kale, torn
- 14oz. coconut milk
- 2tbsp. olive oil
- Salt and black pepper to taste.

DIRECTIONS

1. In a pan that fits your air fryer, mix the kale with the rest of the ingredients and toss
2. Put the pan in the fryer, cook at 380°F for 15 minutes, divide between plates and serve

NUTRITION: Calories: 162; Fat: 4g; Fiber: 1g; Carbs: 3g; Protein: 5g

341. Spicy Olives and Avocado

Preparation Time: 20 minutes • Servings: 4

INGREDIENTS

- 2small avocados, pitted; peeled and sliced
- ¼ cup cherry tomatoes; halved
- 2cups kalamata olives, pitted
- 1tbsp. coconut oil; melted
- juice of 1 lime

DIRECTIONS:

1. In a pan that fits the air fryer, combine the olives with the other ingredients, toss.
2. Put the pan in your air fryer and cook at 370°F for 15 minutes
3. Divide the mix between plates and serve.

NUTRITION: Calories: 153; Fat: 3g; Fiber: 3g; Carbs: 4g; Protein: 6g

342. Lemon Endives

Preparation Time: 20 minutes • Servings: 4

INGREDIENTS

- 12endives, trimmed
- 3tbsp. ghee; melted
- 1tbsp. lemon juice
- A pinch of salt and black pepper

DIRECTIONS

1. take a bowl and mix the endives with the ghee, salt, pepper and lemon juice and toss.
2. put the endives in the fryer's basket and cook at 350°f for 15 minutes
3. divide between plates and serve.

NUTRITION: Calories: 163; Fat: 4g; Fiber: 3g; Carbs: 5g; Protein: 6g

343. Roasted Lemon Cauliflower

Preparation Time: 20 minutes • Servings: 4

INGREDIENTS

- 1medium head cauliflower
- 1medium lemon.
- 2tbsp. salted butter; melted.

- 1tsp. dried parsley.
- ½ tsp. garlic powder.

DIRECTIONS

1. Remove the leaves from the head of cauliflower and brush it with melted butter. Cut the lemon in half and zest one half onto the cauliflower. Squeeze the juice of the zested lemon half and pour it over the cauliflower.
2. Sprinkle with garlic powder and parsley. Place cauliflower head into the air fryer basket. Adjust the temperature to 350 Degrees F and set the timer for 15 minutes
3. Check cauliflower every 5 minutes to avoid overcooking. It should be fork tender.
4. To serve, squeeze juice from other lemon half over cauliflower. Serve immediately.

NUTRITION: Calories: 91; Protein: 3.0g; Fiber: 3.2g; Fat: 5.7g; Carbs: 8.4g

344. Creamy Kale

Preparation Time: 20 minutes • Servings: 4

INGREDIENTS

- 2lb. kale, torn
- 2garlic cloves; minced
- ½ cup parmesan, grated
- 1½ cups coconut cream
- 2tbsp. olive oil
- ½ tsp. nutmeg, ground
- A pinch of salt and black pepper

DIRECTIONS

1. In a pan that fits your air fryer, mix the kale with the rest of the ingredients, toss, introduce the pan in the fryer and cook at 400°F for 15 minutes. Divide between plates and serve

NUTRITION: Calories: 135; Fat: 3g; Fiber: 2g; Carbs: 4g; Protein: 6g

345. Mustard Asparagus

Preparation Time: 17 minutes • Servings: 4

INGREDIENTS

- 1lb. asparagus, trimmed
- ½ cup parmesan, grated
- ¼ cup mustard
- 3garlic cloves; minced
- 2tbsp. olive oil

DIRECTIONS

1. Take a bowl and mix the asparagus with the oil, garlic and mustard and toss really well.
2. Put the asparagus spears in your air fryer's basket and cook at 400°F for 12 minutes
3. Divide between plates, sprinkle the parmesan on top and serve.

NUTRITION: Calories: 162; Fat: 4g; Fiber: 4g; Carbs: 6g; Protein: 9g

346. Kale and Brussels Sprouts

Preparation Time: 20 minutes • Servings: 8

INGREDIENTS

- 1lb. Brussels sprouts, trimmed
- 3oz. mozzarella, shredded
- 2cups kale, torn
- 1tbsp. olive oil
- Salt and black pepper to taste.

DIRECTIONS

1. In a pan that fits the air fryer, combine all the ingredients except the mozzarella and toss.
2. Put the pan in the air fryer and cook at 380°F for 15 minutes
3. Divide between plates, sprinkle the cheese on top and serve.

NUTRITION: Calories: 170; Fat: 5g; Fiber: 3g; Carbs: 4g; Protein: 7g

347. Butter Broccoli

Preparation Time: 20 minutes • Servings: 4

INGREDIENTS

- 1lb. broccoli florets
- ½ tbsp. butter; melted
- 1tsp. sweet paprika
- a pinch of salt and black pepper

DIRECTIONS

1. Take a bowl and mix the broccoli with the rest of the ingredients and toss.
2. Put the broccoli in your air fryer's basket, cook at 350°F for 15 minutes, divide between plates and serve

NUTRITION: Calories: 173; Fat: 5g; Fiber: 3g; Carbs: 5g; Protein: 8g

348. Oregano Kale

Preparation Time: 15 minutes • Servings: 4

INGREDIENTS

- 1lb. kale, torn
- 2tbsp. oregano; chopped
- 1tbsp. olive oil
- A pinch of salt and black pepper

DIRECTIONS

1. In a pan that fits the air fryer, combine all the ingredients and toss.
2. Put the pan in the air fryer and cook at 380°F for 10 minutes. Divide between plates and serve

NUTRITION: Calories: 140; Fat: 3g; Fiber: 2g; Carbs: 3g; Protein: 5g

349. Savoy Cabbage

Preparation Time: 20 minutes • Servings: 4

INGREDIENTS

- 1Savoy cabbage head, shredded
- 1tbsp. dill; chopped.
- 1½ tbsp. ghee; melted
- ¼ cup coconut cream
- Salt and black pepper to taste.

DIRECTIONS

1. In a pan that fits the air fryer, combine all the ingredients except the coconut cream, toss, put the pan in the air fryer and cook at 390°F for 10 minutes
2. Add the cream, toss, cook for 5 minutes more, divide between plates and serve

NUTRITION: Calories: 130; Fat: 3g; Fiber: 3g; Carbs: 4g; Protein: 8g

350. Broccoli and Tomato Sauce

Preparation Time: 20 minutes • Servings: 4

INGREDIENTS

- 1broccoli head, florets separated
- ¼ cup scallions; chopped
- ½ cup tomato sauce
- 1tbsp. olive oil
- 1tbsp. sweet paprika
- Salt and black pepper to taste.

DIRECTIONS

1. In a pan that fits the air fryer, combine the broccoli with the rest of the ingredients, toss.
2. Put the pan in the fryer and cook at 380°F for 15 minutes
3. Divide between plates and serve.

NUTRITION: Calories: 163; Fat: 5g; Fiber: 2g; Carbs: 4g; Protein: 8g

351. Italian Olives

Preparation Time: 20 minutes • Servings: 4

INGREDIENTS

- 12oz. tomatoes; chopped.
- 2cups black olives, pitted and halved
- 4garlic cloves; minced
- 2rosemary springs; chopped.
- 2red bell peppers; sliced
- A handful basil; chopped.
- 2tbsp. olive oil

DIRECTIONS

1. In a pan that fits the air fryer, combine the olives with the rest of the ingredients, toss.
2. Put the pan in the fryer and cook at 380°F for 15 minutes
3. Divide between plates and serve.

NUTRITION: Calories: 173; Fat: 6g; Fiber: 2g; Carbs: 4g; Protein: 5g

352. Kale and Olives

Preparation Time: 20 minutes • Servings: 4

INGREDIENTS

- 1an ½ lb. kale, torn
- 1tbsp. hot paprika
- 2tbsp. olive oil
- 2tbsp. black olives, pitted and sliced
- Salt and black pepper to taste.

DIRECTIONS

1. In a pan that fits the air fryer, combine all the ingredients and toss.
2. Put the pan in your air fryer, cook at 370°F for 15 minutes, divide between plates and serve

NUTRITION: Calories: 154; Fat: 3g; Fiber: 2g; Carbs: 4g; Protein: 6g

353. Broccoli Casserole

Preparation Time: 35 minutes • Servings: 4

INGREDIENTS

- 1lb. broccoli florets
- 15oz. coconut cream
- 2eggs, whisked
- 2cups cheddar, grated
- 1cup parmesan, grated
- 1tbsp. parsley; chopped
- 3tbsp. ghee; melted
- 1tbsp. mustard
- A pinch of salt and black pepper

DIRECTIONS

1. Grease a baking pan that fits the air fryer with the ghee and arrange the broccoli on the bottom.
2. Add the cream, mustard, salt, pepper and the eggs and toss
3. Sprinkle the cheese on top, put the pan in the air fryer and cook at 380°F for 30 minutes
4. Divide between plates and serve.

NUTRITION: Calories: 244; Fat: 12g; Fiber: 3g; Carbs: 5g; Protein: 12g

354. Cheesy Zoodle Bake

Preparation Time: 18 minutes • Servings: 4

INGREDIENTS

- ½ cup heavy whipping cream.
- 2oz. full-fat cream cheese.
- 1cup shredded sharp Cheddar cheese.
- 2medium zucchini, spiralized
- ¼ cup diced white onion

- 2tbsp. salted butter
- ½ tsp. minced garlic

DIRECTIONS

1. In a large saucepan over medium heat, melt butter. Add onion and sauté until it begins to soften, 1–3 minutes. Add garlic and sauté 30 seconds, then pour in cream and add cream cheese
2. Remove the pan from heat and stir in Cheddar. Add the zucchini and toss in the sauce, then put into a 4-cup round baking dish.
3. Cover the dish with foil and place into the air fryer basket. Adjust the temperature to 370 Degrees F and set the timer for 8 minutes
4. After 6 minutes remove the foil and let the top brown for remaining cooking time. Stir and serve.

NUTRITION: Calories: 337; Protein: 9.6g; Fiber: 1.2g; Fat: 28.4g; Carbs: 5.9g

355. Fennel and Collard Greens Sauté

Preparation Time: 17 minutes • Servings: 4

INGREDIENTS

- 1lb. collard greens, trimmed
- ½ cup tomato sauce
- 2fennel bulbs, trimmed and quartered
- 2tbsp. olive oil
- Salt and black pepper to taste.

DIRECTIONS

1. In a pan that fits your air fryer, mix the collard greens with the fennel and the rest of the ingredients, toss, put the pan in the fryer and cook at 350°F for 12 minutes
2. Divide everything between plates and serve.

NUTRITION: Calories: 163; Fat: 4g; Fiber: 3g; Carbs: 5g; Protein: 6g

356. Tomato and Kale Salad

Preparation Time: 20 minutes • Servings: 4

INGREDIENTS

- ½ lb. kale leaves, torn
- ¼ cup veggie stock
- 10cherry tomatoes; halved
- 2tbsp. tomato sauce
- Salt and black pepper to taste.

DIRECTIONS

1. In a pan that fits your air fryer, mix tomatoes with the remaining ingredients, toss.
2. Put the pan in the fryer and cook at 360°F for 15 minutes

3. Divide between plates and serve right away.

NUTRITION: Calories: 161; Fat: 2g; Fiber: 2g; Carbs: 4g; Protein: 6g

357. Beef Stuffed Bell Peppers

Preparation Time: 50 minutes • Servings: 4

INGREDIENTS

- Ground beef – 1 pound
- Ground coriander – 1 tsp
- Medium white onion, peeled and chopped – 1
- Minced garlic – 1 ½ tsp
- Turmeric powder – 1/2 tsp
- Hot curry powder – 1 tbsp
- Olive oil – 2 tbsps
- Grated ginger – 1 tbsp
- Ground cumin – 1/2 tsp
- Salt – 1/2 tsp
- Ground black pepper – 1/2 tsp
- Egg – 1
- Medium green bell peppers; halves and cored – 4
- Raisins – 1/3 cup
- Chopped walnuts – 1/3 cup

DIRECTIONS

1. Place a medium skillet pan over medium- high heat, add oil and when hot, add onion and cook for 4 to 5 minutes or until softened, stirring frequently.
2. Then add garlic and beef, stir well and continue cooking for 10 minutes.
3. Add remaining ingredients except for bell pepper, stir well until combined and remove the pan from heat.
4. Plug in the air fryer, insert fryer basket greased with oil, shut with lid and preheat at 320 0F for 10 minutes.
5. In the meantime, stuff pepper halves with prepared beef mixture.
6. Place stuffed peppers into heated air fryer in a single layer, spray with oil and cook for 20 minutes.
7. Serve straightaway.

NUTRITION: Calories: 170; Fat: 4; Fiber: 3; Carbs: 7; Protein: 12

358. Crispy Leeks with Lemon

Preparation Time: 12 minutes • Servings: 4

INGREDIENTS

- Medium leeks; washed, ends cut off and halved – 4
- Unsalted butter; melted – 1 tbsp
- Salt – ½ tsp
- Ground black pepper – ½ tsp
- Lemon juice – 1 tbsp

DIRECTIONS

1. Plug in the air fryer, insert fryer basket

greased with oil, shut with lid and preheat at 350 0F for 5 minutes.

2. Meanwhile, rub melted butter all over leeks and then season with salt and black pepper.
3. Place leeks into the air fryer and cook for 7 minutes or until done.
4. When done, transfer leeks onto a serving plate, drizzle with lemon juice and serve.

NUTRITION: Calories: 100; Fat: 4; Fiber: 2; Carbs: 6; Protein: 2

359. Okra Salad with Tomato and Corn

Preparation Time: 22 minutes • Servings: 6

INGREDIENTS

- Okra; trimmed – 1 pound
- Scallions; chopped – 6
- Tomatoes; chopped – 28 ounce
- Medium green bell peppers; chopped – 3
- Salt – ½ tsp
- Ground black pepper – ¼ tsp
- Olive oil – 2 tbsps
- Sugar – 1 tsp
- Corn – 1 cup

DIRECTIONS

1. Plug in the air fryer, insert fryer basket, shut with lid and preheat at 360 0F for 10 minutes.
2. In the meantime, place a pan that fits into air fryer over medium heat, add oil and when hot, add scallions and bell pepper and cook for 5 minutes.
3. Then add okra, tomatoes and corn, season with salt and black pepper and stir until mixed.
4. Insert pan into the air fryer and cook for 7 minutes or until done.
5. Serve immediately.

NUTRITION: Calories: 152; Fat: 4; Fiber: 3; Carbs: 18; Protein: 4

360. Cheesy Fennel

Preparation Time: 18 minutes • Servings: 4

INGREDIENTS

- Fennel bulbs; cut into quarters – 2
- Olive oil – 3 tbsps
- Lemon, juiced – 1/2
- Salt – ½ tsp
- Ground black pepper – ¼ tsp
- Minced garlic – ½ tsp
- Red chili pepper; chopped – 1
- Vegetable stock – 3/4 cup
- White wine – 1/4 cup
- Grated parmesan cheese – 1/4 cup

DIRECTIONS

1. Plug in the air fryer, insert fryer basket, shut with lid and preheat at 350 0F for 10 minutes.
2. In the meantime, place a pan that fits into air fryer over medium-high heat, add oil and when hot, add chili peppers and garlic and cook for 2 minutes.
3. Add fennel and parmesan cheese, pour in lemon juice, wine and stock, season with salt and black pepper and stir until mixed.
4. Insert pan into the air fryer and cook for 6 minutes or until done/
5. Serve straightaway.

NUTRITION: Calories: 100; Fat: 4; Fiber: 8; Carbs: 4; Protein: 4

361. Parmesan Swiss Chard with Sausage

Preparation Time: 30 minutes • Servings: 8

INGREDIENTS

- Swiss chard; chopped – 8 cups
- White onion; chopped – 1/2 cup
- Grated parmesan cheese – 1/4 cup
- Sausage; chopped – 1 pound
- Olive oil – 1 tbsp
- Minced garlic – ½ tsp
- Salt – ½ tsp
- Ground black pepper – ¼ tsp
- Eggs – 3
- Ricotta cheese – 2 cups
- Shredded mozzarella cheese – 1 cup
- Ground nutmeg – 1/8 tsp

DIRECTIONS

1. Plug in the air fryer, insert fryer basket, shut with lid and preheat at 320 0F for 10 minutes.
2. In the meantime, place a pan that fits into air fryer over medium heat, add oil and when hot, add Swiss chard, onion, and garlic, season with salt, black pepper and nutmeg and stir until mixed.
3. Cook Swiss chard for 2 minutes, then remove the pan from heat and set aside.
4. Crack eggs in a bowl, add cheeses, whisk until combined, then pour the mixture over Swiss chard's and toss until mixed.
5. Insert pan into the air fryer and cook for 17 minutes or until done.
6. Serve straightaway.

NUTRITION: Calories: 332; Fat: 13; Fiber: 3; Carbs: 14; Protein: 23

362. Beet, Red Onion and Tomato Mix with Goat Cheese

Preparation Time: 44 minutes • Servings: 8

INGREDIENTS

- Small beets; trimmed, peeled and halved– 8
- Medium red onion; peeled and sliced – 1
- Sugar – 2 tbsps

- Mixed cherry tomatoes; halved – 1 pint
- Pecans – 2 ounce
- Olive oil – 2 tbsps
- Goat cheese; crumbled – 4 ounce
- Balsamic vinegar – 1 tbsp
- Salt – ½ tsp
- Ground black pepper – ½ tsp

DIRECTIONS

1. Plug in the air fryer, insert fryer basket greased with oil, shut with lid and preheat at 350 0F for 5 minutes.
2. Then add beets into the air fryer, season with salt and black pepper and cook for 14 minutes or until done.
3. When done, transfer beets into a salad bowl, then add onion, tomatoes, and pecans and toss until mixed.
4. Whisk together sugar, oil, and vinegar into a small bowl until sugar dissolves completely and then drizzle this mixture over salad.
5. Add cheese, toss until mixed and serve.

NUTRITION: Calories: 124; Fat: 7; Fiber: 5; Carbs: 12; Protein: 6

363. Brussels Sprouts with Cherry Tomatoes and Green Onions

Preparation Time: 15 minutes • Servings: 4

INGREDIENTS

- Brussels sprouts; trimmed – 1 pound
- Cherry tomatoes; halved – 6
- Green onions; chopped – 1/4 cup
- Olive oil – 1 tbsp
- Salt – ¾ tsp
- Ground black pepper – ¼ tsp

DIRECTIONS

1. Plug in the air fryer, insert fryer basket greased with oil, shut with lid and preheat at 350 0F for 5 minutes.
2. Add sprouts, season with salt and black pepper and cook for 10 minutes or until done.
3. When done, transfer sprouts into a bowl, add tomatoes, onion, and olive oil and toss until mixed.
4. Serve straightaway.

NUTRITION: Calories: 121; Fat: 4; Fiber: 4; Carbs: 11; Protein: 4

364. Cheesy Radish Hash Browns

Preparation Time: 17 minutes • Servings: 4

INGREDIENTS

- Onion powder – 1/2 tsp
- Grated parmesan cheese – 1/3 cup
- Eggs – 4
- Radishes; sliced – 1 pound

- Garlic powder – 1/2 tsp
- Salt – ½ tsp
- Ground black pepper – ¼ tsp

DIRECTIONS

1. Plug in the air fryer, insert fryer basket, shut with lid and preheat at 350 0F for 5 minutes.
2. Meanwhile, place radish in a bowl, add eggs, onion powder, garlic powder, cheese, then season with salt, black pepper and stir well until combined.
3. Spoon radish into a pan that fits into the air fryer, then insert it into the fryer and cook for 7 minutes or until done.
4. Divide hash evenly and serve.

NUTRITION: Calories: 80; Fat: 5; Fiber: 2; Carbs: 5; Protein: 7

365. Spinach Stuffed Spinach Pie

Preparation Time: 45 minutes • Servings: 4

INGREDIENTS

- Flour – 7 ounce
- Unsalted butter – 2 tbsps
- Spinach – 7 ounce
- Olive oil – 1 tbsp
- Medium white onion; peeled and chopped – 1
- Eggs – 2
- Milk – 2 tbsps
- Cottage cheese – 3 ounce
- Salt – 1 ½ tsp
- Ground black pepper – 1 tsp

DIRECTIONS

1. Place flour in a bowl, season with ¾ tsp salt and ¼ tsp black pepper, add butter, 1 egg and milk and blend using an immersion blender until well combined.
2. Knead the mixture for 5 minutes and then let rest for 10 minutes at room temperature.
3. Then place a skillet pan over medium- high heat, add oil and when hot, add onion and spinach and cook for 2 minutes.
4. Season with remaining salt and black pepper, add cottage cheese and remaining eggs, stir well and remove the pan from heat.
5. Plug in the air fryer, insert fryer basket greased with oil, shut with lid and preheat at 360 0F for 5 minutes.
6. Divide dough evenly into four portions, then roll each dough and place on the bottom of the ramekin and stuff with spinach filling.
7. Place ramekins into the air fryer and cook for 15 minutes until done.
8. Serve straightaway.

NUTRITION: Calories: 250; Fat: 12; Fiber: 2; Carbs: 23; Protein: 12

366. Shrimp Stuffed Peppers

Preparation Time: 16 minutes • Servings: 4

INGREDIENTS:

- Baby bell peppers; cut into halves lengthwise – 12
- Shrimp; cooked, peeled and de-veined – 1 pound
- Red pepper flakes; crushed – 1/4 tsps
- Basil pesto – 6 tbsps
- Lemon juice – 1 tbsp
- Olive oil – 1 tbsp
- Salt – ¾ tsp
- Ground black pepper – ½ tsp
- Chopped parsley – 2 tbsps

DIRECTIONS

1. Plug in the air fryer, insert fryer basket greased with oil, shut with lid and preheat at 320 0F for 5 minutes.
2. Meanwhile, place shrimps in a bowl, add parsley, pesto, lemon juice and oil, season with salt, black pepper, and red pepper flakes and whisk until well combined.
3. Stuff the shrimp mixture into peppers and then place into the fryer, spraying with oil and cook for 6 minutes or until done.
4. Serve straightaway.

NUTRITION: Calories: 130; Fat: 2; Fiber: 1; Carbs: 3; Protein: 15

367. Balsamic Cherry Tomatoes Salad

Preparation Time: 47 minutes• Servings: 4

INGREDIENTS

- Balsamic vinegar – 3 tbsps
- Minced garlic – 1 ½ tsp
- Chopped thyme – 1 tbsp
- Cherry tomatoes – 24
- Olive oil – 2 tbsp
- Salt – 1 tsp
- Ground black pepper – ½ tsp
- For the dressing:
- Balsamic vinegar – 2 tbsps
- Salt – 1/8 tsp
- Ground black pepper – 1/8 tsp
- Olive oil – 4 tbsps

DIRECTIONS

1. Place minced garlic, thyme, oil and vinegar in a bowl, season with salt and black pepper and whisk until well mixed.
2. Then add tomatoes, toss until evenly coated and set aside for 30 minutes.
3. When ready to cook, plug in the air fryer, insert fryer

basket greased with oil, shut with lid and preheat at 360 0F for 5 minutes.

4. In the meantime, thread marinated tomatoes onto skewers.
5. Place tomatoes into the air fryer and cook for 6 minutes.
6. In the meantime, whisk together ingredients for the dressing until combined.
7. When tomatoes are cooked, divide them evenly on a plate, then drizzle with dressing and serve.

NUTRITION: Calories: 140; Fat: 1; Fiber: 1; Carbs: 2; Protein: 7

368. Chinese Broccoli Salad

Preparation Time: 18 minutes • Servings: 4

INGREDIENTS

- Broccoli head; cut into florets – 1
- Chinese rice wine vinegar – 1 tbsp
- Peanut oil – 1 tbsp
- Minced garlic – 3 tsps
- Salt – 1 tsp
- Ground black pepper – ½ tsp

DIRECTIONS

1. Plug in the air fryer, insert fryer basket greased with oil, shut with lid and preheat at 350 0F for 5 minutes.
2. Meanwhile, place broccoli florets in a bowl, add half of the oil, season with salt and black pepper and toss until mixed.
3. Add seasoned broccoli into the air fryer and cook for 8 minutes, shaking halfway through.
4. When done, transfer broccoli to a salad bowl, add remaining ingredients and toss until mixed.
5. Serve straightaway.

NUTRITION: Calories: 121; Fat: 3; Fiber: 4; Carbs: 4; Protein: 4

369. Beet Salad with Parsley Dressing

Preparation Time: 40 minutes • Servings: 4

INGREDIENTS

- Medium beets – 4
- Balsamic vinegar – 2 tbsps
- Bunch of parsley; chopped – 1
- Olive oil – 1 tbsp
- Minced garlic – ½ tsp
- Capers – 2 tbsps
- Salt – ¾ tsp
- Ground black pepper – ½ tsp

DIRECTIONS

1. Plug in the air fryer, insert fryer basket greased with oil, shut with lid and preheat at 360 0F for 5 minutes.

2. Then place beets in a single layer and cook for 14 minutes.
3. In the meantime, stir together garlic, parsley, capers, salt, black pepper, and oil until combined.
4. When beets are done, transfer them onto a cutting board, then let cool for 15 minutes and peel.
5. Cut beets into slices, then place them into a salad bowl, season with capers mixture and drizzle with vinegar.
6. Toss until beets are evenly coated and serve.

NUTRITION: Calories: 70; Fat: 2; Fiber: 1; Carbs: 6; Protein: 4

370. Eggplant and Garlic Sauce Recipe

Preparation Time: 20 minutes • Servings: 4

INGREDIENTS

- Olive oil – 2 tbsps
- Minced garlic – 1 tsp
- Grated ginger – ½ tsp
- Soy sauce – 1 tbsp
- Eggplants; halved and sliced – 3
- Red chili pepper; chopped – 1
- Green onion stalk; chopped – 1
- Balsamic vinegar – 1 tbsp

DIRECTIONS

1. Plug in the air fryer, insert fryer basket greased with oil, shut with lid and preheat at 320 0F for 5 minutes.
2. Meanwhile, take a pan that fits into the air fryer, place it over medium-high heat, then add oil and when hot, add eggplant and cook for 2 minutes per side.
3. Add remaining ingredients, stir well and insert pan into the air fryer.
4. Cook eggplant for 7 minutes or until done and serve.

NUTRITION: Calories: 130; Fat: 2; Fiber: 4; Carbs: 7; Protein: 9

371. Cherry Tomatoes with Basil and Parmesan

Preparation Time: 20 minutes • Servings: 8

INGREDIENTS

- Jalapeno pepper; chopped – 1
- Minced garlic – 2 tsps
- Dried oregano – 1/2 tsp
- Chopped basil – 1/4 cup
- Cherry tomatoes; halved – 2 pounds
- Salt – 1 tsp
- Ground black pepper – ½ tsp
- Olive oil – 1/4 cup
- Grated parmesan cheese – 1/2 cup

DIRECTIONS

1. Plug in the air fryer, insert fryer basket greased with oil, shut with lid and preheat at 380 0F for 5 minutes.
2. Meanwhile, place tomatoes and peppers in a bowl, add garlic and oil, season with salt, black pepper, and oregano and toss until evenly coated.
3. Then place tomatoes into the air fryer and cook for 15 minutes until done.
4. When ready, transfer tomatoes into a salad bowl, add basil and parmesan, toss until coated and serve.

NUTRITION: Calories: 140; Fat: 2; Fiber: 2; Carbs: 6; Protein: 8

372. Lemony Eggplant and Zucchini Mix

Preparation Time: 18 minutes • Servings: 4

INGREDIENTS

- Medium eggplant; roughly cubed – 1
- Medium zucchinis; roughly cubed – 3
- Lemon juice – 2 tbsps
- Dried thyme – 1 tsp
- Salt – 1 tsp
- Ground black – ½ tsp
- Dried oregano – 1 tsp
- Olive oil – 3 tbsps

DIRECTIONS

1. Plug in the air fryer, insert fryer basket, shut with lid and preheat at 360 0F for 5 minutes.
2. Take a pan that fits into an air fryer, place eggplant in the bottom, then add zucchini, drizzle with lemon juice and season with salt, black pepper, thyme, and oregano.
3. Toss until well mixed, then place the pan into the air fryer and cook for 8 minutes until done.
4. When ready, divide evenly between plates and serve.

NUTRITION: Calories: 152; Fat: 5; Fiber: 7; Carbs: 19; Protein: 5

373. Mexican Style Stuffed Bell Peppers

Preparation Time: 35 minutes • Servings: 4

INGREDIENTS:

- Medium green bell peppers; tops cut off and seeds removed – 4
- Tomato juice – 1/2 cup
- Medium white onion; chopped – 1/4 cup
- Green peppers; chopped – /4 cup
- Tomato sauce – 2 cups

- Jalapeno peppers; chopped – 2 tbsps
- Chicken breasts – 4
- Tomatoes; chopped – 1 cup
- Salt – 1 tsp
- Ground black pepper – ½ tsp
- Onion powder – 2 tsps
- Red pepper; crushed – 1/2 tsp
- Red chili powder – 1 tsp
- Garlic powder – 1/2 tsp
- Ground cumin – 1 tsp

DIRECTIONS

1. Plug in the air fryer, insert fryer basket greased with oil, shut with lid and preheat at 350 0F for 5 minutes.
2. Take a pan that fits into air fryer, place chicken in it along with remaining ingredients except for bell peppers and stir until mixed.
3. Insert the pan into the air fryer and cook for 15 minutes or until done.
4. Then shred chicken using two forks, stir well and stuff into bell peppers.
5. Place stuffed bell peppers into the air fryer and cook for 10 minutes at 320 0F.
6. Serve straightaway.

NUTRITION: Calories: 180; Fat: 4; Fiber: 3; Carbs: 7; Protein: 14

374. Balsamic Artichokes with Oregano

Preparation Time: 15 minutes • Servings: 4

INGREDIENTS

- Large artichokes; trimmed – 4
- Lemon juice – 2 tbsps
- Balsamic vinegar – 2 tsps
- Dried oregano – 1 tsp
- Olive oil – 1/4 cup
- Minced garlic – 1 tsp
- Salt – 1 ½ tsp
- Ground black pepper – 1 tsp

DIRECTIONS

1. Plug in the air fryer, insert fryer basket greased with oil, shut with lid and preheat at 360 0F for 5 minutes.
2. Meanwhile, place artichokes in a bowl, season with 1 tsp salt and ½ tsp black pepper, drizzle with half of the lemon juice and oil and toss until evenly coated.
3. Place artichokes into the air fryer and cook for 7 minutes or until done.
4. In the mean time prepare vinaigrette and for this, whisk together remaining oil, lemon juice, salt, and black pepper, add garlic and oregano and stir well until combined.

5. When artichokes are ready, place them on a serving plate, drizzle with prepared vinaigrette and toss until coated.
6. Serve straightaway.

NUTRITION: Calories: 200; Fat: 3; Fiber: 6; Carbs: 12; Protein: 4

375. Artichokes with Anchovy Sauce

Preparation Time: 15 minutes • Servings: 2

INGREDIENTS

- Medium artichokes; trimmed – 2
- Minced garlic – 1 tsp
- Olive oil – ½ tsp
- Lemon juice – 1 tbsp
- For the sauce:
- Anchovy fillets – 3
- Coconut oil – 1/4 cup
- Olive oil – 1/4 cup
- Minced garlic – 1 ½ tsp

DIRECTIONS

1. Plug in the air fryer, insert fryer basket greased with oil, shut with lid and preheat at 360 0F for 5 minutes.
2. Meanwhile, place artichokes in a bowl, add minced garlic, lemon juice, and oil and toss until evenly coated.
3. Place artichokes into the air fryer and cook for 6 minutes or until done.
4. In the meantime prepare sauce and for this, blend all the ingredients for the sauce in a blender for 2 minutes or until smooth.
5. When artichokes are ready, divide evenly between plates, then drizzle with anchovy sauce and serve.

NUTRITION: Calories: 261; Fat: 4; Fiber: 7; Carbs: 20; Protein: 12

376. Beets and Arugula Salad with Cider Dressing

Preparation Time: 20 minutes • Servings: 4

INGREDIENTS

- Beets; peeled and quartered – 1 ½ pound
- Brown sugar – 2 tbsps
- Scallions; chopped – 2
- Mustard – 2 tsps
- Olive oil – 1/8 tsp
- Orange zest; grated – 2 tsps
- Apple cider vinegar – 2 tbsps
- Orange juice – 1/2 cup
- Arugula – 2 cups

DIRECTIONS

1. Plug in the air fryer, insert fryer basket greased with oil, shut with lid and preheat at 360 0F for 5 minutes.
2. Meanwhile, rub each beet with orange juice and oil.
3. Place beets into the air fryer and cook for 10 minutes until done.
4. Then transfer beets into a bowl, add scallion and arugula, sprinkle with orange zest and toss until mixed.
5. Whisk together sugar, vinegar, and mustard until well combined, then drizzle this over beets and toss until evenly coated.
6. Serve straightaway.

NUTRITION: Calories: 121; Fat: 2; Fiber: 3; Carbs: 11; Protein: 4

377. Cheesy Artichokes

Preparation Time: 15 minutes • Servings: 6

INGREDIENTS:

- Artichoke hearts – 14 ounce
- Cream cheese – 8 ounce
- Shredded mozzarella cheese – 8 ounce
- Sour cream – 1/2 cup
- Minced garlic – 1 ½ tsp
- Grated parmesan cheese – 16 ounce
- Spinach – 10 ounce
- Chicken stock – 1/2 cup
- Mayonnaise – 1/2 cup
- Onion powder – 1 tsp

DIRECTIONS

1. Plug in the air fryer, insert fryer basket, shut with lid and preheat at 360 0F for 5 minutes.
2. Meanwhile, take a pan that fits into air fryer, place artichokes in it, add remaining ingredients except for cheeses and stir until mixed.
3. Insert the pan into the air fryer and cook for 6 minutes or until done.
4. When ready, add cheese into artichokes, toss until mixed and serve.

NUTRITION: Calories: 261; Fat: 12; Fiber: 2; Carbs: 12; Protein: 15

378. Parmesan Brussels Sprouts

Preparation Time: 18 minutes • Servings: 4

INGREDIENTS

- Brussels sprouts; washed – 1 pound
- Lemon, juiced – 1

- Unsalted butter – 2 tbsps
- Grated parmesan cheese – 3 tbsps
- Salt – 1 tsp
- Ground black pepper – ½ tsp

DIRECTIONS

1. Plug in the air fryer, insert fryer basket greased with oil, shut with lid and preheat at 350 0F for 5 minutes.
2. Then add Brussels sprouts and cook for 8 minutes until done.
3. Meanwhile, place a skillet pan over medium heat, add butter and when it melts, add salt, black pepper, and lemon juice and whisk well until smooth, remove the pan from heat and set aside.
4. When sprouts are ready, transfer them into a bowl, top with butter sauce and set aside.

NUTRITION: Calories: 152; Fat: 6; Fiber: 6; Carbs: 8; Protein: 12

379. Simple and Sweet Baby Carrots

Preparation Time: 15 minutes • Servings: 4

INGREDIENTS

- Baby carrots – 2 cups
- Salt – 1/8 tsp
- Ground black pepper – 1/8 tsp
- Brown sugar – 1 tbsp
- Butter; melted – 1/2 tbsp

DIRECTIONS

5. Plug in the air fryer, insert fryer basket, shut with lid and preheat at 350 0F for 5 minutes.
6. Meanwhile, take a pan that fits into the air fryer, add carrots in it along with butter, then sprinkle with salt, black pepper and sugar and toss until mixed.
7. Insert pan into the air fryer and cook for 10 minutes or until done.
8. Serve straightaway.

NUTRITION: Calories: 100; Fat: 2; Fiber: 3; Carbs: 7; Protein: 4

CHAPTER 10

SNACKS

380. Sea Salt and Black Pepper Cucumber Chips

Preparation time: 15 minutes • Cooking time: 3 Hours • Servings: 4

INGREDIENTS

- 4cups very thin cucumber slices
- 2Tbsp apple cider vinegar
- 2tsp sea salt
- 1Tsp ground black pepper

DIRECTIONS:

1. Preheat your air fryer to 200 degrees F.
2. Place the cucumber slices on a paper towel and layer another paper towel on top to absorb the moisture in the cucumbers.
3. Place the dried slices in a large bowl and toss with the vinegar, ground black pepper, and salt.
4. Place the cucumber slices on a tray lined with parchment and then bake in the air fryer for 3 hours. The cucumbers will begin to curl and brown slightly.
5. Turn off the air fryer and let the cucumber slices cool inside the fryer (this will help them dry a little more).
6. Enjoy right away or store in an airtight container.

NUTRITION: Calories 16, Total Fat 0g, Saturated Fat 0g, Total Carbs 4g, Net Carbs 3g, Protein 1g, Sugar 2g, Fiber 1g, Sodium 34mg, Potassium 0g

381. Taco Cucumber Chips

Preparation time: 15 minutes • Cooking time: 3 Hours • Servings: 4

INGREDIENTS

- 4cups very thin cucumber slices
- 2Tbsp apple cider vinegar
- 2tsp sea salt
- 2tsp taco seasoning

DIRECTIONS:

1. Preheat your air fryer to 200 degrees F.
2. Place the cucumber slices on a paper towel and layer another paper towel on top to absorb the moisture in the cucumbers.
3. Place the dried slices in a large bowl

and toss with the vinegar, taco seasoning, and salt.

4. Place the cucumber slices on a tray lined with parchment and then bake in the air fryer for 3 hours. The cucumbers will begin to curl and brown slightly.
5. Turn off the air fryer and let the cucumber slices cool inside the fryer (this will help them dry a little more).
6. Enjoy right away or store in an airtight container.

NUTRITION: Calories 23, Total Fat 0g, Saturated Fat 0g, Total Carbs 4g, Net Carbs 3g, Protein 1g, Sugar 2g, Fiber 1g, Sodium 38mg, Potassium 0g

382. Dilly Almonds

Preparation time: 5 minutes • Cooking time: 10 minutes • Servings: 6

INGREDIENTS

- 1egg white
- 3cups whole almonds
- 2tsp salt
- 2tsp dried dill
- ½ tsp ground black pepper

DIRECTIONS:

1. Preheat your air fryer to 325 degrees F and prepare the air fryer tray with parchment paper.
2. Place the egg whites in a large bowl and whip until stiff peaks form.
3. Add the almonds and toss to coat.
4. Sprinkle with the seasonings and then place the almonds on the tray, laying them out as evenly as possible on the tray.
5. Bake in the air fryer for 10 minutes. The almonds should be golden brown.
6. Remove from the air fryer and let cool.

NUTRITION: Calories 414, Total Fat 34g, Saturated Fat 8g, Total Carbs 14g, Net Carbs 7g, Protein 14, Sugar 2g, Fiber 8g, Sodium 210mg, Potassium 0g

383. Garlic Almonds

Preparation time: 5 minutes • Cooking time: 10 minutes • Servings: 6

INGREDIENTS

- 1egg white
- 3cups whole almonds
- 2tsp salt
- 2tsp garlic powder
- ½ tsp ground black pepper

DIRECTIONS:

1. Preheat your air fryer to 325 degrees F and prepare the air fryer tray with parchment paper.

2. Place the egg whites in a large bowl and whip until stiff peaks form.
3. Add the almonds and toss to coat.
4. Sprinkle with the seasonings and then place the almonds on the tray, laying them out as evenly as possible on the tray.
5. Bake in the air fryer for 10 minutes. The almonds should be golden brown.
6. Remove from the air fryer and let cool.

NUTRITION: Calories 412, Total Fat 34g, Saturated Fat 8g, Total Carbs 14g, Net Carbs 7g, Protein 14, Sugar 2g, Fiber 8g, Sodium 212mg, Potassium 0g

384. Sweet and Salty Almonds

Preparation time: 5 minutes • Cooking time: 10 minutes • Servings: 6

INGREDIENTS

- 1egg white
- 3cups whole almonds
- 2tsp salt
- 1Tbsp swerve sweetener
- ½ tsp ground black pepper

DIRECTIONS:

1. Preheat your air fryer to 325 degrees F and prepare the air fryer tray with parchment paper.
2. Place the egg whites in a large bowl and whip until stiff peaks form.
3. Add the almonds and toss to coat.
4. Sprinkle with the salt, swerve and ground black pepper, and then place the almonds on the tray, laying them out as evenly as possible on the tray.
5. Bake in the air fryer for 10 minutes. The almonds should be golden brown.
6. Remove from the air fryer and let cool.

NUTRITION: Calories 409, Total Fat 34g, Saturated Fat 8g, Total Carbs 14g, Net Carbs 7g, Protein 14, Sugar 2g, Fiber 8g, Sodium 201mg, Potassium 0g

385. Cayenne Almonds

Preparation time: 5 minutes • Cooking time: 10 minutes • Servings: 6

INGREDIENTS

- 1egg white
- 3cups whole almonds
- 2tsp salt
- 2tsp cayenne pepper
- ½ tsp ground black pepper

DIRECTIONS:

1. Preheat your air fryer to 325 degrees F and prepare the air fryer tray with parchment paper.
2. Place the egg whites in a large bowl and whip until stiff peaks form.
3. Add the almonds and toss to coat.
4. Sprinkle with the seasonings and then place the almonds on the tray, laying them out as evenly as possible on the tray.
5. Bake in the air fryer for 10 minutes. The almonds should be golden brown.
6. Remove from the air fryer and let cool.

NUTRITION: Calories 414, Total Fat 34g, Saturated Fat 8g, Total Carbs 14g, Net Carbs 7g, Protein 14, Sugar 2g, Fiber 8g, Sodium 210mg, Potassium 0g

386. Black Pepper Almonds

Preparation time: 5 minutes • Cooking time: 10 minutes • Servings: 6

INGREDIENTS

- 1egg white
- 3cups whole almonds
- 2tsp salt
- 1tsp ground black pepper

DIRECTIONS:

1. Preheat your air fryer to 325 degrees F and prepare the air fryer tray with parchment paper.
2. Place the egg whites in a large bowl and whip until stiff peaks form.
3. Add the almonds and toss to coat.
4. Sprinkle with the salt and pepper and then place the almonds on the tray, laying them out as evenly as possible on the tray.
5. Bake in the air fryer for 10 minutes. The almonds should be golden brown.
6. Remove from the air fryer and let cool.

NUTRITION: Calories 414, Total Fat 34g, Saturated Fat 8g, Total Carbs 14g, Net Carbs 7g, Protein 14, Sugar 2g, Fiber 8g, Sodium 210mg, Potassium 0g

387. Sweet Candied Pecans

Preparation time: 5 minutes • Cooking time: 10 minutes • Servings: 6

INGREDIENTS

- 1egg white
- 3cups whole pecans
- 2tsp salt
- 1Tbsp swerve

DIRECTIONS:

1. Preheat your air fryer to 325 degrees F and prepare the air fryer tray with parchment paper.
2. Place the egg whites in a large bowl and whip until stiff peaks form.
3. Add the almonds and toss to coat.
4. Sprinkle with the swerve and salt and then place the almonds on the tray, laying them out as evenly as possible on the tray.
5. Bake in the air fryer for 10 minutes. The almonds should be golden brown.
6. Remove from the air fryer and let cool.

NUTRITION: Calories 409, Total Fat 34g, Saturated Fat 8g, Total Carbs 14g, Net Carbs 7g, Protein 14, Sugar 2g, Fiber 8g, Sodium 201mg, Potassium 0g

388. Garlicky Cauliflower Crunch

Preparation time: 5 minutes • Cooking time: 6 Hours • Servings: 4

INGREDIENTS

- 4cups cauliflower florets, chopped into bite sized pieces
- 1Tbsp olive oil
- 1tsp sea salt
- 1tsp garlic powder

DIRECTIONS:

1. Preheat your air fryer to 135 degrees F.
2. Wash and drain the cauliflower florets.
3. Place the cauliflower in a large bowl and toss with the olive oil and sea salt.
4. Add the cauliflower to the basket of your air fryer or spread them in a flat layer on the tray of your air fryer (either option will work!).
5. Cook in the air fryer for about 6 hours, tossing the cauliflower every hour or so to cook evenly. Essentially, you will be dehydrating the cauliflower.
6. Once the cauliflower is fully dried, remove it from the air fryer, toss it with the garlic powder, and then let cool. It will keep crisping as it cools.
7. Enjoy fresh or store in an airtight container for up to a month.

NUTRITION: Calories 57, Total Fat 3g, Saturated Fat 0g, Total Carbs 4g, Net Carbs 3g, Protein 1g, Sugar 2g, Fiber 1g, Sodium 619mg, Potassium 320g

389. Cajun Cauliflower Crunch

Preparation time: 5 minutes • Cooking time: 6 Hours • Servings: 4

INGREDIENTS

- 4cups cauliflower florets, chopped into bite sized pieces
- 1Tbsp olive oil
- 1tsp sea salt
- 1tsp Cajun seasoning

DIRECTIONS:

1. Preheat your air fryer to 135 degrees F.
2. Wash and drain the cauliflower florets.
3. Place the cauliflower in a large bowl and toss with the olive oil and sea salt.
4. Add the cauliflower to the basket of your air fryer or spread them in a flat layer on the tray of your air fryer (either option will work!).
5. Cook in the air fryer for about 6 hours, tossing the cauliflower every hour or so to cook evenly. Essentially, you will be dehydrating the cauliflower.
6. Once the cauliflower is fully dried, remove it from the air fryer, toss with the Cajun seasoning, and then let cool. It will keep crisping as it cools.
7. Enjoy fresh or store in an airtight container for up to a month.

NUTRITION: Calories 59, Total Fat 3g, Saturated Fat 0g, Total Carbs 4g, Net Carbs 3g, Protein 1g, Sugar 2g, Fiber 1g, Sodium 621mg, Potassium 320g

390. Air Fried Red Cabbage, Garlic-flavored

Preparation Time: 25 Minutes • Servings: 4

INGREDIENTS

- Seasoning- Salt and black pepper to the taste
- Apple cider vinegar-1 tbsps
- Chopped red cabbage-6 cups
- Veggie stock-1 cup
- Applesauce-1 cup
- Olive oil-1 tbsps Chopped Yellow onion-½ cup
- 4Minced garlic cloves

DIRECTIONS

1. Combine and mix cabbage with onion, garlic, oil, stock, vinegar, applesauce in a heatproof dish that fits into your air fryer, seasoned with salt and pepper; toss well.
2. Transfer dish into your air fryer's basket and cook for 15minutes at a temperature of 380°F.
3. Share between plates and serve.

391. Healthy Italian Parmesan Mushrooms

Preparation Time: 25 Minutes • Servings: 3

INGREDIENTS

- Italian seasoning-1 tsp
- Melted butter-1 tbsps
- 1egg white
- Mushroom caps-9 button
- 3Crumbled cream cracker slices
- Grated Parmesan -2 tbsps
- Seasoning-A pinch of salt and black pepper

DIRECTIONS

1. Combine and mix crackers with egg white, parmesan, Italian seasoning, butter in a bowl, season with salt and pepper; stir well and stuff mushrooms with this mix
2. Place mushrooms in your air fryer's basket in an orderly manner, cook for 15minutes at a temperature of 360°F.
3. Share among plates and serve.

392. Sweet Tomatoes, Garlic-Herbed Dish

Preparation Time: 25 Minutes • Servings: 4

INGREDIENTS

- 4big tomatoes halved and insides scooped out
- 2minced garlic cloves
- Chopped thyme-½ tsp
- Olive oil-1 tbsps
- Seasoning- Salt and black pepper to the taste

DIRECTIONS

- 4potatoes scrubbed, peeled into thin chips, soaked in water for 30 minutes, drained and pat dried
- Chopped rosemary-2 tsp

DIRECTIONS

1. Combine and mix potato chips with salt and oil in a bowl toss to coat.
2. Transfer into your air fryer's basket and cook for 30minutes at a temperature of 330°F.
3. Share among plates; drizzle rosemary all over and serve.

393. Herbed Roasted Carrots

Preparation Time: 30 Minutes • Servings: 4

INGREDIENTS

- Orange juice-4 tbsps
- Baby carrots-1-lbs
- Olive oil-2 tsp
- Herbs de Provence-1 tsp

DIRECTIONS

1. Combine and mix carrots with herbs de Provence, oil and orange juice in your air fryer's basket, then toss well.

2. Cook for 20 minutes at a temperature of 320°F.
3. Share among plates and serve.

394. Sweet Potato Chips

Preparation Time: 60 Minutes • Servings: 4

INGREDIENTS

- Olive oil-1 tbsps
- Salt to taste
- 4potatoes scrubbed, peeled into thin chips, soaked in water for 30 minutes, drained and pat dried
- Chopped rosemary-2 tsp

DIRECTIONS

1. Combine and mix potato chips with salt and oil in a bowl toss to coat.
2. Transfer into your air fryer's basket and cook for 30minutes at a temperature of 330°F.
3. Share among plates; drizzle rosemary all over and serve.

395. Awesome Barley Risotto Recipe

Preparation Time: 40 Minutes • Servings: 8

INGREDIENTS

- Veggie stock-5 cups
- Olive oil-3 tbsps
- 2Chopped yellow onions
- 2Minced garlic cloves
- Chopped and peeled Sweet potato-2- lbss
- Barley-3/4-lbs
- Sliced mushrooms-3-ounce
- skim milk-2-ounces
- Seasoning -Salt and black pepper to the taste
- Dried Thyme-1 tsp
- Dried Tarragon-1 tsp

DIRECTIONS

1. Add stock in a pot, put barley, stir well, with medium temperature bring to a boil and cook for 15 minutes.
2. Heat up your air fryer at a temperature of 350°F, add oil and heat it up
3. Put the following ingredients: barley, onions, garlic, mushrooms, milk, salt, pepper, tarragon, and sweet potato, stir and cook for another 15 minutes.
4. Share among plates and serve.

396. Healthy Cauliflower and Broccoli

Preparation Time: 17 Minutes • Servings: 4

INGREDIENTS:

- 2cauliflower heads florets separated and steamed

- 1broccoli head florets separated and steamed
- Chopped capers-1 tbsps
- Juice from 1 orange
- A pinch of hot pepper flakes
- Seasoning -Salt and black pepper to the taste
- Olive oil-4 tbsps
- 4anchovies
- Zest from 1 orange grated

DIRECTIONS

1. Combine and mix the orange zest with orange juice, pepper flakes, anchovies, capers salt, pepper and olive oil in a bowl, whisk well.
2. Put broccoli and cauliflower ensure it is tossed well.
3. Transfer into your air fryer's basket and cook for 7minutes at a temperature of 400°F.
4. Share among plates, drizzle all over with some orange vinaigrette and serve.

397. Garlic-Herbed Mayonnaise Brussels Sprouts Dish

Preparation Time: 25 Minutes • Servings: 4

INGREDIENTS

- Mayonnaise-½ cup
- Brussels sprouts trimmed and halved - 1-lbs
- Olive oil-6 tsp
- Chopped Thyme-½ tsp
- Seasoning-Salt and black pepper to the taste
- Crushed Roasted garlic -2 tbsps

DIRECTIONS

1. Combine and mix Brussels sprouts with salt, pepper, and oil in a clean bowl, toss well, cook for 15minutes at a temperature of 390°F.
2. In a separate bowl, mix thyme with mayo and garlic and ensure it is well whisked.
3. Share Brussels sprouts between plates, sprinkle garlic sauce on top and serve.

398. Unusual Risotto Recipe

Preparation Time: 40 Minutes • Servings: 4

INGREDIENTS

- Dried Basil-1 tsp
- Dried oregano-1 tsp
- Rice-1 ½ Cups
- Olive oil-2 tbsps
- 2Chopped yellow onions.
- Beer-2 cups
- Chicken stock-2 cups

- Butter-1 tbsps
- Sliced mushrooms-1 cup
- Grated parmesan-½ cup

DIRECTIONS

1. Combine and mix oil with onions, mushrooms, basil and oregano in a dish that fits your air fryer and stirs well.
2. Add rice, beer, butter, stock, and butter; stir carefully again.
3. Transfer in your air fryer's basket and cook for 30minutes at a temperature of 350°F.
4. Share among plates, add grated parmesan on top and serve.

399. Lip-smacking Buttermilk-Biscuits

Preparation Time: 30 Minutes • Servings: 8

INGREDIENTS

- Buttermilk-1 ⅓ cup
- ½ cup butter+ 1 tbsps melted
- Self-rising flour-2 ⅓ cup
- Grated Cheddar cheese-½ cup
- Flour-1 cup
- Sugar-2 tbsps

DIRECTIONS

1. Combine and mix self-rising flour with ½ cup butter, sugar, cheddar cheese and buttermilk in a bowl, stir well until you obtain a dough
2. Prepare a clean working surface and spread 1 cup of flour on it, roll dough, flatten it, cut 8 circles with a cookie cutter and coat them with flour.
3. Line your air fryer's basket with tin foil, put biscuits, brush them with melted butter and cook for 20 minutes at a temperature of 380°F.
4. Share between plates and serve as a side dish.

400. Spicy Eggplant Dish

Preparation Time: 20 Minutes • Servings: 4

INGREDIENTS

- Tomato paste-1 tbsps
- 1green bell pepper chopped
- Chopped coriander-1 bunch
- Chopped Tomato- 1quantity
- A pinch of dried oregano
- 8baby eggplants; scoopedin the center and pulp reserved
- Seasoning- Salt and black pepper to the taste
- Garlic powder-½ tsp
- Olive oil-1 tbsps
- Chopped yellow onion- 1 quantity

DIRECTIONS

1. With medium temperature, heat the oil in a pan, add onion; stir well and cook for 1 minute.
2. Seasoned with salt and pepper, add eggplant pulp, oregano, green bell pepper, tomato paste, garlic powder, coriander, and tomato; stir carefully, and cook for another 2 minutes more, put off heat and cool down.
3. Eggplants should be stuffed with this mix, transfer them in your air fryer's basket and cook for 8 minutes at a temperature of 360°F.
4. Share eggplants between plates and serve.

401. Lip-smacking Mushroom Recipe

Preparation Time: 20 Minutes • Servings: 6

INGREDIENTS

- Seasoning-Salt and black pepper to the taste
- 1green bell pepper chopped
- Mushrooms with stems removed – 24 quantity
- 1Grated carrot
- 2Chopped bacon strips
- 1yellow onion chopped
- Grated Cheddar cheese - 1 cup
- Sour cream-½ cup

DIRECTIONS

1. With medium-high temperature, heat up a pan add bacon, onion, bell pepper, and carrot; stir well and cook for 1 minute.
2. Put salt, pepper, and sour cream, stir well and cook for a minute more put off heat and cool down.
3. Mushrooms should be stuffed with this mix, drizzle cheese on top and cook for 8minutes at a temperature 360°F.
4. Share between plates and serve.

402. Simple Creamy Fried Potato Dish

Preparation Time: 1 hour and 30 Minutes • Servings: 2

INGREDIENTS

- Seasoning-Salt and black pepper to the taste

- 2bacon strips cooked and chopped
- Olive oil-1 tsp
- Big potato- 1 quantity
- Shredded cheddar cheese-1/3 cup
- Butter-1 tbsps
- Chopped Green onions-1 tbsps
- Heavy cream-2 tbsps

DIRECTIONS

1. Polish potato with oil, season with salt and pepper, transfer in a preheated air fryer and cook for 30 minutes at a temperature of 400°F.
2. Flip potato on both sides, cook for another 30 minutes, transfer to a clean cutting board, cool it down then slice in half lengthwise and scoop pulp in a bowl
3. Put bacon, cheese, butter, heavy cream, green onions, then seasoned with salt and pepper, stir well and stuff potato skins with this mix.
4. Put potatoes back to your air fryer and cook for 20minutes at a temperature of 400°F.
5. Share between

plates and serve.

403. Nice Veggie Fries Dish

Preparation Time: 40 Minutes • Servings: 4

INGREDIENTS

- Parsnips cut into medium sticks-4 quantity
- 2sweet potatoes cut into medium sticks
- Chopped rosemary-2 tbsps
- Olive oil-2 tbsps
- Seasoning-Salt and black pepper to the taste
- 4mixed carrots cut into medium sticks
- Flour-1 tbsps
- Garlic powder-½ tsp

DIRECTIONS

1. In a bowl put veggie fries, add oil, garlic powder, seasoned with salts and pepper, add flour and rosemary, toss well to coat
2. In your preheated air fryer put sweet potatoes, cook them for 10 minutes at a temperature of 350°F and transfer into a platter.
3. Also, in your air fryer put parsnip, and cook for 5 minutes then transfer over potato fries.
4. More also, put carrot fries in your air fryer, cook for 15 minutes at a temperature of 350°F and transfer to the platter with the other fries.
5. Share veggie fries on plates and serve.

404. Enjoyable Green Beans Dish

Preparation Time: 35 Minutes • Servings: 4

INGREDIENTS

- 1½-lbs Green beans trimmed and steamed for 2 minutes

- Olive oil-2 tbsps
- Chopped Shallots-½-lbs
- Toasted Almonds-1/4 cup
- Seasoning-Salt and black pepper to the taste

DIRECTIONS

1. Mix green beans with salt, pepper, shallots, almonds, and oil in your air fryer's basket; toss well and cook for 25 minutes at a temperature of 400°F.
2. Share between plates and serve.

405. Healthy Cinnamon Roasted Pumpkin

Preparation Time: 22 Minutes • Servings: 4

INGREDIENTS

- A pinch of nutmeg ground
- Pumpkin de seeded, slic ed and roughly chopped-1½ lbs
- 3garlic cloves; minced
- A pinch of brown sugar
- A pinch of sea salt
- Olive oil-1 tbsps
- A pinch of cinnamon powder

DIRECTIONS

1. Combine and mix, pumpkin with garlic, oil, salt, brown sugar, cinnamon and nutmeg in your air fryer's basket, toss well, cover and cook for 12minutes at a temperature of 370°F.
2. Share between plates and serve.

406. Cinnamon-Mayonnaise-Potato Fries

Preparation Time: 30 Minutes • Servings: 2

INGREDIENTS

- 2sweet potatoes peeled and cut into medium fries
- Mayonnaise -2 tbsps
- Ketchup-1/4 cup
- Olive oil-2 tbsps
- A pinch of ginger powder
- Cumin ground-½ tsp
- A pinch of cinnamon powder
- Curry powder-½ tsp
- Coriander ground-1/4 tsp
- Seasoning-Salt and black pepper to the taste

DIRECTIONS

1. Combine and mix sweet potato fries with salt, pepper, coriander, curry powder and oil in your air fryer's basket,

toss well and cook for 20minutes at a temperature of 370°F, flip potatoes once.
2. Meanwhile, in a separate bowl, mix ketchup with mayo, cumin, ginger, and cinnamon then whisk well.
3. Share fries on plates, sprinkle ketchup mix on top and serve.

407. Delicious Cauliflower Cakes

Preparation Time: 20 Minutes • Servings: 6

INGREDIENTS

- Parmesan; grated-½ cup
- 2eggs
- White flour-1/4 cup
- Cauliflower rice-3 ½ cups
- Seasoning-Salt and black pepper to the taste
- Cooking spray

DIRECTIONS

1. Mix cauliflower rice with salt and pepper in a bowl, stir well and squeeze excess water.
2. Put cauliflower into another bowl, put eggs, salt, and pepper, flour, and parmesan stir really well and shape your cakes.
3. Polish your air fryer with cooking spray, heat it up to a temperature of 400°F, put cauliflower cakes and cook for 10 minutes, flipping them halfway.
4. Share cakes on plates and serve.

408. Tasty Button Mushroom Dish Recipe

Preparation Time: 18 Minutes • Servings: 4

INGREDIENTS

- 10button mushrooms; stems removed
- Italian seasoning -1 tbsps
- Grated Cheddar cheese-2 tbsps
- Olive oil-1 tbsps
- Seasoning-Salt and black pepper to the taste
- Grated Mozzarella-2 tbsps
- Chopped dill-1 tbsps

DIRECTIONS

1. Combine and Mix mushrooms with Italian seasoning, seasoned with salt and pepper, oil and dill in a bowl and rub well.
2. Place mushrooms in your air fryer's basket in an orderly manner; sprinkle mozzarella and cheddar in each.
3. Cook them for 8minutes at a temperature of 360°F.
4. Share between plates and serve.

409. Sweet Buttermilk-Tomatoes

Preparation Time: 15 Minutes • Servings: 4

INGREDIENTS

- Creole seasoning-½ tbsps
- Flour -½ cup
- 2green tomatoes; sliced
- Seasoning-Salt and black pepper to the taste
- Cooking spray
- Buttermilk-1 cup
- Panko bread crumbs-1 cup

DIRECTIONS:

1. Tomato slices should be seasoned with salt and pepper.
2. In three separate bowl, Put flour in one; buttermilk in second and panko crumbs and Creole seasoning in a third one.
3. Tomato slices should be dredged in flour, then in buttermilk and panko bread crumbs.
4. Transfer into your air fryer's basket polished with cooking spray and cook for 5minutes at a temperature of 400°F.
5. Share among plates and serve.

410. Delicious Garlic Potatoes

Preparation Time: 30 Minutes Servings: 6

INGREDIENTS

- Dried basil-½ tsp
- Dried oregano-½ tsp
- Chopped parsley-2 tbsps
- Olive oil-2 tbsps
- Seasoning-Salt and black pepper to the taste
- 5garlic cloves minced
- Butter-2 tbsps
- Grated parmesan-1/3 cup
- 3-lbs red potatoes; halved
- Dried thyme

DIRECTIONS

1. Combine and mix potato halves with parsley, garlic, basil, oregano, thyme, oil, butter, seasoned with salt and pepper in a bowl.
2. Toss the mixture really well and transfer to your air fryer's basket to cook.
3. Cover with lid and cook for 20 minutes with a temperature of 400°F, flipping them once and drizzle with parmesan on top.
4. Share potatoes between plates and serve.

411. Sweet Eggplant Dish with Garlic flavor

Preparation Time: 30 Minutes • Servings: 6

INGREDIENTS

- Onion powder-1 tsp
- Juice from ½ lemon
- 2bay leaves

- Garlic powder-1 tsp
- Olive oil-1 tbsps
- Cubed eggplant-1 ½-lbs
- Za'atar-2 tsp
- Sumac-1 tsp

DIRECTIONS

1. Combine and mixture eggplant cubes with oil, garlic powder, onion powder, sumac, za'atar, lemon juice, and bay leaves in your air fryer.
2. Toss well and cook for 20 minutes at a temp at a temperature of 370°F. Share among plates and serve.

412. Nice Cauliflower Healthy Dish

Preparation Time: 20 Minutes • Servings: 4

INGREDIENTS

- Turmeric powder-1/4 tsp
- Lemon juice-2 tsp
- Seasoning-Salt and black pepper to the taste
- Cooking spray
- Steamed florets-12 cauliflower
- White flour-3 tbsps
- Grated Ginger-1 tbsps
- Water - 2 tbsps
- Corn flour-½ tsp
- Red chili powder-1½ tsp

DIRECTIONS

1. Combine and mix chili powder with turmeric powder, ginger paste, salt, pepper, lemon juice, white flour, corn flour and water in a bowl, stir carefully.
2. Put cauliflower, toss well and transfer them to your air fryer's basket and Coat them with cooking spray.
3. Cook for 10 minutes at a temperature of 400°F. Share among plates and serve.

413. Sweet Cauliflower Rice Dish

Preparation Time: 50 Minutes • Servings: 8

INGREDIENTS

- 3garlic cloves; minced
- 1cauliflower head; riced
- 1Whisked egg
- Drained water chestnuts-9-ounce
- Peas-3/4 cup
- Grated Ginger-1 tbsps
- Juice from ½ lemon
- Soy sauce-4 tbsps
- Peanut oil-1 tbsps
- Sesame oil-1 tbsps
- Chopped mushrooms-15-ounce

DIRECTIONS

1. Combine and mix cauliflower rice with peanut oil, sesame oil, soy sauce, garlic, ginger and lemon juice in your air fryer; stir well.
2. Cover with lid and cook for 20 minutes at a temperature of 350°F.
3. Put chestnuts, peas, mushrooms, and egg; toss and cook for another 20 minutes at a temperature of 360°F.
4. Share among plates and serve for breakfast

414. Tasty Hassel-Back Potatoes

Preparation Time: 30 Minutes • Servings: 2

INGREDIENTS

- Sweet paprika-½ tsp
- Olive oil - 2 tbsps
- 2potatoes peeled and thinly sliced almost all the way horizontally
- Dried oregano-½ tsp
- Dried basil-½ tsp
- Minced Garlic-1 tsp
- Seasoning- Salt and black pepper to the taste

DIRECTIONS

1. Combine and mix oil with garlic, salt, pepper, oregano, basil, and paprika in a bowl and whisk really well
2. Grease potatoes with this mix, place them in your air fryer's basket and fry them for 20 minutes at a temperature of 360°F.
3. Share between plates and serve.

415. Easy Buttered-Mushroom Cakes

Preparation Time: 18 Minutes • Servings: 8

INGREDIENTS

- Flour-1 ½ tbsps
- Bread crumbs-1 tbsps
- Milk-14-ounces
- Chopped mushrooms-4-ounce
- 1yellow onion; chopped.
- Ground Nutmeg-½ tsp
- Olive oil-2 tbsps
- Butter-1 tbsps
- Seasoning-Salt and black pepper to the taste

DIRECTIONS:

1. With medium-high temperature, Heat up the butter in a pan, put onion and mushrooms; stir well, cook for 3 minutes, add flour then stir well again and put off the heat.
2. Put milk gradually, seasoned with salt, pepper, and nutmeg, stir carefully and set aside to cool down completely.
3. Mix oil with bread crumbs and whisk in a bowl.
4. A spoonful of the mushroom

filling should be added to breadcrumbs mix, coat well, shape patties out of this mix.

5. Transfer them in your air fryer's basket
and cook for 8 minutes at 400°F.

6. Share among plates
and serve.

416. Delicious Beet Wedges Dish

Preparation Time: 25 Minutes • Servings: 4

INGREDIENTS

- 4beets washed, peeled and cut into large wedges
- Lemon juice-1 tsp
- Seasoning-Salt and black to the taste
- Olive oil-1 tbsps
- 2garlic cloves; minced

DIRECTIONS

1. Combine and mix beets with oil, salt, pepper, garlic and lemon juice in a bowl; toss well,
2. Place mixture in your air fryer's basket and cook for 15minutes at a temperature of 400°F.
3. Share beets wedges on
plates and serve.

417. Tasty Roasted Peppers Dish

Preparation Time: 20 Minutes • Servings: 4

INGREDIENTS

- 1lettuce head; cut into strips
- Seasoning-Salt and black pepper to the taste
- Lemon juice-1 tbsps
- Greek yogurt-3 tbsps
- Olive oil-2 tbsps
- Yellow bell pepper-2 tbsps
- Red bell pepper – 1 Quantity
- Green bell pepper-1 Quantity
- Rocket leaves -1-ounce

DIRECTIONS

1. Transfer bell peppers in your air fryer's basket and cook for 10 minutes at a temperature of 400°F.
2. Transfer bell pepper into a bowl, set aside for 10 minutes, peel and discard seeds, cut them into strips, transfer to a larger bowl.
3. Add rocket leaves and lettuce strips and toss
4. In a separate bowl, combine and mix oil with lemon juice, yogurt, salt, and pepper, then whisk well. Put this over bell peppers mix, toss well to coat.
5. Share among plates and serve as a side
salad.

418. Nice Vermouth-White Mushrooms Recipe

Preparation Time: 35 Minutes • Servings: 4

INGREDIENTS

- Olive oil-1 tbsps
- Herbs de Provence-2 tsp
- 2Minced garlic cloves.
- White mushrooms-2-lbs
- White vermouth-2 tbsps

DIRECTIONS

1. In your air fryer; Combine and mix oil with mushrooms, herbs de Provence and garlic in a bowl, then ensure its tossed well.
2. Cook for 20 minutes at a temperature of 350° F, add vermouth, toss and cook for another 5 minutes more.
3. Share among plates and serve as a side dish

419. Sweet Pumpkin Rice Dish

Preparation Time: 35 Minutes • Servings: 4

INGREDIENTS

- Allspice-½ tsp
- heavy cream-4-ounce
- Chicken stock-4 cups
- Pumpkin puree-6-ounce
- Olive oil-2 tbsps 2 garlic cloves; minced
- Nutmeg-½ tsp
- White rice-12-ounce
- Chopped thyme-1 tsp
- Grated ginger-½ tsp
- Cinnamon powder-½ tsp
- 1small yellow onion chopped

DIRECTIONS

1. Combine and mix oil with garlic, onion, stock, rice, pumpkin puree, nutmeg, ginger, thyme, cinnamon, allspice and cream in a dish that fits your air fryer, stir well.
2. Transfer dish in your air fryer's basket and
cook for 30 minutes at 360°F.
3. Share among plates and serve.

420. Delicious Fried Creamy Cabbage

Preparation Time: 30 Minutes • Servings: 4

INGREDIENTS:

- 1green cabbage head chopped
- Whipped cream-1 cup
- 4bacon slices chopped.
- Seasoning-Salt and black pepper to the taste

- Cornstarch-2 tbsps
- 1yellow onion; chopped

DIRECTIONS

1. Put cabbage, bacon, and onion in your air fryer
2. Combine and mix cornstarch with cream, salt, and pepper in a bowl, stir well and add over cabbage. Toss carefully.
3. Cook for 20 minutes at a temperature of 400°F. Share among plates and serve.

421. Delicious Onion Rings Dish

Preparation Time: 20 Minutes • Servings: 3

INGREDIENTS

- White flour-1¼ cups
- Baking powder-1 tsp
- 1onion cut into medium slices and rings separated
- Egg- 1 quantity
- Milk-1 cup
- A pinch of salt
- Bread crumbs-3/4 cup

DIRECTIONS:

1. Combine and mix flour with salt and baking powder in a bowl, stir well.
2. Onion rings should be dredged in this mix and transfer them on a separate plate.
3. Put milk and egg to the flour mix and whisk well
4. Onion rings should be dipped in this mix, then they should be dredge in breadcrumbs, then place them in your air fryer's basket.
5. Cook for 10 minutes at a temperature of 360°F.
6. Share among plates and serve as a side dish for a steak

422. Pleasant Cajun Onion Wedges Dish

Preparation Time: 25 Minutes • Servings: 4

INGREDIENTS

- 2eggs
- Cajun seasoning -½ tsp
- Panko-1/3 cup
- A drizzle of olive oil
- Salt and black pepper to the taste
- 2big white onions; cut into wedges
- Milk-1/4 cup
- Paprika-1 ½ tsp
- Garlic powder-1 tsp

DIRECTIONS

1. Mix panko with Cajun seasoning and oil in a bowl and stir carefully.

2. In a separate bowl, Combine and mix the egg with milk, seasoned with salt and pepper then stir carefully again.
3. With paprika and garlic powder, drizzle onion wedges, dip them in egg mix, then in bread crumbs mix.
4. Place in your air fryer's basket, cook for 10 minutes at a temperature of 360°F. also, flip and cook for another 5 minutes.
5. Share among plates and serve as a side dish.

423. Sweet Tortilla Chips

Preparation Time: 16 Minutes • Servings: 4

INGREDIENTS

- A pinch of sweet paprika
- A pinch of garlic powder
- 8 corn tortillas; cut into triangles
- Olive oil-1 tbsps
- Salt and black pepper to the taste

DIRECTIONS

1. Combine and mix tortilla chips with oil, add salt, pepper, garlic powder, and paprika in a bowl, Carefully.
2. Transfer to your air fryer's basket and cook for 6 minutes at a temperature of 400°F.
3. Share among plates then Serve them as a side for a fish dish

424. Rice and Sausage Dish Recipe

Preparation Time: 30 Minutes • Servings: 4

INGREDIENTS

- Already Boiled White rice -2 cups
- Butter-1 tbsps
- 4garlic cloves; minced
- Grated cheddar cheese-3 tbsps
- 1pork sausage chopped
- Seasoning-Salt and black pepper to the taste
- Chopped carrot-2 tbsps
- Shredded mozzarella cheese-2 tbsps

DIRECTIONS

1. Ensure your air fryer is heated up to a temperature of 350°F, put butter, melt it, then add garlic, stir carefully and brown for 2 minutes.
2. Put the following ingredients; sausage, salt, pepper, carrots and rice; stir and also cook for 10 minutes at 350°F.
3. Lastly, put cheddar and mozzarella, toss well, then share among plates and serve as a side dish.

425. Coconut-Potatoes Recipes

Preparation Time: 30 Minutes • Servings: 4

INGREDIENTS

- 2Whisked eggs
- Grated cheddar cheese
- Coconut cream-4-ounce
- Seasoning-Salt and black pepper to the taste
- Flour-1 tbsps
- 2Sliced potatoes

DIRECTIONS

1. In your air fryer's basket, put potato slices and cook for 10 minutes at a temperature of 360°F.
2. In a clean bowl, Combine and mix eggs with coconut cream, salt, pepper, and flour.
3. Put potatoes in your air fryer's pan in an orderly manner, put coconut cream mix over them, then sprinkle cheese all over.
4. Transfer to air fryer's basket and cook for another 10 minutes at a temperature of 400°F.
5. Share among plates then serve.

426. Sweet Glazed Beets Recipe

Preparation Time: 50 Minutes • Servings: 8

INGREDIENTS

- Trimmed Small beets-3-lbss
- Duck fat-1 tbsps
- Maple syrup-4 tbsps

DIRECTIONS

1. Preheat your air fryer at a temperature of 360°F, put duck fat and heat up.
2. Put beets and maple syrup, then toss carefully.
3. Cook for 40 minutes, then share among plates and serve.

427. Veggie Rice Recipe

Preparation Time: 35 Minutes • Servings: 4

INGREDIENTS

- Cumin seeds-1 tbsps
- Butter-2 tbsps
- 1tsp cinnamon powder
- Sugar-1 tbsps
- Bay leaves-2 quantity
- Water-2 cups
- Minced Green chili-½ tsp
- Grated ginger-½ tsp
- Black peppercorns- 5 quantity
- 2whole cardamoms
- 3whole cloves
- 3garlic cloves minced
- Salt to the taste
- 1cup mixed carrots peas, corn, and green beans
- Basmati rice-2 cups

DIRECTIONS

1. In a heatproof dish that fits your air fryer, pour the water.
2. Put rice and the following ingredients; mixed veggies, green chili, grated ginger, garlic cloves, cinnamon, cloves, butter, cumin seeds, bay leaves, cardamoms, black peppercorns, seasoned with salt and sugar; stir carefully, then put in your air fryer's basket and cook for 25 minutes at a temperature of 370°F.
3. Share among plates and serve.

CHAPTER 11

DESSERT

428. Cashew Dip

Preparation time: 5 minutes• Cooking time: 12 minutes • Servings: 6

INGREDIENTS

- 1cup cashews, soaked in water for 4 hours and drained
- 1cup heavy cream
- 1tablespoon lemon zest, grated
- 1tablespoon lemon juice
- A pinch of salt and black pepper
- 1tablespoon chives, chopped

DIRECTIONS

1. In a blender, combine all the ingredients, pulse well and transfer to a ramekin.
2. Put the ramekin in your air fryer's basket and cook at 350 degrees F for 12 minutes.
3. Serve as a party dip.

NUTRITION: Calories 144, Fat 2, Fiber 1, Carbs 3, Protein 4

429. Smoked Salmon Salad

Preparation time: 5 minutes • Cooking time: 10 minutes • Servings: 4

INGREDIENTS:

- 4ounces smoked salmon, skinless, boneless and cubed
- 1cup kalamata olives, pitted and halved
- 1cup corn
- 1cup baby spinach
- 2tablespoons lemon juice
- 1teaspoon avocado oil
- 1tablespoon chives, chopped
- A pinch of salt and black pepper

DIRECTIONS

1. In the air fryer's pan, mix the salmon with the olives and the other ingredients, put the pan in the machine and cook at 350 degrees F for 10 minutes.
2. Divide into bowls and serve as an appetizer.

NUTRITION: Calories 100, Fat 2, Fiber 1, Carbs 2, Protein 2

430. Salmon Meatballs

Preparation time: 5 minutes • Cooking time: 20 minutes • Servings: 6

INGREDIENTS

- 1pound salmon fillets, boneless, skinless and ground
- 2eggs, whisked
- ¼ cup almond flour

- ½ teaspoon sweet paprika
- 1teaspoon garlic powder
- A pinch of salt and black pepper
- 1tablespoon parsley, chopped
- Cooking spray

DIRECTIONS

1. In a bowl, mix the salmon with the eggs and the other ingredients except the cooking spray, stir well and shape medium meatballs out of this mix.
2. Pace them in your lined air fryer's basket, grease with cooking spray and cook at 360 degrees F for 20 minutes.
3. Serve as an appetizer.

NUTRITION: Calories 180, Fat 5, Fiber 2, Carbs 5, Protein 7

431. Chicken Meatballs

Preparation time: 5 minutes • Cooking time: 20 minutes • Servings: 8

INGREDIENTS

- 1and ½ pounds chicken breast, skinless, boneless and ground
- 2eggs, whisked
- 1tablespoon oregano, chopped
- 1tablespoon chives, chopped
- ¼ cup almond flour
- A pinch of salt and black pepper
- 2garlic cloves, minced
- 2spring onions, chopped
- Cooking spray

DIRECTIONS

1. In a bowl, mix the meat with the eggs and the other ingredients except the cooking spray, stir well and shape medium meatballs out of this mix.
2. Arrange the meatballs in your air fryer's basket, grease them with cooking spray and cook at 360 degrees F for 20 minutes.
3. Serve as an appetizer.

NUTRITION: Calories 257, Fat 14, Fiber 1, Carbs 3, Protein 17

432. Ginger Dip

Preparation time: 5 minutes • Cooking time: 20 minutes • Servings: 6

INGREDIENTS

- 1cup Greek yogurt
- ½ cup heavy cream
- 2tablespoons ginger, grated

- 2shallots, chopped
- 1tablespoon chives, chopped
- A pinch of salt and black pepper
- Cooking spray

DIRECTIONS:

1. In the air fryer's pan, mix the cream with the yogurt and the other ingredients, put the pan in the machine and cook at 380 degrees F for 20 minutes.
2. Serve as a party dip.

NUTRITION: Calories 200, Fat 12, Fiber 2, Carbs 3, Protein 14

433. Asparagus and Olives Bowls

Preparation time: 5 minutes • Cooking time: 15 minutes • Servings: 8

INGREDIENTS

- ½ pound asparagus, roughly chopped
- 1cup black olives, pitted and halved
- 1cup kalamata olives, pitted and halved
- 1cup baby spinach
- Juice of 1 lime
- 2tablespoons olive oil
- A pinch of salt and black pepper

DIRECTIONS

1. In the air fryer's pan, mix the asparagus with the olives and the other ingredients, put the pan in the machine and cook at 390 degrees F for 15 minutes.
2. Divide into bowls and serve as an appetizer.

NUTRITION: Calories 173, Fat 4, Fiber 2, Carbs 3, Protein 6

434. Walnuts and Radish Bites

Preparation time: 5 minutes • Cooking time: 15 minutes • Servings: 4

INGREDIENTS

- 1pound radishes, halved
- 1cup walnuts
- 1teaspoon chili powder
- 1teaspoon sweet paprika
- A pinch of salt and black pepper
- 2tablespoons avocado oil

DIRECTIONS:

1. In the air fryer's basket, mix the radishes with the walnuts and the other ingredients, toss and cook at 400 degrees F for 15 minutes.
2. Serve as a snack.

NUTRITION: Calories 174, Fat 5, Fiber 1, Carbs 3, Protein 6

435. Olives Spread

Preparation time: 5 minutes • Cooking time: 5 minutes • Servings: 6

INGREDIENTS

- 1cup black olives, pitted and chopped
- 1cup kalamata olives, pitted and chopped
- 1cup green olives, pitted and chopped
- 1cup Greek yogurt
- 1tablespoon olive oil
- 3tablespoons lemon juice
- 1cup basil, chopped
- A pinch of salt and black pepper

DIRECTIONS

1. In a blender, combine the olives with the yogurt and the other ingredients, pulse well and transfer to a ramekin.
2. Place the ramekin in your air fryer's basket and cook at 350 degrees F for 5 minutes.
3. Serve as a party spread.

NUTRITION: Calories 120, Fat 5, Fiber 2, Carbs 3, Protein 7

436. Melon Salsa

Preparation time: 5 minutes • Cooking time: 5 minutes • Servings: 4

INGREDIENTS:

- 1cup watermelon, peeled and cubed
- 1cup cherry tomatoes, halved
- 1cup corn
- 1cup baby spinach
- 2spring onions, chopped
- 2tablespoons lime juice
- 1tablespoon avocado oil
- 2teaspoons parsley, chopped
- Cooking spray

DIRECTIONS

1. In the air fryer's pan, mix the watermelon with the tomatoes and the other ingredients and toss.
2. Introduce the pan in the machine and cook at 360 degrees F for 5 minutes.
3. Divide into bowls and serve as an appetizer.

NUTRITION: Calories 148, Fat 1, Fiber 2, Carbs 3, Protein 5

437. Shrimp Spread

Preparation time: 5 minutes • Cooking time: 6 minutes • Servings: 4

INGREDIENTS

- 1cup cream cheese, soft
- Juice of 1 lime
- Zest of 1 lime, grated
- 1pound shrimp, peeled, deveined and minced
- A pinch of salt and black pepper
- 1tablespoon chives, chopped

DIRECTIONS

1. In a bowl, mix all the ingredients, whisk them really well, transfer the mix to a ramekin, place it in your air fryer's basket and cook at 370 degrees F for 6 minutes.
2. Serve as a party spread.

NUTRITION: Calories 180, Fat 7, Fiber 1, Carbs 5, Protein 7

438. Pork Dip

Preparation time: 10 minutes • Cooking time: 20 minutes • Servings: 4

INGREDIENTS

- 1pound pork stew meat, ground
- 1tablespoon olive oil
- 1red onion, chopped
- ¼ teaspoon rosemary, dried
- ½ teaspoon coriander, ground
- 1cup heavy cream
- 1tablespoon cilantro, chopped
- 2garlic cloves, minced
- A pinch of salt and black pepper

DIRECTIONS

1. Preheat the air fryer with the oil at 370 degrees F, add the meat and cook for 5 minutes.
2. Add the rest of the ingredients, cook for 15 minutes more, divide into bowls and serve as a party dip.

NUTRITION: Calories 249, Fat 16, Fiber 2, Carbs 3, Protein 17

439. Spinach Dip

Preparation time: 6 minutes • Cooking time: 20 minutes • Servings: 6

INGREDIENTS

- 1cup cream cheese, soft
- 1cup mozzarella, shredded
- 2cups baby spinach
- 1cup heavy cream

- A pinch of salt and black pepper
- 2tablespoons butter, melted

DIRECTIONS

1. In the air fryer's pan, mix the cream cheese with the mozzarella and the other ingredients, put the pan in the machine and cook at 360 degrees F for 20 minutes.
2. Serve as a party dip.

NUTRITION: Calories 210, Fat 8, Fiber 1, Carbs 3, Protein 8

440. Pork and Spinach Bowls

Preparation time: 10 minutes • Cooking time: 20 minutes • Servings: 6

INGREDIENTS

- 1pound pork stew meat, cut into strips
- 1cup baby spinach
- 1cup cherry tomatoes, halved
- 1tablespoon balsamic vinegar
- 2tablespoons olive oil
- 1teaspoon sweet paprika
- A pinch of salt and black pepper
- 1tablespoon chives, chopped

DIRECTIONS

1. In the air fryer's pan, mix the meat with the spinach and the other ingredients, put the pan in the machine and cook at 360 degrees F for 20 minutes.
2. Divide into bowls and serve as a snack.

NUTRITION: Calories 251, Fat 14, Fiber 3, Carbs 5, Protein 18

441. Tomato and Radish Bowls

Preparation time: 5 minutes •
Cooking time: 20 minutes •
Servings: 6

INGREDIENTS

- 1pound cherry tomatoes, halved
- 2cups radishes, halved
- 1cup baby kale
- 1cup carrots, peeled and grated
- 1tablespoon olive oil
- Juice of 1 lime
- 2ounces watercress
- A pinch of salt and black pepper
- 1tablespoon chives, chopped

DIRECTIONS

1. In the air fryer's pan, mix the tomatoes with the radishes and the other ingredients, put the pan in the machine and cook at 360 degrees F for 20 minutes.
2. Divide into bowls and serve.

NUTRITION: Calories 131, Fat 7, Fiber 2, Carbs 4, Protein 7

442. Green Beans Bites

Preparation time: 5 minutes • Cooking time: 15 minutes • Servings: 4

INGREDIENTS

- 12ounces green beans, trimmed and halved
- 1teaspoon sweet paprika
- A drizzle of olive oil
- ½ teaspoon coriander, ground
- 1egg, whisked
- A pinch of salt and black pepper

DIRECTIONS

1. In a bowl, mix the green beans with the other ingredients except the egg and toss.
2. Put the egg in a separate bowl,
3. Dredge the green beans in the egg mix, arrange the green beans in your air fryer's basket and cook at 380 degrees F for 12 minutes.
4. Serve as a snack.

NUTRITION: Calories 112, Fat 6, Fiber 1, Carbs 2, Protein 9

443. Rosemary Shrimp Platter

Preparation time: 5 minutes • Cooking time: 10 minutes • Servings: 4

INGREDIENTS

- 1pound shrimp, peeled and deveined
- 2tablespoons avocado oil
- 1tablespoon rosemary, chopped
- Juice of ½ lemon
- A pinch of salt and black pepper

DIRECTIONS

1. In a pan that fits your air fryer, mix the shrimp with the oil and the other ingredients, toss, introduce in the fryer and cook at 370 degrees F for 10 minutes.
2. Serve as an appetizer.

NUTRITION: Calories 242, Fat 14, Fiber 2, Carbs 3, Protein 17

444. Chocolate Cake

Preparation time: 30 minutes • Cooking time: 30 minutes • Servings: 12

INGREDIENTS

- 2½ cups almond flour
- ¼ cup coconut flour

- ¼ cup chocolate protein powder
- ½ tsp salt
- ¼ cup unsweetened cocoa powder
- 1Tbsp baking powder
- 2/3 cup granulated erythritol
- ½ cup butter
- ¾ cup whole milk
- 1tsp vanilla
- 4whole eggs

DIRECTIONS:

1. Preheat your air fryer to 325 degrees F and grease and 8" cake pan.
2. Place the butter in a mixing bowl along with the erythritol and beat until fluffy.
3. In a separate bowl, mix the eggs, milk and vanilla together.
4. In a third bowl, combine the remaining dry ingredients.
5. Add half of the wet mixture to the bowl with the fluffy butter and beat together slowly.
6. Add half of the dry mix to the bowl and beat again until smooth.
7. Add the remaining wet ingredients, mix and add the remaining dry ingredients and blend until a smooth batter forms.
8. Pour the cake batter into the prepared pan and place in the air fryer to cook for 30 minutes. The cake will be golden brown and a toothpick will come out cleanly when inserted into the center of the cake.
9. Remove from the air fryer and cool in the pan for 20 minutes. Flip the cake out of the pan, slice and enjoy! You can also frost the cake however you'd like with a tasty keto frosting.

NUTRITION: Calories 348, Total Fat 36g, Saturated Fat 16g, Total Carbs 9g, Net Carbs 4g, Protein 11g, Sugar 4g, Fiber 5g, Sodium 321mg, Potassium 63g

445. Peanut Butter Cake

Preparation time: 30 minutes • Cooking time: 30 minutes • Servings: 12

INGREDIENTS

- 2½ cups almond flour
- ¼ cup coconut flour
- ¼ cup vanilla protein powder
- ½ tsp salt
- 1Tbsp baking powder
- 2/3 cup granulated erythritol
- ¼ cup butter
- ¼ cup peanut butter
- ¾ cup whole milk
- 1tsp vanilla
- 4whole eggs

DIRECTIONS:

1. Preheat your air fryer to 325 degrees F and grease and 8" cake pan.
2. Place the butter and peanut butter in a mixing bowl along with the erythritol and beat until fluffy.
3. In a separate bowl, mix the eggs, milk and vanilla together.
4. In a third bowl, combine the remaining dry ingredients.
5. Add half of the wet mixture to the bowl with the fluffy butter and beat together slowly.
6. Add half of the dry mix to the bowl and beat again until smooth.
7. Add the remaining wet ingredients, mix and add the remaining dry ingredients and blend until a smooth batter forms.
8. Pour the cake batter into the prepared pan and place in the air fryer to cook for 30 minutes. The cake will be golden brown and a toothpick will come out cleanly when inserted into the center of the cake.
9. Remove from the air fryer and cool in the pan for 20 minutes. Flip the cake out of the pan, slice and enjoy!

NUTRITION: Calories 351, Total Fat 36g, Saturated Fat 19g, Total Carbs 10g, Net Carbs 6g, Protein 10g, Sugar 5g, Fiber 4g, Sodium 483mg, Potassium 89g

446. Hazelnut Cake

Preparation time: 30 minutes • Cooking time: 30 minutes • Servings: 12

INGREDIENTS

- 2cups almond flour
- ¾ cup hazelnut flour
- ¼ cup vanilla protein powder
- ½ tsp salt
- 1Tbsp baking powder
- 2/3 cup granulated erythritol
- ¼ cup butter
- ¼ cup hazelnut butter
- ¾ cup whole milk
- 1tsp vanilla
- 4whole eggs

DIRECTIONS:

1. Preheat your air fryer to 325 degrees F and grease and 8" cake pan.
2. Place the butter and hazelnut butter in a mixing bowl along with the erythritol and beat until fluffy.
3. In a separate bowl, mix the eggs, milk and vanilla together.
4. In a third bowl, combine the remaining dry ingredients.
5. Add half of the wet mixture to the bowl with the fluffy butter and beat together slowly.
6. Add half of the dry mix to the bowl and beat again until smooth.
7. Add the remaining wet ingredients, mix and add the remaining dry ingredients and blend until a smooth batter forms.
8. Pour the cake batter into the prepared pan and place in the air fryer to cook for

30 minutes. The cake will be golden brown and a toothpick will come out cleanly when inserted into the center of the cake.

9. Remove from the air fryer and cool in the pan for 20 minutes. Flip the cake out of the pan, slice and enjoy!

NUTRITION: Calories 429, Total Fat 43g, Saturated Fat 24g, Total Carbs 14g, Net Carbs 9g, Protein 10g, Sugar 5g, Fiber 5g, Sodium 477mg, Potassium 97g

447. Walnut Cake

Preparation time: 30 minutes • Cooking time: 30 minutes • Servings: 12

INGREDIENTS

- 2cups almond flour
- ¾ cup walnut flour
- ¼ cup vanilla protein powder
- ½ tsp salt
- 1Tbsp baking powder
- 2/3 cup granulated erythritol
- ½ cup butter
- ¾ cup whole milk
- 1tsp vanilla
- 4whole eggs

DIRECTIONS:

1. Preheat your air fryer to 325 degrees F and grease and 8" cake pan.
2. Place the butter and in a mixing bowl along with the erythritol and beat until fluffy.
3. In a separate bowl, mix the eggs, milk and vanilla together.
4. In a third bowl, combine the remaining dry ingredients.
5. Add half of the wet mixture to the bowl with the fluffy butter and beat together slowly.
6. Add half of the dry mix to the bowl and beat again until smooth.
7. Add the remaining wet ingredients, mix and add the remaining dry ingredients and blend until a smooth batter forms.
8. Pour the cake batter into the prepared pan and place in the air fryer to cook for
30 minutes. The cake will be golden brown and a toothpick will come out cleanly when inserted into the center of the cake.
9. Remove from the air fryer and cool in the pan for 20 minutes. Flip the cake out of the pan, slice and enjoy!

NUTRITION: Calories 357, Total Fat 38g, Saturated Fat 21g, Total Carbs 11g, Net Carbs 6g, Protein 11g, Sugar 5g, Fiber 5g, Sodium 483mg, Potassium 102g

448. NY Keto Cheesecake

Preparation time: 15 minutes • Cooking time: 1 hour 15 minutes • Servings: 12

INGREDIENTS

- 1½ pounds cream cheese
- 5Tbsp butter
- 1cup powdered erythritol
- 3eggs

- 1½ tsp vanilla extract
- ¾ cup sour cream

DIRECTIONS:

1. Preheat your air fryer to 275 degrees F and grease an 8" spring form cake pan. Place a piece of parchment in the bottom of the pan as well.
2. Place the cream cheese and butter in a large bowl and beat until combined.
3. Add the powdered erythritol and beat again until smooth.
4. Add the eggs, one at a time, allowing them to fully mix in after each addition.
5. Add the sour cream and vanilla extract and stir one last time, making sure the batter is smooth and all the ingredients are well blended.
6. Pour the batter into the prepared cake pan and then place the pan on a larger tray with high sides that will fit in the air fryer. Fill the pan with water, creating a water bath for the cheese cake.
7. Place in the pre heated air fryer and bake for an hour and 15 minutes. The cheesecake will be mostly set but may have a very slight jiggle in the center.
8. Allow the cheesecake to cool for 3 hours in the fridge before removing from the pan and serving.

NUTRITION: Calories 287, Total Fat 26g, Saturated Fat 14g, Total Carbs 3g, Net Carbs 1g, Protein 5g, Sugar 1g, Fiber 2g, Sodium 192mg, Potassium 80g

449. Strawberry Cheesecake

Preparation time: 15 minutes • Cooking time: 1 hour 15 minutes • Servings: 12

INGREDIENTS

- 1½ pounds cream cheese
- 5Tbsp butter
- 1cup powdered erythritol
- 3eggs
- 1½ tsp vanilla extract
- ¾ cup sour cream
- ¾ cup chopped, fresh strawberries

DIRECTIONS:

1. Preheat your air fryer to 275 degrees F and grease an 8" spring form cake pan. Place a piece of parchment in the bottom of the pan as well.
2. Place the cream cheese and butter in a large bowl and beat until combined.
3. Add the powdered erythritol and beat again until smooth.
4. Add the eggs, one at a time, allowing them to fully mix in after each addition.
5. Add the sour cream and vanilla extract and stir one last time, making sure the batter is smooth and all the ingredients are well blended.

6. Fold in the chopped strawberries
7. Pour the batter into the prepared cake pan and then place the pan on a larger tray with high sides that will fit in the air fryer. Fill the pan with water, creating a water bath for the cheese cake.
8. Place in the pre heated air fryer and bake for an hour and 15 minutes. The cheesecake will be mostly set but may have a very slight jiggle in the center.
9. Allow the cheesecake to cool for 3 hours in the fridge before removing from the pan and serving.

NUTRITION: Calories 315, Total Fat 26g, Saturated Fat 14g, Total Carbs 8g, Net Carbs 6g, Protein 5g, Sugar 5g, Fiber 2g, Sodium 192mg, Potassium 110g

450. Blueberry Cheesecake

Preparation time: 15 minutes • Cooking time: 1 hour 15 minutes • Servings: 12

INGREDIENTS

- 1½ pounds cream cheese
- 5Tbsp butter
- 1cup powdered erythritol
- 3eggs
- 1½ tsp vanilla extract
- ¾ cup sour cream
- 1cup fresh blueberries

DIRECTIONS:

1. Preheat your air fryer to 275 degrees F and grease an 8" spring form cake pan. Place a piece of parchment in the bottom of the pan as well.
2. Place the cream cheese and butter in a large bowl and beat until combined.
3. Add the powdered erythritol and beat again until smooth.
4. Add the eggs, one at a time, allowing them to fully mix in after each addition.
5. Add the sour cream and vanilla extract and stir one last time, making sure the batter is smooth and all the ingredients are well blended.
6. Fold in the blueberries gently.
7. Pour the batter into the prepared cake pan and then place the pan on a larger tray with high sides that will fit in the air fryer. Fill the pan with water, creating a water bath for the cheese cake.
8. Place in the pre heated air fryer and bake for an hour and 15 minutes. The cheesecake will be mostly set but may have a very slight jiggle in the center.
9. Allow the cheesecake to cool for 3 hours in the fridge before removing from the pan and serving.

NUTRITION: Calories 322, Total Fat 26g, Saturated Fat 14g, Total Carbs 9g, Net Carbs 7g, Protein 5g, Sugar 6g, Fiber 2g, Sodium 192mg, Potassium 125g

451. Raspberry Cheesecake

Preparation time: 15 minutes • Cooking time: 1 hour 15 minutes • Servings: 12

INGREDIENTS:

- 1½ pounds cream cheese
- 5Tbsp butter
- 1cup powdered erythritol
- 3eggs
- 1½ tsp vanilla extract
- ¾ cup sour cream
- 1cup fresh raspberries

DIRECTIONS:

1. Preheat your air fryer to 275 degrees F and grease an 8" spring form cake pan. Place a piece of parchment in the bottom of the pan as well.
2. Place the cream cheese and butter in a large bowl and beat until combined.
3. Add the powdered erythritol and beat again until smooth.
4. Add the eggs, one at a time, allowing them to fully mix in after each addition.
5. Add the sour cream and vanilla extract and stir one last time, making sure the batter is smooth and all the ingredients are well blended.
6. Fold in the raspberries gently.
7. Pour the batter into the prepared cake pan and then place the pan on a larger tray with high sides that will fit in the air fryer. Fill the pan with water, creating a water bath for the cheese cake.
8. Place in the pre heated air fryer and bake for an hour and 15 minutes. The cheesecake will be mostly set but may have a very slight jiggle in the center.
9. Allow the cheesecake to cool for 3 hours in the fridge before removing from the pan and serving.

NUTRITION: Calories 319, Total Fat 26g, Saturated Fat 14g, Total Carbs 9g, Net Carbs 7g, Protein 5g, Sugar 6g, Fiber 2g, Sodium 192mg, Potassium 121g

452. Cinnamon Cheesecake

Preparation time: 15 minutes • Cooking time: 1 hour 15 minutes • Servings: 12

INGREDIENTS

- 1½ pounds cream cheese
- 5Tbsp butter
- 1cup powdered erythritol
- 1tsp ground cinnamon
- 3eggs
- 1½ tsp vanilla extract
- ¾ cup sour cream

DIRECTIONS:

1. Preheat your air fryer to 275 degrees F and grease an 8" spring form cake pan. Place a piece of parchment in the bottom of the pan as well.
2. Place the cream cheese and butter in a large bowl and beat until combined.
3. Add the powdered erythritol, cinnamon and beat again until smooth.
4. Add the eggs, one at a time, allowing them to fully mix in after each addition.
5. Add the sour cream and vanilla extract and stir one last time, making sure the batter is smooth and all the ingredients are well blended.
6. Pour the batter into the prepared cake pan and then place the pan on a larger tray with high sides that will fit in the air fryer. Fill the pan with water, creating a water bath for the cheese cake.
7. Place in the pre heated air fryer and bake for an hour and 15 minutes. The cheesecake will be mostly set but may have a very slight jiggle in the center.
8. Allow the cheesecake to cool for 3 hours in the fridge before removing from the pan and serving.

NUTRITION: Calories 292, Total Fat 26g, Saturated Fat 14g, Total Carbs 3g, Net Carbs 1g, Protein 5g, Sugar 1g, Fiber 2g, Sodium 192mg, Potassium 80g

453. Chocolate Keto Cheesecake

Preparation time: 15 minutes • Cooking time: 1 hour 15 minutes • Servings: 12

INGREDIENTS

- 1½ pounds cream cheese
- 5Tbsp butter
- 1cup powdered erythritol
- ¼ cup unsweetened cocoa powder
- 3eggs
- 1½ tsp vanilla extract
- ¾ cup sour cream

DIRECTIONS:

1. Preheat your air fryer to 275 degrees F and grease an 8" spring form cake pan. Place a piece of parchment in the bottom of the pan as well.
2. Place the cream cheese and butter in a large bowl and beat until combined.
3. Add the powdered erythritol, cocoa powder and beat again until smooth.
4. Add the eggs, one at a time, allowing them to fully mix in after each addition.
5. Add the sour cream and vanilla extract and stir one last time, making sure the batter is smooth and all the ingredients are well blended.

6. Pour the batter into the prepared cake pan and then place the pan on a larger tray with high sides that will fit in the air fryer. Fill the pan with water, creating a water bath for the cheese cake.
7. Place in the pre heated air fryer and bake for an hour and 15 minutes. The cheesecake will be mostly set but may have a very slight jiggle in the center.
8. Allow the cheesecake to cool for 3 hours in the fridge before removing from the pan and serving.

NUTRITION: Calories 302, Total Fat 34g, Saturated Fat 18g, Total Carbs 4g, Net Carbs 2g, Protein 5g, Sugar 2g, Fiber 2g, Sodium 192mg, Potassium 80g

454. Chocolate Chip Cheesecake

Preparation time: 15 minutes • Cooking time: 1 hour 15 minutes • Servings: 12

INGREDIENTS

- 1½ pounds cream cheese
- 5Tbsp butter
- 1cup powdered erythritol
- 3eggs
- 1½ tsp vanilla extract
- ¾ cup sour cream
- 1cup dark chocolate chips

DIRECTIONS:

1. Preheat your air fryer to 275 degrees F and grease an 8" spring form cake pan. Place a piece of parchment in the bottom of the pan as well.
2. Place the cream cheese and butter in a large bowl and beat until combined.
3. Add the powdered erythritol and beat again until smooth.
4. Add the eggs, one at a time, allowing them to fully mix in after each addition.
5. Add the sour cream and vanilla extract and stir one last time, making sure the batter is smooth and all the ingredients are well blended.
6. Fold in the dark chocolate chips.
7. Pour the batter into the prepared cake pan and then place the pan on a larger tray with high sides that will fit in the air fryer. Fill the pan with water, creating a water bath for the cheesecake.
8. Place in the pre heated air fryer and bake for an hour and 15 minutes. The cheesecake will be mostly set but may have a very slight jiggle in the center.
9. Allow the cheesecake to cool for 3 hours in the fridge before removing from the pan and serving.

NUTRITION: Calories 364, Total Fat 36g, Saturated Fat 20g, Total Carbs 8g, Net Carbs 6g, Protein 5g, Sugar 3g, Fiber 2g, Sodium 190mg, Potassium 102g

455. Pumpkin Spice Cheesecake

Preparation time: 15 minutes • Cooking time: 1 hour 15 minutes • Servings: 12

INGREDIENTS

- 1½ pounds cream cheese
- 5Tbsp butter
- 1cup powdered erythritol
- 2tsp pumpkin spice
- 3eggs
- 1½ tsp vanilla extract
- ¾ cup sour cream

DIRECTIONS:

1. Preheat your air fryer to 275 degrees F and grease an 8" spring form cake pan. Place a piece of parchment in the bottom of the pan as well.
2. Place the cream cheese and butter in a large bowl and beat until combined.
3. Add the powdered erythritol and pumpkin spice and beat again until smooth.
4. Add the eggs, one at a time, allowing them to fully mix in after each addition.
5. Add the sour cream and vanilla extract and stir one last time, making sure the batter is smooth and all the ingredients are well blended.
6. Pour the batter into the prepared cake pan and then place the pan on a larger tray with high sides that will fit in the air fryer. Fill the pan with water, creating a water bath for the cheese cake.
7. Place in the pre heated air fryer and bake for an hour and 15 minutes. The cheesecake will be mostly set but may have a very slight jiggle in the center.
8. Allow the cheesecake to cool for 3 hours in the fridge before removing from the pan and serving.

NUTRITION: Calories 293, Total Fat 26g, Saturated Fat 14g, Total Carbs 3g, Net Carbs 1g, Protein 5g, Sugar 1g, Fiber 2g, Sodium 195mg, Potassium 83g

456. Lemon Cheesecake

Preparation time: 15 minutes • Cooking time: 1 hour 15 minutes • Servings: 12

INGREDIENTS

- 1½ pounds cream cheese
- 5Tbsp butter
- 1cup powdered erythritol
- 3eggs
- 1½ tsp vanilla extract
- ¾ cup sour cream
- 1tsp lemon zest

DIRECTIONS:

1. Preheat your air fryer to 275 degrees F and grease an 8" spring form cake pan. Place a piece of parchment in the bottom of the pan as well.
2. Place the cream cheese and butter in a large bowl and beat until combined.
3. Add the powdered erythritol and beat again until smooth.
4. Add the eggs, one at a time, allowing them to fully mix in after each addition.
5. Add the sour cream, lemon zest and vanilla extract and stir one last time, making sure the batter is smooth and all the ingredients are well blended.
6. Pour the batter into the prepared cake pan and then place the pan on a larger tray with high sides that will fit in the air fryer. Fill the pan with water, creating a water bath for the cheese cake.
7. Place in the pre heated air fryer and bake for an hour and 15 minutes. The cheesecake will be mostly set but may have a very slight jiggle in the center.
8. Allow the cheesecake to cool for 3 hours in the fridge before removing from the pan and serving.

Nutrition: Calories 294, Total Fat 27g, Saturated Fat 14g, Total Carbs 5g, Net Carbs 1g, Protein 5g, Sugar 3g, Fiber 2g, Sodium 198mg, Potassium 87g

457. Gingerbread Cheesecake

Preparation time: 15 minutes • Cooking time: 1 hour 15 minutes • Servings: 12

INGREDIENTS

- 1½ pounds cream cheese
- 5Tbsp butter
- 1cup powdered erythritol
- ½ tsp ground ginger
- ¼ tsp ground cinnamon
- 3eggs
- 1½ tsp vanilla extract
- ¾ cup sour cream

DIRECTIONS:

1. Preheat your air fryer to 275 degrees F and grease an 8" spring form cake pan. Place a piece of parchment in the bottom of the pan as well.
2. Place the cream cheese and butter in a large bowl and beat until combined.
3. Add the powdered erythritol, cinnamon, ginger and beat again until smooth.
4. Add the eggs, one at a time, allowing them to fully mix in after each addition.
5. Add the sour cream and vanilla extract and stir one last time, making sure the batter is smooth and all the ingredients are well blended.
6. Pour the batter into the

prepared cake pan and then place the pan on a larger tray with high sides that will fit in the air fryer. Fill the pan with water, creating a water bath for the cheesecake.

7. Place in the pre heated air fryer and bake for an hour and 15 minutes. The cheesecake will be mostly set but may have a very slight jiggle in the center.
8. Allow the cheesecake to cool for 3 hours in the fridge before removing from the pan and serving.

NUTRITION: Calories 293, Total Fat 26g, Saturated Fat 14g, Total Carbs 3g, Net Carbs 1g, Protein 5g, Sugar 1g, Fiber 2g, Sodium 195mg, Potassium 82g

458. Mascarpone Cheesecake

Preparation time: 15 minutes • Cooking time: 1 hour 15 minutes • Servings: 12

INGREDIENTS

- 1pound cream cheese
- ½ pound mascarpone cheese
- 5Tbsp butter
- 1cup powdered erythritol
- 3eggs
- 1½ tsp vanilla extract
- ¾ cup sour cream

DIRECTIONS:

1. Preheat your air fryer to 275 degrees F and grease an 8" spring form cake pan. Place a piece of parchment in the bottom of the pan as well.
2. Place the cream cheese, mascarpone and butter in a large bowl and beat until combined.
3. Add the powdered erythritol and beat again until smooth.
4. Add the eggs, one at a time, allowing them to fully mix in after each addition.
5. Add the sour cream and vanilla extract and stir one last time, making sure the batter is smooth and all the ingredients are well blended.
6. Pour the batter into the prepared cake pan and then place the pan on a larger tray with high sides that will fit in the air fryer. Fill the pan with water, creating a water bath for the cheese cake.
7. Place in the pre heated air fryer and bake for an hour and 15 minutes. The cheesecake will be mostly set but may have a very slight jiggle in the center.
8. Allow the cheesecake to cool for 3 hours in the fridge before removing from the pan and serving.

NUTRITION: Calories 295, Total Fat 31g, Saturated Fat 19g, Total Carbs 4g, Net Carbs 2g, Protein 5g, Sugar 2g, Fiber 2g, Sodium 198mg, Potassium 86g

459. Coconut Cheesecake

Preparation time: 15 minutes • Cooking time: 1 hour 15 minutes • Servings: 12

INGREDIENTS

- 1½ pounds cream cheese

- 5Tbsp butter
- 1cup powdered erythritol
- 3eggs
- 1½ tsp coconut extract
- ¾ cup sour cream
- ½ cup unsweetened coconut flakes

DIRECTIONS:

1. Preheat your air fryer to 275 degrees F and grease an 8" spring form cake pan. Place a piece of parchment in the bottom of the pan as well.
2. Place the cream cheese and butter in a large bowl and beat until combined.
3. Add the powdered erythritol and beat again until smooth.
4. Add the eggs, one at a time, allowing them to fully mix in after each addition.
5. Add the sour cream and coconut extract and stir one last time, making sure the batter is smooth and all the ingredients are well blended.
6. Fold in the unsweetened coconut flakes
7. Pour the batter into the prepared cake pan and then place the pan on a larger tray with high sides that will fit in the air fryer. Fill the pan with water, creating a water bath for the cheese cake.
8. Place in the pre heated air fryer and bake for an hour and 15 minutes. The cheesecake will be mostly set but may have a very slight jiggle in the center.
9. Allow the cheesecake to cool for 3 hours in the fridge before removing from the pan and serving.

NUTRITION: Calories 311, Total Fat 29g, Saturated Fat 17g, Total Carbs 6g, Net Carbs 4g, Protein 5g, Sugar 3g, Fiber 2g, Sodium 192mg, Potassium 80g

460. Fudge Brownies

Preparation time: 15 minutes • Cooking time: 20 minutes • Servings: 16

INGREDIENTS

- ½ cup melted butter
- 2/3 cup swerve
- ½ tsp vanilla extract
- 3room temperature eggs
- ½ cup almond flour
- 1/3 cup unsweetened cocoa powder
- 1Tbsp plain, unsweetened gelatin
- ½ tsp salt
- ½ tsp baking powder
- ¼ cup water

DIRECTIONS:

1. Preheat your air fryer to 325 degrees F and grease an 8x8 inch square baking pan.
2. Combine the eggs, vanilla extract, swerve, and melted butter in a bowl and whisk

together well.
3. Add the cocoa powder, almond flour, baking powder, gelatin, and salt and whisk again until smooth.
4. Add the water and stir again.
5. Pour the batter into the greased baking pan and place in the preheated air fryer. Bake for 15 minutes. The center will seem a little wet while the edges will be more firm- this is perfect.
6. Let the brownies cool in the pan before slicing and serving.

NUTRITION: Calories 110, Total Fat 10g, Saturated Fat 4g, Total Carbs 4g, Net Carbs 1g, Protein 3g, Sugar 1g, Fiber 3g, Sodium 283mg, Potassium 316g

461. Double Chocolate Brownies

Preparation time: 15 minutes • Cooking time: 20 minutes • Servings: 16

INGREDIENTS

- ½cup melted butter
- 2/3 cup swerve
- ½ tsp vanilla extract
- 3room temperature eggs
- ½ cup almond flour
- 1/3 cup unsweetened cocoa powder
- 1Tbsp plain, unsweetened gelatin
- ½ tsp salt
- ½ tsp baking powder
- ¼ cup water
- ½ cup dark chocolate chips, unsweetened

DIRECTIONS:

1. Preheat your air fryer to 325 degrees F and grease an 8x8 inch square baking pan.
2. Combine the eggs, vanilla extract, swerve, and melted butter in a bowl and whisk together well.
3. Add the cocoa powder, almond flour, baking powder, gelatin, and salt and whisk again until smooth.
4. Add the water and stir again.
5. Fold in the chocolate chips.
6. Pour the batter into the greased baking pan and place in the preheated air fryer. Bake for 15 minutes. The center will seem a little wet while the edges will be more firm- this is perfect.
7. Let the brownies cool in the pan before slicing and serving.

NUTRITION: Calories 193, Total Fat 10g, Saturated Fat 4g, Total Carbs 6g, Net Carbs 3g, Protein 3g, Sugar 3g, Fiber 3g, Sodium 299mg, Potassium 322g

Chocolate Walnuts Brownies

Preparation time: 15 minutes • Cooking time: 20 minutes • Servings: 16

INGREDIENTS

- ½ cup melted butter
- 2/3 cup swerve
- ½ tsp vanilla extract
- 3room temperature eggs
- ½ cup almond flour
- 1/3 cup unsweetened cocoa powder
- 1Tbsp plain, unsweetened gelatin
- ½ tsp salt
- ½ tsp baking powder
- ¼ cup water
- ½ cup chopped walnuts

DIRECTIONS:

1. Preheat your air fryer to 325 degrees F and grease an 8x8 inch square baking pan.
2. Combine the eggs, vanilla extract, swerve, and melted butter in a bowl and whisk together well.
3. Add the cocoa powder, almond flour, baking powder, gelatin, and salt and whisk again until smooth.
4. Add the water and stir again.
5. Fold in walnuts.
6. Pour the batter into the greased baking pan and place in the preheated air fryer. Bake for 15 minutes. The center will seem a little wet while the edges will be more firm- this is perfect.
7. Let the brownies cool in the pan before slicing and serving.

NUTRITION: Calories 178, Total Fat 19g, Saturated Fat 5g, Total Carbs 8g, Net Carbs 4g, Protein 3g, Sugar 2g, Fiber 4g, Sodium 283mg, Potassium 322g

462. Peanut Butter Brownies

Preparation time: 15 minutes • Cooking time: 20 minutes • Servings: 16

INGREDIENTS

- ½ cup peanut butter
- 2/3 cup swerve
- ½ tsp vanilla extract
- 3room temperature eggs
- ½ cup almond flour
- 1/3 cup unsweetened cocoa powder
- 1Tbsp plain, unsweetened gelatin
- ½ tsp salt
- ½ tsp baking powder
- ¼ cup water

DIRECTIONS:

1. Preheat your air fryer to 325 degrees F and grease an 8x8 inch square baking pan.

2. Combine the peanut butter, vanilla extract, swerve, and eggs in a bowl and whisk together well.
3. Add the cocoa powder, almond flour, baking powder, gelatin, and salt and whisk again until smooth.
4. Add the water and stir again.
5. Pour the batter into the greased baking pan and place in the preheated air fryer. Bake for 15 minutes. The center will seem a little wet while the edges will be more firm- this is perfect.
6. Let the brownies cool in the pan before slicing and serving.

NUTRITION: Calories 131, Total Fat 11g, Saturated Fat 5g, Total Carbs 6g, Net Carbs 3g, Protein 6g, Sugar 4g, Fiber 3g, Sodium 283mg, Potassium 324g

463. Almond Brownies

Preparation time: 15 minutes • Cooking time: 20 minutes • Servings: 16

INGREDIENTS

- ½ cup melted butter
- 2/3 cup swerve
- ½ tsp almond extract
- 3room temperature eggs
- ½ cup almond flour
- 1/3 cup unsweetened cocoa powder
- 1Tbsp plain, unsweetened gelatin
- ½ tsp salt
- ½ tsp baking powder
- ¼ cup water

DIRECTIONS:

1. Preheat your air fryer to 325 degrees F and grease an 8x8 inch square baking pan.
2. Combine the eggs, almond extract, swerve, and melted butter in a bowl and whisk together well.
3. Add the cocoa powder, almond flour, baking powder, gelatin, and salt and whisk again until smooth.
4. Add the water and stir again.
5. Pour the batter into the greased baking pan and place in the preheated air fryer. Bake for 15 minutes. The center will seem a little wet while the edges will be more firm- this is perfect.
6. Let the brownies cool in the pan before slicing and serving.

NUTRITION: Calories 110, Total Fat 10g, Saturated Fat 4g, Total Carbs 4g, Net Carbs 1g, Protein 3g, Sugar 1g, Fiber 3g, Sodium 283mg, Potassium 316g

464. Chocolate Coconut Brownies

Preparation time: 15 minutes • Cooking time: 20 minutes • Servings: 16

INGREDIENTS

- ½ cup melted butter
- 2/3 cup swerve

- ½ tsp vanilla extract
- 3room temperature eggs
- ½ cup almond flour
- 1/3 cup unsweetened cocoa powder
- 1Tbsp plain, unsweetened gelatin
- ½ tsp salt
- ½ tsp baking powder
- ¼ cup water
- ½ cup unsweetened shredded coconut

DIRECTIONS:

1. Preheat your air fryer to 325 degrees F and grease an 8x8 inch square baking pan.
2. Combine the eggs, vanilla extract, swerve, and melted butter in a bowl and whisk together well.
3. Add the cocoa powder, almond flour, baking powder, gelatin, and salt and whisk again until smooth.
4. Add the water and stir again.
5. Fold in the shredded coconut.
6. Pour the batter into the greased baking pan and place in the preheated air fryer. Bake for 15 minutes. The center will seem a little wet while the edges will be more firm- this is perfect.
7. Let the brownies cool in the pan before slicing and serving.

NUTRITION: Calories 218, Total Fat 22g, Saturated Fat 8g, Total Carbs 9g, Net Carbs 5g, Protein 3g, Sugar 3g, Fiber 4g, Sodium 283mg, Potassium 389g

465. Chocolate Mint Brownies

Preparation time: 15 minutes • Cooking time: 20 minutes • Servings: 16

INGREDIENTS

- ½ cup melted butter
- 2/3 cup swerve
- ½ tsp peppermint extract
- 3room temperature eggs
- ½ cup almond flour
- 1/3 cup unsweetened cocoa powder
- 1Tbsp plain, unsweetened gelatin
- ½ tsp salt
- ½ tsp baking powder
- ¼ cup water

DIRECTIONS:

1. Preheat your air fryer to 325 degrees F and grease an 8x8 inch square baking pan.

2. Combine the eggs, peppermint extract, swerve, and melted butter in a bowl and whisk together well.
3. Add the cocoa powder, almond flour, baking powder, gelatin, and salt and whisk again until smooth.
4. Add the water and stir again.
5. Pour the batter into the greased baking pan and place in the preheated air

fryer. Bake for 15 minutes. The center will seem a little wet while the edges will be more firm- this is perfect.
6. Let the brownies cool in the pan before slicing and serving.

NUTRITION: Calories 110, Total Fat 10g, Saturated Fat 4g, Total Carbs 4g, Net Carbs 1g, Protein 3g, Sugar 1g, Fiber 3g, Sodium 283mg, Potassium 316g

466. Hazelnut Brownies

Preparation time: 15 minutes • Cooking time: 20 minutes • Servings: 16

INGREDIENTS

- ½ cup melted butter
- 2/3 cup swerve
- ½ tsp vanilla extract
- 3room temperature eggs
- ½ cup almond flour
- 1/3 cup unsweetened cocoa powder
- 1Tbsp plain, unsweetened gelatin
- ½ tsp salt
- ½ tsp baking powder
- ¼ cup water
- ½ cup chopped hazelnuts

DIRECTIONS:

1. Preheat your air fryer to 325 degrees F and grease an 8x8 inch square baking pan.
2. Combine the eggs, vanilla extract, swerve, and melted butter in a bowl and whisk together well.
3. Add the cocoa powder, almond flour, baking powder, gelatin, and salt and whisk again until smooth.
4. Add the water and stir again.
5. Pour the batter into the greased baking pan, sprinkle with the chopped hazelnuts and place in the preheated air fryer. Bake for 15 minutes. The center will seem a little wet while the edges will be more firm- this is perfect.
6. Let the brownies cool in the pan before slicing and serving.

NUTRITION: Calories 152, Total Fat 23g, Saturated Fat 6g, Total Carbs 8g, Net Carbs 2g, Protein 3g, Sugar 1g, Fiber 6g, Sodium 292mg, Potassium 489g

467. Espresso Brownies

Preparation time: 15 minutes • Cooking time: 20 minutes • Servings: 16

INGREDIENTS

- ½ cup melted butter
- 2/3 cup swerve
- ½ tsp vanilla extract
- 3room temperature eggs
- ½ cup almond flour
- 1/3 cup unsweetened cocoa powder
- 1Tbsp plain, unsweetened gelatin
- ½ tsp salt
- ½ tsp baking powder
- ¼ cup brewed espresso

DIRECTIONS:

1. Preheat your air fryer to 325 degrees F and grease an 8x8 inch square baking pan.
2. Combine the eggs, vanilla extract, swerve, and melted butter in a bowl and whisk together well.
3. Add the cocoa powder, almond flour, baking powder, gelatin, and salt and whisk again until smooth.
4. Add the brewed espresso and stir again.
5. Pour the batter into the greased baking pan and place in the preheated air fryer. Bake for 15 minutes. The center will seem a little wet while the edges will be more firm- this is perfect.
6. Let the brownies cool in the pan before slicing and serving.

NUTRITION: Calories 116, Total Fat 10g, Saturated Fat 4g, Total Carbs 4g, Net Carbs 1g, Protein 3g, Sugar 1g, Fiber 3g, Sodium 283mg, Potassium 316g

468. Caramel Fudge Brownies

Preparation time: 15 minutes • Cooking time: 20 minutes • Servings: 16

INGREDIENTS

- ½ cup melted butter
- 2/3 cup swerve
- ½ tsp vanilla extract
- 3room temperature eggs
- ½ cup almond flour
- 1/3 cup unsweetened cocoa powder
- 1Tbsp plain, unsweetened gelatin
- ½ tsp salt
- ½ tsp baking powder
- ¼ cup water
- ½ cup keto caramel sauce

DIRECTIONS:

1. Preheat your air fryer to 325 degrees F and grease an 8x8 inch square baking pan.
2. Combine the eggs, vanilla extract, swerve, and melted butter in a bowl and whisk together well.
3. Add the cocoa powder, almond flour, baking powder, gelatin, and salt and whisk again until smooth.
4. Add the water and stir again.
5. Pour the batter into the greased baking pan and swirl in the caramel sauce.
6. Place the pan in the preheated air fryer. Bake for 15 minutes. The center will seem a little wet while the edges will be more firm- this is perfect.
7. Let the brownies cool in the pan before slicing and serving.

NUTRITION: Calories 208, Total Fat 11g, Saturated Fat 4g, Total Carbs 10g, Net Carbs 7g, Protein 3g, Sugar 5g, Fiber 3g, Sodium 383mg, Potassium 316g

469. Raspberry Brownies

Preparation time: 15 minutes • Cooking time: 20 minutes • Servings: 16

INGREDIENTS

- ½ cup melted butter
- 2/3 cup swerve
- ½ tsp vanilla extract
- 3room temperature eggs
- ½ cup almond flour
- 1/3 cup unsweetened cocoa powder
- 1Tbsp plain, unsweetened gelatin
- ½ tsp salt
- ½ tsp baking powder
- ¼ cup water
- ½ cup fresh raspberries, cut in half

DIRECTIONS:

1. Preheat your air fryer to 325 degrees F and grease an 8x8 inch square baking pan.
2. Combine the eggs, vanilla extract, swerve, and melted butter in a bowl and whisk together well.
3. Add the cocoa powder, almond flour, baking powder, gelatin, and salt and whisk again until smooth.
4. Add the water and stir again.
5. Fold in the fresh raspberries.
6. Pour the batter into the greased baking pan and place in the preheated air fryer. Bake for 15 minutes. The center will seem a little wet while the edges will be more firm- this is perfect.
7. Let the brownies cool in the pan before slicing and serving.

NUTRITION: Calories 170, Total Fat 10g, Saturated Fat 4g, Total Carbs 9g, Net Carbs 3g, Protein 3g, Sugar 3g, Fiber 6g, Sodium 283mg, Potassium 368g

470. Cauliflower Rice and Plum Pudding

Preparation Time: 30 minutes • Servings: 4

INGREDIENTS

- 4plums, pitted and roughly chopped.
- 1½ cups cauliflower rice
- 2cups coconut milk
- 2tbsp. ghee; melted
- 3tbsp. stevia

DIRECTIONS

1. Take a bowl and mix all the ingredients, toss, divide into ramekins, put them in the air fryer and cook at 340°F for 25 minutes. Cool down and serve

NUTRITION: Calories: 221; Fat: 4g; Fiber: 1g; Carbs: 3g; Protein: 3g

471. Creamy Chia Seeds Pudding

Preparation Time: 35 minutes • Servings: 6

INGREDIENTS

- 2cups coconut cream
- ¼ cup chia seeds
- 6egg yolks, whisked
- 1tbsp. ghee; melted
- 2tbsp. stevia
- 2tsp. cinnamon powder

DIRECTIONS:

1. Take a bowl and mix all the ingredients, whisk, divide into 6 ramekins, place them all in your air fryer and cook at 340°F for 25 minutes. Cool the puddings down and serve

NUTRITION: Calories: 180; Fat: 4g; Fiber: 2 carbs 5g; Protein: 7g

472. Ginger Cookies

Preparation Time: 25 minutes • Servings: 12

INGREDIENTS

- ¼ cup butter; melted
- 2cups almond flour
- 1cup swerve
- 1egg
- ¼ tsp. nutmeg, ground
- ¼ tsp. cinnamon powder
- 2tsp. ginger, grated
- 1tsp. vanilla extract

DIRECTIONS

1. Take a bowl and mix all the ingredients and whisk well.
2. Spoon small balls out of this mix on a lined baking sheet that fits the air fryer lined with parchment paper and flatten them
3. Put the sheet in the fryer and cook at 360°F for 15 minutes
4. Cool the cookies down and serve.

NUTRITION: Calories: 220; Fat: 13g; Fiber: 2g; Carbs: 4g; Protein: 3g

473. Spiced Avocado Pudding

Preparation Time: 30 minutes • Servings: 6

INGREDIENTS

- 4small avocados, peeled, pitted and mashed
- 2eggs, whisked
- ¾ cup swerve
- 1cup coconut milk
- 1tsp. cinnamon powder
- ½ tsp. ginger powder

DIRECTIONS:

1. Take a bowl and mix all the ingredients and whisk well.
2. Pour into a pudding mould, put it in the air fryer and cook at 350°F for 25 minutes
3. Servings warm

NUTRITION: Calories: 192; Fat: 8g; Fiber: 2g; Carbs: 5g; Protein: 4g

474. Coconut Bars

Preparation Time: 45 minutes • Servings: 12

INGREDIENTS

- 1¼ cups almond flour
- ½ cup coconut cream
- 1½ cups coconut, flaked
- 1egg yolk
- ¾ cup walnuts; chopped.
- 1cup swerve
- 1cup butter; melted
- ½ tsp. vanilla extract

DIRECTIONS

1. Take a bowl and mix the flour with half of the swerve and half of the butter, stir well and press this on the bottom of a baking pan that fits the air fryer.
2. Introduce this in the air fryer and cook at 350°F for 15 minutes
3. Meanwhile, heat up a pan with the rest of the butter over medium heat, add the remaining swerve and the rest of the ingredients, whisk, cook for 1-2 minutes, take off the heat and cool down
4. Spread this well over the crust, put the pan in the air fryer again and cook at 350°F for 25 minutes. Cool down; cut into bars and serve.

NUTRITION: Calories: 182; Fat: 12g; Fiber: 2g; Carbs: 4g; Protein: 4g

475. Plum Cream

Preparation Time: 25 minutes • Servings: 4

INGREDIENTS

- 1lb. plums, pitted and chopped.
- 1½ cups heavy cream
- ¼ cup swerve
- 1tbsp. lemon juice

DIRECTIONS

1. Take a bowl and mix all the ingredients and whisk really well.
2. Divide this into 4 ramekins, put them in the air fryer and cook at 340°F for 20 minutes
3. Servings cold

NUTRITION: Calories: 171; Fat: 4g; Fiber: 2g; Carbs: 4g; Protein: 4g

476. Raspberry Muffins

Preparation Time: 30 minutes • Servings: 8

INGREDIENTS

- ¾ cup raspberries
- ½ cup swerve
- ¼ cup coconut flour
- ¼ cup ghee; melted
- 1egg
- 3tbsp. cream cheese
- 2tbsp. almond meal
- ½ tsp. baking soda
- ½ tsp. baking powder
- 1tsp. cinnamon powder
- Cooking spray

DIRECTIONS

1. Take a bowl and mix all the ingredients except the cooking spray and whisk well.
2. Grease a muffin pan that fits the air fryer with the cooking spray
3. Pour the raspberry mix, put the pan in the machine and cook at 350°F for 20 minutes
   Servings the muffins cold

NUTRITION: Calories: 223; Fat: 7g; Fiber: 2g; Carbs: 4g; Protein: 5g

477. Cinnamon Plums

Preparation Time: 25 minutes • Servings: 4

INGREDIENTS

- 4plums; halved
- 3tbsp. swerve
- 4tbsp. butter; melted
- 2tsp. cinnamon powder

DIRECTIONS

1. In a pan that fits your air fryer, mix the plums with the rest of the ingredients, toss, put the pan in the air fryer and cook at 300°F for 20 minutes
2. Divide into cups and serve cold.

NUTRITION: Calories: 162; Fat: 3g; Fiber: 2g; Carbs: 4g; Protein: 5g

478. Strawberry Cake

Preparation Time: 45 minutes • Servings: 6

INGREDIENTS

- 1lb. strawberries; chopped.
- 1egg, whisked
- 1cup almond flour
- ¼ cup swerve
- 1cup cream cheese, soft

- 3tbsp. coconut oil; melted
- 1tbsp. lime juice
- 1tsp. vanilla extract
- 2tsp. baking powder

DIRECTIONS

1. Take a bowl and mix all the ingredients, stir well and pour this into a cake pan lined with parchment paper.
2. Put the pan in the air fryer, cook at 350°F for 35 minutes, cool down, slice and serve

NUTRITION: Calories: 200; Fat: 6g; Fiber: 2g; Carbs: 4g; Protein: 6g

479. Chocolate Pudding

Preparation Time: 30 minutes • Servings: 6

INGREDIENTS

- 24oz. cream cheese, soft
- 12oz. dark chocolate; melted
- ½ cup heavy cream
- ¼ cup erythritol
- 3eggs, whisked
- 1tbsp. vanilla extract
- 2tbsp. almond meal

DIRECTIONS

1. In a bowl mix all the ingredients and whisk well.
2. Divide this into 6 ramekins, put them in your air fryer and cook at 320°F for 20 minutes.
3. Keep in the fridge for 1 hour before serving

NUTRITION: Calories: 200; Fat: 7g; Fiber: 2g; Carbs: 4g; Protein: 6g

480. Cream Cheese Brownies

Preparation Time: 35 minutes • Servings: 6

INGREDIENTS

- 3eggs, whisked
- ¼ cup almond flour
- ¼ cup coconut flour
- ½ cup almond milk
- 2tbsp. cocoa powder
- 3tbsp. swerve
- 6tbsp. cream cheese, soft
- 3tbsp. coconut oil; melted
- 1tsp. vanilla extract
- ¼ tsp. baking soda
- Cooking spray

DIRECTIONS

1. Grease a cake pan that fits the air fryer with the cocking spray.
2. Take a bowl and mix rest of the ingredients, whisk well and pour into the pan
3. Put the pan in your air fryer, cook at 370°F for 25 minutes, cool the brownies down, slice and serve.

NUTRITION: Calories: 182; Fat: 12g; Fiber: 2g; Carbs: 4g; Protein: 6g

481. Lemon Coconut Pie

Preparation Time: 45 minutes • Servings: 8

INGREDIENTS

- 4oz. coconut, shredded
- 2eggs, whisked
- ¼ cup coconut flour
- ¾ cup swerve
- 2tbsp. butter; melted
- 1tsp. lemon zest, grated
- 1tsp. baking powder
- 1tsp. vanilla extract
- ½ tsp. lemon extract
- Cooking spray

DIRECTIONS

1. In a bowl, combine all the ingredients except the cooking spray and stir well.
2. Grease a pie pan that fits the air fryer with the cooking spray
3. Pour the mixture inside, put the pan in the air fryer and cook at 360°F for 35 minutes. Slice and serve warm.

NUTRITION: Calories: 212; Fat: 15g; Fiber: 2g; Carbs: 6g; Protein: 4g

482. Almond Butter Cookies

Preparation Time: 17 minutes • Servings: 12

INGREDIENTS

- 1cup almond butter, soft
- 1egg
- 2tbsp. erythritol
- 1tsp. vanilla extract

DIRECTIONS

1. Take a bowl and mix all the ingredients and whisk really well.
2. Spread this on a cookie sheet that fits the air fryer lined with parchment paper, introduce in the fryer and cook at 350°F and bake for 12 minutes. Cool down and serve

NUTRITION: Calories: 130; Fat: 12g; Fiber: 1g; Carbs: 3g; Protein: 5g

483. Avocado Granola

Preparation Time: 12 minutes • Servings: 6

INGREDIENTS

- 1cup avocado, peeled, pitted and cubed
- ¼ cup walnuts; chopped.
- ¼ cup almonds; chopped.
- ½ cup coconut flakes

- 2tbsp. stevia
- 2tbsp. ghee; melted

DIRECTIONS

1. In a pan that fits your air fryer, mix all the ingredients, toss, put the pan in the fryer and cook at 320°F for 8 minutes
2. Divide into bowls and serve right away.

NUTRITION: Calories: 170; Fat: 3g; Fiber: 2g; Carbs: 4g; Protein: 3g

484. Blackberry Chia Jam

Preparation Time: 40 minutes • Servings: 12

INGREDIENTS

- ¼ cup swerve
- 3cups blackberries
- 4tbsp. chia seeds
- 4tbsp. lemon juice

DIRECTIONS

1. In a pan that fits the air fryer, combine all the ingredients and toss.
2. Put the pan in the machine and cook at 300°F for 30 minutes. Divide into cups and serve cold

NUTRITION: Calories: 100; Fat: 2g; Fiber: 1g; Carbs: 3g; Protein: 1g

485. Lemon Bars

Preparation Time: 45 minutes • Servings: 8

INGREDIENTS

- 1¾ cups almond flour
- 3eggs, whisked
- ½ cup butter; melted
- 1cup erythritol
- Zest of 1 lemon, grated
- Juice of 3 lemons

DIRECTIONS

1. Take a bowl and mix 1 cup flour with half of the erythritol and the butter, stir well and press into a baking dish that fits the air fryer lined with parchment paper
2. Put the dish in your air fryer and cook at 350°F for 10 minutes.
3. Meanwhile, in a bowl, mix the rest of the flour with the remaining erythritol and the other ingredients and whisk well
4. Spread this over the crust, put the dish in the air fryer once more and cook at 350°F for 25 minutes
5. Cool down; cut into bars and serve.

NUTRITION: Calories: 210; Fat: 12g; Fiber: 1g; Carbs: 4g; Protein: 8g

486. Strawberries Stew

Preparation Time: 30 minutes • Servings: 4

INGREDIENTS

- 1lb. strawberries; halved
- 1½ cups water
- 1tbsp. lemon juice
- 4tbsp. stevia

DIRECTIONS

1. In a pan that fits your air fryer, mix all the ingredients, toss, put it in the fryer and cook at 340°F for 20 minutes
2. Divide the stew into cups and serve cold.

NUTRITION: Calories: 176; Fat: 2g; Fiber: 1g; Carbs: 3g; Protein: 5g

487. Blueberries and Chocolate Cream

Preparation Time: 25 minutes • Servings: 4

INGREDIENTS

- 2cups blueberries
- 3tbsp. cream cheese, soft
- 4tbsp. erythritol
- 3tbsp. chocolate; melted

DIRECTIONS

1. In a pan that fits the air fryer, combine all the ingredients, whisk.
2. Put the pan in the fryer and cook at 340°F for 20 minutes
3. Divide into bowls and serve cold.

NUTRITION: Calories: 200; Fat: 6g; Fiber: 2g; Carbs: 4g; Protein: 5g

488. Cocoa Cake

Preparation Time: 25 minutes • Servings: 8

INGREDIENTS

- 2egg
- ¼ cup coconut milk
- 4tbsp. almond flour
- 1tbsp. cocoa powder
- 3tbsp. swerve
- 3tbsp. coconut oil; melted
- ½ tsp. baking powder

DIRECTIONS

1. Take a bowl and mix all the ingredients and stir well.
2. Pour this into a cake pan that fits the air fryer, put the pan in the machine and cook at 340°F for 20 minutes

NUTRITION: Calories: 191; Fat: 12g; Fiber: 2g; Carbs: 4g; Protein: 6g

489. Mini Lava Cakes

Preparation Time: 30 minutes • Servings: 4

INGREDIENTS

- 3oz. dark chocolate; melted
- 2eggs, whisked
- ¼ cup coconut oil; melted
- 1tbsp. almond flour
- 2tbsp. swerve
- ¼ tsp. vanilla extract
- Cooking spray

DIRECTIONS

1. In bowl, combine all the ingredients except the cooking spray and whisk really well.
2. Divide this into 4 ramekins greased with cooking spray, put them in the fryer and cook at 360°F for 20 minutes

NUTRITION: Calories: 161; Fat: 12g; Fiber: 1g; Carbs: 4g; Protein: 7g

490. Avocado Brownies

Preparation Time: 40 minutes Servings: 12

INGREDIENTS

- 1cup avocado; peeled and mashed
- 2eggs, whisked
- ½ cup dark chocolate, unsweetened and melted
- ¾ cup almond flour
- 3tbsp. coconut oil; melted
- 4tbsp. cocoa powder
- 1tsp. baking powder
- 1tsp. stevia
- ½ tsp. vanilla extract
- ¼ tsp. baking soda

DIRECTIONS

1. Take a bowl and mix the flour with stevia, baking powder and soda and stir.
2. Add the rest of the ingredients gradually, whisk and pour into a cake pan that fits the air fryer after you lined it with parchment paper
3. Put the pan in your air fryer and cook at 350°F for 30 minutes. Cut into squares and serve cold.

NUTRITION: Calories: 155; Fat: 6g; Fiber: 2g; Carbs: 6g; Protein: 4g

491. Baked Plums

Preparation Time: 25 minutes • Servings: 6

INGREDIENTS

- 6plums; cut into wedges
- 10drops stevia
- Zest of 1 lemon, grated

- 2tbsp. water
- 1tsp. ginger, ground
- ½ tsp. cinnamon powder

DIRECTIONS

1. In a pan that fits the air fryer, combine the plums with the rest of the ingredients, toss gently.
2. Put the pan in the air fryer and cook at 360°F for 20 minutes
3. Servings cold

NUTRITION: Calories: 170; Fat: 5g; Fiber: 1g; Carbs: 3g; Protein: 5g

492. Lime Berry Pudding

Preparation Time: 20 minutes • Servings: 6

INGREDIENTS

- 1/3 cup blueberries
- 2cups coconut cream
- 1/3 cup blackberries
- Zest of 1 lime, grated
- 3tbsp. swerve

DIRECTIONS

1. In a blender, combine all the ingredients and pulse well.
2. Divide this into 6 small ramekins, put them in your air fryer and cook at 340°F for 15 minutes
3. Servings cold

NUTRITION: Calories: 173; Fat: 3g; Fiber: 1g; Carbs: 4g; Protein: 4g

493. Currant Pudding

Preparation Time: 25 minutes • Servings: 6

INGREDIENTS:

- 1cup red currants, blended
- 1cup coconut cream
- 1cup black currants, blended
- 3tbsp. stevia

DIRECTIONS

1. In a bowl, combine all the ingredients and stir well.
2. Divide into ramekins, put them in the fryer and cook at 340°F for 20 minutes
3. Serve the pudding cold.

NUTRITION: Calories: 200; Fat: 4g; Fiber: 2g; Carbs: 4g; Protein: 6g

494. Cocoa and Nuts Bombs

Preparation Time: 13 minutes • Servings: 12

INGREDIENTS

- 2cups macadamia nuts; chopped.
- ¼ cup cocoa powder
- 1/3 cup swerve

- 4tbsp. coconut oil; melted
- 1tsp. vanilla extract

DIRECTIONS

1. Take a bowl and mix all the ingredients and whisk well.
2. Shape medium balls out of this mix, place them in your air fryer and cook at 300°F for 8 minutes Servings cold

NUTRITION: Calories: 120; Fat: 12g; Fiber: 1g; Carbs: 2g; Protein: 1g

495. Blueberry Cream

Preparation Time: 24 minutes • Servings: 6

INGREDIENTS

- 2cups blueberries
- 2tbsp. swerve
- 2tbsp. water
- 1tsp. vanilla extract
- Juice of ½ lemon

DIRECTIONS

1. Take a bowl and mix all the ingredients and whisk well.
2. Divide this into 6 ramekins, put them in the air fryer and cook at 340°F for 20 minutes.
3. Cool down and serve

NUTRITION: Calories: 123; Fat: 2g; Fiber: 2g; Carbs: 4g; Protein: 3g

496. Strawberry Jam

Preparation Time: 30 minutes • Servings: 12

INGREDIENTS

- 8oz. strawberries; sliced
- ¼ cup swerve
- ¼ cup water
- 1tbsp. lemon juice

DIRECTIONS

1. In a pan that fits the air fryer, combine all the ingredients.
2. Put the pan in the machine and cook at 380°F for 20 minutes
3. Divide the mix into cups, cool down and serve.

NUTRITION: Calories: 100; Fat: 1g; Fiber: 0g; Carbs: 1g; Protein: 1g

497. Butter Cookies

Preparation Time: 30 minutes • Servings: 12

INGREDIENTS

- 2eggs, whisked
- 2¾ cup almond flour

- ¼ cup swerve
- ½ cup butter; melted
- 1tbsp. heavy cream
- 2tsp. vanilla extract
- Cooking spray

DIRECTIONS

1. Take a bowl and mix all the ingredients except the cooking spray and stir well.
2. Shape 12 balls out of this mix, put them on a baking sheet that fits the air fryer greased with cooking spray and flatten them
3. Put the baking sheet in the air fryer and cook at 350°F for 20 minutes
4. Serve the cookies cold.

NUTRITION: Calories: 234; Fat: 13g; Fiber: 2g; Carbs: 4g; Protein: 7g

498. Cream Cheese and Zucchinis Bars

Preparation Time: 25 minutes • Servings: 12

INGREDIENTS

- 3oz. zucchini, shredded
- 4oz. cream cheese
- 6eggs
- 2tbsp. erythritol
- 3tbsp. coconut oil; melted
- 2tsp. vanilla extract
- ½ tsp. baking powder

DIRECTIONS

1. In a bowl, combine all the ingredients and whisk well.
2. pour this into a baking dish that fits your air fryer lined with parchment paper, introduce in the fryer and cook at 320°F, bake for 15 minutes. Slice and serve cold

NUTRITION: Calories: 178; Fat: 8g; Fiber: 3g; Carbs: 4g; Protein: 5g

499. Coconut Cookies

Preparation Time: 20 minutes • Servings: 8

INGREDIENTS

- 1½ cups coconut, shredded
- 2eggs, whisked
- 2tbsp. erythritol
- ¼ tsp. almond extract
- ½ tsp. baking powder

DIRECTIONS

1. Take a bowl and mix all the ingredients and whisk well.
2. Scoop 8 servings of this mix on a baking sheet that fits the air fryer which you've lined with parchment paper.
3. Put the baking sheet in your air fryer and cook at 350°F for 15 minutes
4. Servings cold

NUTRITION: Calories: 125; Fat: 7g; Fiber: 1g; Carbs: 5g; Protein: 4g

500. Lemon Cookies

Preparation Time: 30 minutes • Servings: 12

INGREDIENTS

- ¼ cup cashew butter, soft
- 1egg, whisked
- ¾ cup swerve
- 1cup coconut cream
- Juice of 1 lemon
- 1tsp. baking powder
- 1tsp. lemon peel, grated

DIRECTIONS

1. In a bowl, combine all the ingredients gradually and stir well.
2. Spoon balls this on a cookie sheet lined with parchment paper and flatten them.
3. Put the cookie sheet in the fryer and cook at 350°F for 20 minutes
4. Servings the cookies cold

NUTRITION: Calories: 121; Fat: 5g; Fiber: 1g; Carbs: 4g; Protein: 2g

501. Delicious cheesecake

Preparation Time: 25 Minutes • Servings: 15

INGREDIENTS

- Cream cheese: 1 lb
- Vanilla extract: ½ tbsp
- Graham crackers: 1 cup crumbled
- Butter: 2 tbsp
- Eggs: 2
- Sugar: 4 tbsp

DIRECTIONS

1. Mix crackers and butter in a bowl
2. Press the mix on a lined cake pan
3. Preheat your fryer to 350 ° F
4. Place the pan the air fryer. Cook for 4 minutes
5. In another bowl, mix sugar, cream cheese, eggs and vanilla while stirring
6. Spread them onto the crackers. Cook at 310 ° F for 15 minutes.
7. Cool it in the fridge for 15 minutes
8. Servings

NUTRITION: Calories: 245; Fat: 12; Protein: 3; Carbohydrates: 20; Fiber: 1

502. Macaroons

Preparation Time: 18 Minutes • Servings: 20

INGREDIENTS

- Sugar 2 tbsp
- Coconut: 2 cups shredded
- Egg whites: 2
- Vanilla extract: 1 tbsp

DIRECTIONS

1. Beat egg whites with stevia in a bowl
2. While stirring, add coconut and vanilla extract
3. Shape them into balls
4. Place them in the air fryer. Cook until 340 ° F and let it cook at this temperature for8 minutes
5. Servings

NUTRITION: Calories: 55; Fat: 6; Protein: 1; Carbohydrates: 2; Fiber: 1

503. Orange cake

Preparation Time: 42 Minutes • Servings: 12

INGREDIENTS

- Orange: 1 peeled and cut to quarters
- Vanilla extract: 1 tbsp
- Eggs: 6
- Orange zest: 2 tbsp
- Cream cheese: 4 oz.
- Baking powder: 1 tbsp
- Flour: 9 oz.
- Sugar: 2 oz. and 2 tbsp
- Yogurt: 4 oz.

DIRECTIONS

1. Pulse the orange in a food processor
2. Pour in the flour, 2 tbsp sugar, baking powder, eggs and vanilla extract. Pulse it again
3. Place it in 2 spring-form pans.
4. Place it in the air fryer then heat it to 330° F after which let it cook for 16 minutes.
5. In another bowl, mix cream cheese, orange zest, yogurt and the remaining sugar while stirring
6. Sandwich half of the contents of the bowl between the two cake layers from each spring pan. Spread the half that remained on top of the cake. Serve.

NUTRITION: Calories: 200; Fat: 13; Protein: 8; Carbohydrates: 9; Fiber: 2

504. Amaretto and bread dough

Preparation Time: 22 Minutes • Servings: 12

INGREDIENTS

- Bread dough: 1 lb
- Heavy cream: 1 cup

- Chocolate chips: 12 oz.
- Sugar: 1 cup
- Butter: 1 cup melted
- Amaretto liqueur: 2 tbsp

DIRECTIONS

1. Roll the dough on a working surface. Cut it into 20 slices. Further cut the 20 slices into halves
2. Brush each dough piece with butter then sprinkle sugar on it
3. Brush the air fryer with some butter
4. Place the dough pieces in the pan. Cook at 350 ° F for 5 minutes.
5. Flip them and let them cook for 3 minutes
6. Place the heavy cream in a pan. Heat over medium meat.
7. Carefully add the chocolate chips and let them melt.
8. Add liqueur, stir then transfer them to a bowl. Serve.

NUTRITION: Calories: 200; Fat: 1; Protein: 6; Carbohydrates: 6; Fiber: 0

505. Carrot cake

Preparation Time: 55 Minutes • Servings: 6

INGREDIENTS

- Flour: 5 oz.
- Baking powder: ¾ tbsp
- Nutmeg: ¼ tbsp
- Cinnamon powder: ½ tbsp
- Sugar: ½ cup
- Carrots: 1/3 cup grated
- Pecans: 1/3 cup toasted and chopped
- Pineapple juice: ¼ cup
- Allspice: ½ tbsp
- Egg: 1
- Yogurt: 3 tbsp
- Sunflower oil
- Coconut flakes: 1/3 cup shredded
- Cooking spray

DIRECTIONS

1. Mix flour, allspice, baking powder, baking soda, salt, cinnamon and nutmeg in a bowl A then stir
2. In another bowl B mix egg, yogurt, sugar, pineapple juice, oil, carrots, pecans and coconut flakes while stirring
3. While stirring, mix bowl A and bowl B
4. Pour contents in bowl C into a greased pan. Cook them for 45 minutes at 320°F
5. Let it cool. Serve.

NUTRITION: Calories: 200; Fat: 6; Protein: 4; Carbohydrates: 22; Fiber: 20

506. Banana bread

Preparation Time: 50 Minutes • Servings: 6

INGREDIENTS

- Sugar: ¾ cup
- Butter: 1/3 cup

- Milk: 1/3 cup
- Vanilla extract: 1 tbsp
- Egg: 1
- Baking powder: 1 tbsp
- Flour: 1 ½ cups
- Baking soda: ½ tbsp
- Cream of tartar: 1 ½ tbsp
- Cooking spray

DIRECTIONS

1. While stirring, mix milk, cream of tartar, sugar, butter, egg, vanilla and bananas in a bowl A
2. In another bowl B mix flour, baking powder and baking soda
3. Combine bowl B and bowl A while stirring
4. Place it in a greased pan
5. Place it in an air fryer and cook for 40 minutes at 320 ° F
6. Let it cool then serve.

NUTRITION: Calories: 292; Fat: 7; Protein: 4; Carbohydrates: 28; Fiber: 8

507. Granola

Preparation Time: 45 Minutes • Servings: 4

INGREDIENTS

- Coconut: 1 cup shredded
- Almonds: ½ cup
- Pecans: ½ cup chopped
- Sugar: 2 tbsp
- Pumpkin seeds: ½ cup
- Sunflower seeds: ½ cup
- Sunflower oil: 2 tbsp
- Nutmeg: 1 tbsp ground
- Apple pie spice mix: 1 tbsp

DIRECTIONS

1. While stirring, mix almonds, pecans, pumpkin seeds, sunflower seeds, coconut, nutmeg and apple pie spice in a bowl
2. Heat a greased pan over medium heat
3. Add sugar and stir
4. Pour the bowl mixture in the pan and stir. Let it sit for a few minutes
5. Gently spread it on a baking sheet that has been lined
6. Place the baking sheet in the air fryer and bake for 25 minutes at 300 ° F
7. Let it cool then serve.

NUTRITION: Calories: 322; Fat: 7; Protein: 7; Carbohydrates: 12; Fiber: 8

508. Espresso cream and pears

Preparation Time: 40 Minutes • Servings: 4

INGREDIENTS

- Pears: 4 halved and cored
- Water: 2 tbsp
- Lemon juice: 2 tbsp

- Sugar: 1 tbsp
- Butter: 2 tbsp
- Cream Ingredients:
- Whipping cream: 1 cup
- Cold espresso: 1 tbsp
- Mascarpone: 1 cup
- Sugar: 1/3 cup

DIRECTIONS

1. Mix pears halves, lemon juice, 1 tbsp. sugar, butter and water in a bowl then toss well
2. Place them in an air fryer and cook for 30 minutes at 360 ° F
3. Mix whipping cream, mascarpone, ⅓ cup sugar and espresso in a bowl A and whisk them well
4. Place bowl A in the fridge until the food in the air dryer is cooked. Serve.

NUTRITION: Calories: 211; Fat: 5; Protein: 7; Carbohydrates: 8; Fiber: 7

509. Banana cake

Preparation Time: 40 Minutes • Servings: 4

INGREDIENTS

- Soft butter: 1tbsp
- Brown sugar: 1/3 cup
- Egg: 1
- Baking powder: 1 tbsp
- Cooking spray

DIRECTIONS

1. Grease a cake pan
2. Mix butter, sugar, banana, honey, egg, cinnamon, baking powder and flour in a bowl and whisk
3. Pour them in the pan and cook for 30 minutes in the air fryer at 350 ° F
4. Let it cool then serve.

NUTRITION: Calories: 232; Fat: 4; Protein: 4; Carbohydrates: 34; Fiber: 1

510. Fried banana

Preparation Time: 25 Minutes • Servings: 4

INGREDIENTS:

- Butter: 3 tbsp
- Cinnamon sugar: 3 tbsp
- Panko: 1 cup
- Eggs: 2
- Bananas: 8 peeled and halved
- Corn flour: ½ cup

DIRECTIONS:

1. Heat a greased pan over medium heat

2. Add panko in the pan then stir
3. Mix flour, eggs and panko
4. Roll the mixture and dust it with cinnamon
5. Place the rolls in the air fryer and cook for 10 minutes at 280 °F. Serve

NUTRITION: Calories: 164; Fat: 1; Protein: 4; Carbohydrates: 32; Fiber: 4

511. Coffee cheesecakes

Preparation Time: 30 Minutes • Servings: 6

INGREDIENTS

- Butter: 2 tbsp
- Eggs: 3
- Sugar: 1/3 cup
- Cream cheese: 8 oz.
- Coffee: 3 tbsp
- Caramel syrup: 1 tbsp
- Frosting Ingredients:
- Caramel syrup: 3 tbsp
- Soft mascarpone cheese: 8 oz.
- Butter: 3 tbsp
- Sugar: 2 tbsp

DIRECTIONS

1. Mix cream cheese, eggs, 2 tbsp. butter, coffee, 1 tbsp. caramel syrup and ⅓ cup sugar in a blender then pulse
2. Spoon it into cupcake pans and cook them for 20 minutes at 320 ° F
3. After it cools down, place it in the freezer for 3 hours
4. Mix 3 tbsp. butter, 3 tbsp. caramel syrup, 2 tbsp. sugar and mascarpone in a bowl and blend
5. Spread this mixture over the cheesecakes. Then serve.

NUTRITION: Calories: 254; Fat: 23; Protein: 5; Carbohydrates: 21; Fiber: 0

512. Cinnamon rolls served with Cream cheese

Preparation Time: 2 hours 15 Minutes • Servings: 8

INGREDIENTS

- Bread.dough.1.1b
- Brown sugar 3/4
- melted butter 1/4
- cinnamon 1 ½ tbsp. ground
- Cream cheese ingredients
- Butter 2 tbsp
- Sugar 1. ¼ tbsp
- Vanilla ½ tbsp
- Cream Cheese 4 oz

DIRECTIONS

1. On a working surface, roll the

dough and shape it rectangular
2. Brush the dough with ¼ tbsp butter
3. In a bowl, mix cinnamon and sugar and stir
4. Sprinkle contents of the bowl over the dough
5. Roll the dough into a log then seal it and cut it to 8 pieces. Leave them aside for 2 hours to rise
6. Place them in the air fryer then cook them for 4 minutes at 350 ° F. Flip them and let them cook for 4 minutes
7. Mix cream cheese, butter, sugar and vanilla in a bowl then whisk them well. Serve it with the cinnamon rolls.

NUTRITION: Calories: 200; Fat: 1; Protein: 6; Carbohydrates: 5; Fiber: 0

513. Pumpkin cookies

Preparation Time: 25 Minutes • Servings: 24

INGREDIENTS

- Flour: 2 ½ cups
- Baking soda: ½ tbsp
- Butter: 2 tbsp
- Vanilla extract: 1 tbsp
- Flax seed: 1tbsp ground
- Water: 3 tbsp
- Pumpkin flesh: 1/2 cup mashed
- Honey: ¼ cup
- Dark chocolate chips: ½ cup

DIRECTIONS

1. In a bowl A, mix flax seed and water then stir. Leave it aside for a few minutes.
2. Take a bowl B and mix flour, salt and baking powder
3. Mix honey, pumpkin puree, butter, vanilla extract and flax-seed in another bowl C
4. Mix contents in bowl B, A and bowl C to form cookie dough
5. Take 1 tbsp of cookie dough and arrange them in the air fryer. Cook them for 15 minutes at 350 ° F
6. Let it cool then serve

NUTRITION: Calories: 140; Fat: 2; Protein: 10; Carbohydrates: 7; Fiber: 2

514. Apple bread

Preparation Time: 50 Minutes • Servings: 6

INGREDIENTS

- Apples: 3 cups cored and cubed
- Sugar: 1 tbsp

- Baking powder: 1 tbsp
- Butter: 1 stick
- Vanilla: 1 tbsp
- Eggs: 2
- Apple pie spice: 1 tbsp
- White flour: 2 cups
- Water: 1 cup

DIRECTIONS

1. Mix egg, 1 butter stick, apple pie spice and sugar in a bowl A then stir using your mixer
2. While stirring, add apples
3. Mix baking powder and flour in another bowl B
4. Combine contents in bowl A and bowl B then stir
5. Pour them into a pan in such a way that they make a spring shape. Cook it in the air fryer for 40 minutes at 320°F then serve.

NUTRITION: Calories: 192; Fat: 6; Protein: 7; Carbohydrates: 14; Fiber: 7

515. Strawberry pie

Preparation Time: 30 Minutes • Servings: 12

INGREDIENTS

- Coconut: 1 cup shredded
- Butter: ¼ cup
- Sunflower seeds: 1 cup
- Filling Ingredients:
- Gelatin: 1 tbsp
- Cream cheese: 8 oz.
- Lemon juice: ½ tbsp
- Ste-via: ¼ tbsp
- Strawberries: 4 oz.
- Water: 4 tbsp
- Heavy cream: ½ cup
- Strawberries: 8 oz. chopped for serving

DIRECTIONS

1. Mix sunflower seeds, coconut, a pinch of salt and butter in a food processor then pulse it
2. Press it on the bottom of your cake pan then heat the pan over medium heat
3. Slowly add gelatin and stir. Cook for a few minutes then leave it aside to cool
4. Place it to your food processor, and 4 oz. strawberries, cream cheese, lemon juice and Ste via. Blend it
5. Add heavy cream and stir.
6. Spread it over the crust top it with 4 oz. strawberries and cook in the air fryer for 15 minutes at 330 ° F
7. Keep it in the fridge, then serve when needed.

NUTRITION: Calories: 234; Fat: 23; Protein: 7; Carbohydrates: 6; Fiber: 2

516. Bread pudding

Preparation Time: 1 hour 10 Minutes • Servings: 4

INGREDIENTS

- Glazed doughnuts: 6 crumbled

- Cherries: 1 cup
- Egg yolks: 4
- Sugar: ¼ tbsp
- Chocolate chips: ½ cup.
- Whipping cream: 1 ½ cups
- Raisins: ½ cup

DIRECTIONS

1. Mix cherries, egg yolks and whipping cream in a bowl A then stir well.
2. Mix raisins, sugar, chocolate chips and doughnuts in another bowl B and stir
3. Combine the contents of bowl A and bowl B
4. Place them in a greased pan and cook for 1 hour at 310 ° F let it cool then serve.

NUTRITION: Calories: 302; Fat: 8; Protein: 10; Carbohydrates: 23; Fiber: 2

517. Pomegranate and chocolate bars

Preparation Time: 2 hours 10 Minutes • Servings: 6

INGREDIENTS

- Milk: ½ cup
- Almonds: ½ cup chopped
- Vanilla extract: 1 tbsp
- Dark chocolate: 1 ½ cup chopped
- Pomegranate seeds: ½ cup

DIRECTIONS

1. Pour milk in a pan. Heat it over medium heat
2. B Add chocolate and stir for 5 minutes then turn off the heat
3. C Add vanilla extract, half of the pomegranate seeds and half of the nuts then stir
4. D Pour it into a lined baking pan
5. Add a pinch of salt, the rest of the pomegranate and the rest of the nuts. Cook it for 4 minutes at 300°F in the air fryer
6. Place it in the fridge for 2 hours then serve.

NUTRITION: Calories: 68; Fat: 1; Protein: 1; Carbohydrates: 6; Fiber: 4

518. Crisp apples

Preparation Time: 20 Minutes • Servings: 4

INGREDIENTS

- 1Cinnamon powder: 2 tbsp
- Apples: 5 cored and cut into chunks
- Butter: 4 tbsp
- Flour: ¼ cup
- Old fashioned rolled oats: ¾ cup
- Nutmeg powder: ½ tbsp

- Maple syrup: 1 tbsp
- Water: ½ cup
- Brown sugar: ¼ cup

DIRECTIONS

1. Place the apples in a pa
2. Add cinnamon, nutmeg, maple syrup and water
3. Mix butter, oats, sugar, salt and flour in bowl and stir
4. Place 3 spoonfuls of the bowl contents on the apples. Cook for 10 minutes at 350 ° F in the air fryer. Serve while hot or warm.

NUTRITION: Calories: 200; Fat: 6; Protein: 12; Carbohydrates: 29; Fiber: 8

519. Chocolate cookies

Preparation Time: 35 Minutes • Servings: 12

INGREDIENTS:

- Vanilla extract: 1 tbsp
- Flour: 2 cups
- Butter: 1/2 cup
- Egg: 1
- Sugar: 4 tbsp
- Unsweetened chocolate chips: ½ cup

DIRECTIONS

1. Place butter in a pan and heat it over medium heat
2. Mix egg, vanilla extract and sugar in a bowl while stirring
3. Add melted butter, flour and half f the chocolate chips. Stir it well
4. Transfer them to the air fryer, add the remaining chocolate chips and bake for 25 minutes at 330 ° F. Serve when cold.

Nutrition: Calories: 230; Fat: 12; Protein: 5; Carbohydrates: 4; Fiber: 2

DAY MEAL PLAN

DAY	BREAKFAST	MAINS	DESSERTS
1.	Stuffed Portobello Mushrooms with Ground Beef	Indian Chickpeas	Butter Cookies
2.	Basil-Spinach Quiche	White Beans with Rosemary	Cream Cheese and Zucchinis Bars
3.	Stuffed Chicken Roll with Mushrooms	Squash Bowls	Coconut Cookies
4.	Eggs on Avocado Burgers	Cauliflower Stew with Tomatoes and Green Chilies	Lemon Cookies
5.	Applesauce Mash with Sweet Potato	Simple Quinoa Stew	Delicious cheesecake
6.	Bacon and Kale Breakfast Salad	Green Beans with Carrot	Macaroons
7.	Fish Fritatta	Chickpeas and Lentils Mix	Amaretto and bread dough
8.	Spinach Frittata	Garlic Pork Chops	Orange cake
9.	Kale Quiche with Eggs	Honey Ginger Salmon Steaks	Apple bread
10.	Olives Rice Mix	Mustard Pork Balls	Strawberry pie

11.	Sweet Quinoa Mix	Beef Meatballs in Tomato Sauce	Bread pudding
12.	Creamy Almond Rice	Green Stuffed Peppers	Pomegranate and chocolate bars
13.	Chives Quinoa Bowls	Sweet & Sour Chicken Skewer	Crisp apples
14.	Potato Casserole	Lamb Meatballs	Cocoa cookies
15.	Turkey and Peppers Bowls	Spiced Green Beans with Veggies	Strawberry shortcakes
16.	Turkey Tortillas	Chipotle Green Beans	Lentils and dates brownies
17.	Avocado Eggs Mix	Tomato and Cranberry Beans Pasta	Chocolate cookies
18.	Maple Apple Quinoa	Mexican Casserole	Mini lava cakes
19.	Chopped Kale with Ground Beef	Spicy Herb Chicken Wings	Banana bread
20.	Bacon Wrapped Chicken Fillet	Roasted Cauliflower with Nuts & Raisins	Granola
21.	Egg Whites with Sliced Tomatoes	Red Potatoes with Green Beans and Chutney	Tomato cake
22.	Beef Balls with Sesame and Dill	Simple Italian Veggie Salad	Chocolate cake
23.	Zucchini Rounds with Ground Chicken	Spiced Brown Rice with Mung Beans	Coffee cheesecakes
24.	Meatball Breakfast Salad	Eggplant and Tomato Sauce	Fried banana

25.	Tomatoes with Chicken	Lemony Endive Mix	Banana cake
26.	Cherry Tomatoes Fritatta	Lentils and Spinach Casserole	Espresso cream and pears
27.	Whisked Eggs with Ground Chicken	Scallions and Endives with Rice	Lime cheesecakes Wrapped Pears
28.	Breakfast Bacon Hash	Cabbage and Tomatoes	Strawberry cobbler
29.	Eggplant and Sweet Potato Hash	Lemon Halibut	Almond and cocoa bars
30.	Eggs in Avocado	Medium-Rare Beef Steak	Ginger cheesecake
31.	Spaghetti Squash Casserole Cups	Fried Cod & Spring Onion	Plum cake

CONCLUSION

I hope this book was able to help you to understand the benefits of an Air Fryer and the basics on how to use it. The next step is to plan your meals and gather the ingredients. This appliance is easy to use and you will eventually get the hang of the process. Once you have tried several recipes, you can already start tweaking the ingredients to create variations or start making your own.

Enjoy the process of preparing your meals in a healthier way using this innovation when it comes to cooking.

CPSIA information can be obtained
at www.ICGtesting.com
Printed in the USA
LVHW060053030221
678158LV00009B/208

9 781801 590976